Philosophical Perspective on Cinema

Politics, Literature, & Film

Series Editor: Lee Trepanier, Samford University

The Politics, Literature Film series is an interdisciplinary examination of the intersection of politics with literature and/or film. The series is receptive to works that use a variety of methodological approaches, focus on any period from antiquity to the present, and situate their analysis in national, comparative, or global contexts. Politics, Literature, & Film seeks to be truly interdisciplinary by including authors from all the social sciences and humanities, such as political science, sociology, psychology, literature, philosophy, history, religious studies, and law. The series is open to both American and non-American literature and film. By putting forth bold and innovative ideas that appeal to a broad range of interests, the series aims to enrich our conversations about literature, film, and their relationship to politics.

Advisory Board

Richard Avaramenko, University of Wisconsin-Madison
Linda Beail, Point Loma Nazarene University
Claudia Franziska Brühwiler, University of St. Gallen
Timothy Burns, Baylor University
Paul A. Cantor, University of Virginia
Joshua Foa Dienstag, University of California at Los Angeles
Lilly Goren, Carroll University
Natalie Taylor, Skidmore College
Ann Ward, Baylor University
Catherine Heldt Zuckert, University of Notre Dame
Kimberly Hurd Hale, Coastal Carolina University
Sara MacDonald, Huron University
Steven J. Michels, Sacred Heart University
Andrew Moore, St. Thomas University
Recent Titles
Philosophical Perspective on Film by Pedro Blas González
Between Empire and Republic: America in the Colonial Canadian Imagination by Oana Godeanu-Kenworthy

Sorcerer: William Friedkin and the New Hollywood by Mark Wheeler
Nikolai Chernyshevskii and Ayn Rand: Russian Nihilism Travels to America by Aaron Weinacht
Out of the Gray Fog: Ayn Rand's Europe by Claudia Franziska Bruehwiler
Politics, Literature, and Film in Conversation: Essays in Honor of Mary P. Nichols edited by Matthew D. Dinan, Natalie Taylor, Denise Schaeffer, and Paul E. Kirkland
Defenses Against the Dark Arts: The Political Education of Harry Potter and His Friends by John S Nelson
Between Science and Society: Charting the Space of Science Fiction by Douglas A. Van Belle
Pedagogic Encounters: Master and Disciple in the American Novel After the 1980s by Aristi Trendel
Why Moralize upon It?: Democratic Education through American Literature and Film by Brian Danoff
The Unknown Satanic Verses Controversy on Race and Religion by Üner Daglier
Science Fiction and Political Philosophy: From Bacon to Black Mirror edited by Steven Michels and Timothy McCranor

Philosophical Perspective on Cinema

Pedro Blas González

LEXINGTON BOOKS
Lanham • Boulder • New York • London

Published by Lexington Books
An imprint of The Rowman & Littlefield Publishing Group, Inc.
4501 Forbes Boulevard, Suite 200, Lanham, Maryland 20706
www.rowman.com

86-90 Paul Street, London EC2A 4NE

Copyright © 2022 by The Rowman & Littlefield Publishing Group, Inc.

All rights reserved. No part of this book may be reproduced in any form or by any electronic or mechanical means, including information storage and retrieval systems, without written permission from the publisher, except by a reviewer who may quote passages in a review.

British Library Cataloguing in Publication Information Available

Library of Congress Cataloging-in-Publication Data

Names: Gonzalez, Pedro Blas, 1964- author.
  Title: Philosophical perspective on cinema / Pedro Blas González.
  Description: Lanham : Lexington Books, [2022] | Series: Politics, literature, & film | Includes bibliographical references and index. | Summary: "Philosophical Perspective on Cinema addresses the relationship between human existence and sensual reality. Applying metaphysical/existential reflection to cinema, the author explores the philosophical clarity that cinema can offer reflective persons about the human experience"-- Provided by publisher.
  Identifiers: LCCN 2022004072 (print) | LCCN 2022004073 (ebook) | ISBN 9781666906226 (cloth) | ISBN 9781666906240 (paperback) | ISBN 9781666906233 (epub)
  Subjects: LCSH: Motion pictures--Philosophy.
  Classification: LCC PN1995 .G5774 2022 (print) | LCC PN1995 (ebook) | DDC 791.4301--dc23/eng/20220331
  LC record available at https://lccn.loc.gov/2022004072
  LC ebook record available at https://lccn.loc.gov/2022004073

∞™ The paper used in this publication meets the minimum requirements of American National Standard for Information Sciences—Permanence of Paper for Printed Library Materials, ANSI/NISO Z39.48-1992.

*To my wife, Anne, in love, devotion, and appreciation. And to my children,
Isabell Sophia and Marcus Julian, for the joy you have brought to my life.
Para mis padres, Pedro y Nelida, por todo el amor y dedicación.*

Contents

Introduction: Cinema as Humanism Seeking Transcendence   xi

Chapter One: *2001*: An Existential Odyssey   1

Chapter Two: Andrei Tarkovsky: Truth Endorsed by Life   11

Chapter Three: *Fahrenheit 451*: A Brave New World for the New Man   25

Chapter Four: *Citizen Kane*: Biography and the Unfinished Sentence   41

Chapter 5: *Treasure of the Sierra Madre*: Socrates in the Desert   51

Chapter 6: Jean-Pierre Melville: Encounters with Conscience   63

Chapter 7: *Seven Thieves*: Making the World Gasp   85

Chapter 8: *Curse of the Demon*: Evil, Myth, and Reason   97

Chapter 9: *The Uninvited* and *Dead of Night*: The Transcendent Other   111

Chapter 10: Jacques Tati: Last Bastion of Innocence in Modernity   125

Conclusion   137

Appendix   139

Films Cited   147

Bibliography   159

Index   163

About the Author   167

Introduction

Cinema as Humanism Seeking Transcendence

Indomitable.

Perhaps no other word describes human reality more accurately.

Reality, like a beast of burden, possesses a stubborn quality about it that does not flinch, regardless of our spirited protestations. Reality does not easily give away its secrets. This is because human reality confronts us with universal metaphysical/existential categories that must be appropriated by individuals in their respective capacity. This forces thoughtful persons to reflect on experience, as lived. In spite of our limited perspective, whether individually or as cultures or civilizations, reality remains steadfast in its refusal to become deformed. However, this does not negate the possibility that, even though reality presents itself in sizable snippets, what appear as fragmented aspects of human experience, human understanding cannot attain objective knowledge.

Existential thinkers string together aspects of reality that become manifest, and which affect concrete human existence directly. This is not a theoretical, but rather vital task that enables the human person to comprehend human experience. Man's aesthetic vision, then, is rooted in our refusal to be seduced by the merely sensual—by the utilization of selective aspects of reality taken in isolation. This reflectively creative process adheres to a vital will that seeks understanding, if for no other reason than as a service to life.

ESSENCE AND METAPHYSICAL/EXISTENTIAL APPROPRIATION OF HUMAN REALITY

Like the mariner who seeks the prominent direction of a feeble wind, so too, the thinker has a vital need to decipher the often cryptic and always ambiguous nature of human reality. This is the human pole of this cosmic equation. The other is objective reality, which by its very nature objectivizes human experience. The seizure of understanding is a desperate act of salvation, a vital fusing of the varied essences that inform reality on an objective plain, and the concrete, existential drive that situates human existence in objective reality. This is the metaphysical/existential perspective that can best appropriate the existential makeup of the films that *Philosophical Perspective on Cinema* addresses.

This reflective process is the work of thoughtful existential vocation—one that must equally take into consideration spiritual, intuitive, as well as a moral impulse. The metaphysical/existential perspective brings to light the essences that inform the structure of human reality. In short, metaphysical/existential reflection is a philosophy of life that eschews doctrine.

The first order that the latter demands is that philosophical reflection take into account sensual experience. Through paying allegiance to sensual experience, metaphysical/existential thought remains authentic in its approach to essence. For this reason, the union of objective essences and a phenomenological, metaphysical/existential perspective enable the human person to comprehend the dual aspects of human reality: objective essences and the existential concentration that delivers man to a comprehensive understanding of existence as lived experience.

METAPHYSICAL/EXISTENTIAL APPROACH TO HUMAN EXPERIENCE THROUGH CINEMA

When most people think of cinema today, the immediate overall picture that comes to mind is that of moving images, audio-visual effects, and gimmickry of an unprecedented magnitude in human history. Missing from a popular assessment of cinema is coherence in storytelling, vital emotional output—genuine sentiment—and the essences that inform, structure, and regulate human existence.

The average film operates on an entertainment level, one that is more accessible to human reality than perhaps any other artistic or visual medium. This is important, if cinema pretends to communicate any worthwhile truths about the human condition.

But reality, in this sense, ought not to be taken to mean a mere photographic suspended animation that captures human experience in space and time. Cinema and other art forms can truly reproduce intuitive components of human reality, exhaustively. In other words, no art form can reproduce life as lived experience. It goes without saying that cinema does not have an artistic or moral obligation to depict human reality in its totality. The latter is the purview and purpose of metaphysical/existential reflection, a task that is the responsibility of individuals.

A great number of people enjoy cinema for its escapist quality, their sole demand being to become at once removed from the Herculean task of having to bear too much reality—to take a respite from what Gabriel Marcel has aptly called "the bite of reality." Yet this is only one aspect of cinema that should not curtail the artistic and metaphysical/existential potential of the cinematic medium.

Pictorial depictions of reality often enjoy an advantage over conceptual and moral attempts at making sense of the visible world. What is missed at a conceptual level can often be alluded to with sensual, albeit vague impressions. This is no different than in our personal lives. Yet a strictly sensual approach to life, given its biological limitations, cancels the possibility of experiencing the nuanced, essential details of the lived experience that place man in a better position to understand the complexity of human reality.

For instance, theoretical conceptions of death are hardly equivalent to witnessing it firsthand. However, where cinema is concerned, realistic accuracy alone does not make a work of art. It is impossible to faithfully re-create what the immediate lived experience alone can convey. One of the merits of cinema as an art form is its ability to present diverse aspects of reality through allegory and metaphor.

By realism, then, I do not mean to suggest solely an overwhelming loyalty to reality in the subject matter of cinema. Instead, by realism we can understand a general understanding of the human condition in a representative fashion—commentary on human reality is perhaps a clearer and sounder way of defining this task. In other words, cinema can be an effective medium to comprehend the lived experience as encountered by concrete individuals.

The lived representation of the human world, that is, vital life as we experience it daily, surpasses and transcends the sense of reality that mere pictures may suggest. Cinema is an art form that is motivated by an optical illusion—tricks played on the human eye by still pictures that create the deception of motion. Yet this process can often reach lyrical and metaphorical heights.

When viewing a film, we often see other people, much like ourselves, involved in circumstances and dealing with specific problems, concerns, and dilemmas. We see people engulfed by events and surrounded by circumstances, some that we, too, have experienced, can experience, or would like to participate in.

Thus, the immediate sense of representational realism that most films depict is our own human world replete with familiar surroundings. This is the case even in surreal scenarios that, at first glance, appear vastly removed from human experience. This is so because, ultimately, cinema is created by and for people. "Picture-taking" can be viewed as a triumph over naive realism, as this concerns the everyday world that makes up most people's experience of reality.

The representational value of cinema is such that some cultural historians find an intrinsic value in film, if for no other reason than its ability to record the photographic look of the past. Films that take place in the present day have an almost magical ability to take a snapshot of our manners, customs, idioms, clothes, automobiles, furniture, architecture, and the overall look and feel of things at any given time.

This celluloid sense of reality ought not to be taken lightly; it glances at the world and ourselves in a detached manner. We tend to pay more attention to things when seen outside of their immediacy, that is, from an objective distance. This redemptive attitude, while in some respects allows us to fantasize, and remove us from reality, also makes us the center of the reality that we often neglect in our subjective existence: The value of human existence as viewed from the inside out. The real-time representational qualities of cinema enable this art form to exist as a visual reminder of the vitality, purpose, and inherent meaning of human existence.

Somerset Maugham is correct in his assessment in *The Summing Up* that philosophers are responsible for offering the "plain man a vision and suitable, even if tentative, answer to human concerns." The most effective way to achieve this is through a metaphysical/existential approach to human reality.

Maugham argues that to evade this aspect of the discipline is to neglect a central aspect of philosophical vocation. Maugham adds: "But the plain man's interest in philosophy is practical. He wants to know what the value of life is, how he should live and what sense he can ascribe to the universe. When philosophers stand back and refuse to give even tentative answers to these questions they shirk responsibilities."

Some critics argue that cinema is an escapist medium. In many regards, this is true. Yet it also serves as an opportunity to display the immediate and transparent lived experience before us. Perhaps we should be sincere and remind ourselves that, in a truer sense, all entertainment is escapist. Yet human forms of entertainment can be imaginative and instructive.

We must add the relevant qualification that all forms of entertainment are ecstatic—to use the ancient notion of being outside ourselves—that is, they help to situate our existence in the world at large, as it were.

Cinema is valuable as an artistic form on its own right because it acts as a kind of representation of human life. Part of the reason for this—as is also the case in personal life—is that the greatest heuristic lessons that reality proper convey often go unnoticed in the immediacy of the lived experience. Let us not forget that experience alone teaches us nothing. We must reflect on the meaning of the lived experience in order to create perspective about our circumstances.

Failure to reflect on the meaning and value of our experiences keeps us from taking inventory of the lived experience. This is perhaps where the work of the thoughtful commentator can find its strongest justification.

From a strictly philosophical perspective, realism, the attempt to see things as they really are without idealization and overintellectualization, should in principle, serve as the fulcrum from which the thoughtful person can access the meaning of any given film.

Raw reality—what can be referred to as the immediacy of lived experience—can never be surpassed. Ironically, it is precisely because of reality's translucent quality that we often take life for granted. In other words, reflective viewers can act as students of reality who try to reconstruct vital reality through cinema.

The appeal of cinema for most people resides in its apparent portrayal of reality and its power to transform aspects of human existence into entertainment value. For the philosophical commentator, this quality can be brought to life through a film's structural narrative and the lingering impressions, emotions, and thoughts that it can give rise to.

The most interesting dilemma for thoughtful students of human reality is that the objects of knowledge—as these exist in their immediacy—often absorb us in such a manner that we tend to forget ourselves. Though, this is hardly a bad thing. Isn't this perhaps a description of human life itself?

This process necessitates a lapse in time that is necessary in order for reflection to occur, much like the light of a dead star that will continue to be seen for the duration of the time that it takes light to travel the distance between the star and Earth.

However, cinema finds itself in a historically precarious situation today. Much like many aspects of postmodern life, it has been cheapened, robbed of inherent redemptive value. The problem is that in many cases cinema has become entertainment for the sake of entertainment, or what is essentially a dispensable and disposable medium.

Cinema has traditionally showcased its unique and privileged capability in its regard for secular and religious humanism. For instance, this understated humanism is evidenced in the camaraderie that is effectively placed on display in William Wellman's film *Battleground*, as well as in the surreal inner vitality felt by Bertrand in François Truffaut's *The Man Who Loved Women*.

Equally ennobling is Nick Charles's sophisticated and urbane wit in *The Thin Man* series, and the ethereal weightlessness and fanciful mayhem of Frank Capra's *You Can't Take It With You*. These films embrace profound depictions of fundamental aspects of the lived existence, which are made poignant through a metaphysical/existential perspective.

Few other aspects of human existence are as exalting as laughter—the act of celebrating life by keeping proper perspective—a form of checks and balances over the trivial and mundane. We encounter fine examples of this in the cathartic and joyful innocence of children in Albert Lamorisse's *Red Balloon,* the out-of-this-world mayhem of Eliseo Subiela's *Hombre mirando al sudeste*, and Jacques Tati's films. A metaphysical/existential approach to cinema can help us understand the lived experience of concrete individuals.

Chapter One

2001

An Existential Odyssey

SYNOPSIS

2001: A Space Odyssey is a science fiction film that confronts viewers with perennial questions of the origin of man, the infinite, and the order of human reality in relation to the cosmic. The film is also a nuanced reflection on the nature of intelligence and personal immortality. As far as science is concerned, *2001* offers a look at man's future and the possibility of man's living beyond the Earth.

We should not be quick to dismiss the idea that form is not a limitless, bottomless well of inspiration. Form is an objective reservoir that meets man's most pressing aesthetic and metaphysical/existential concerns on its own terms. By definition, if form is the architectonic that structures reality, it can be recognized. This means that it can also be de-formed, thus making form lose its efficacy. Ancient Greek thinkers like Pythagoras, Parmenides, and Plato argued that form is best recognized by people who seek it. Postmodernity's hyperactive domain of sensual whims and desires pays little heed to the nature of form.

Cinema is a fine example of a field that, from its earliest and rudimentary beginning, has evolved beyond the wildest expectations of its originators. Even an informal survey of the thousands of films that have been made makes one privy to the qualitative complexities that creative vision encounters.

In the early days of cinema, when there was very little to rely on by way of technology, directors mostly embraced imagination and the inherent value of storytelling. With the advent and frantic pace of technological development in the twentieth century, more directors have come to rely less on storytelling and more on technology. It is fair to say that today a great number of films exemplify a sophomoric dare to prove that special effects alone can create cinema.

While the use of special effects in cinema is a perpetual temptation for some directors, this does not preclude the desire of some directors to forgo its use, as special effects can often interfere with the creative process. We can consider a number of great directors and their successful films, and how they did very well by keeping special effects at bay. We can point out the lyrical qualities of John Ford's films, the life-affirming nuances that Jacques Tati showcases in his body of work, Jean-Pierre Melville's profoundly existential dramas, and Hitchcock's use of suggestive horror. These are some of many poignant exceptions.

Cinema can be an enlightening humanistic art.[1] It is because of its entrancing entertainment qualities that the aforementioned can be convincingly argued. Undoubtedly, the moral and existential condition of man in the first decade of the twenty-first century is dominated by a profound lack of curiosity and wonder—what can be characterized as debilitating existential boredom. This boredom partly originates as the result of a surplus of visual images. Practically speaking, my suggestion is simply that man's intellectual, spiritual, and moral makeup may very well be exhaustible. By this, I mean to stress that innovation can only take us so far before it begins to collapse under the exigencies of its own weight.

Might it not be the case that technological development has delivered us to a state of technological ennui? Is our postmodern predicament a spiritual and moral condition, or are we merely the victims of technological advancement? One possible answer, though perhaps somewhat naive, is that we would not embrace any technological advancement that we weren't ready to accept morally. If we use the telephone "caller identification" excessively, it is because we find this a useful way of not having to talk to certain callers. According to some statistics, thirty-six percent of the population has a television on during every waking hour as companion background noise, this may be a strong indicator of some people's aversion to silence and solitude.

A surplus of images may be exactly what the doctor ordered for an age that is existentially superficial and morally saturated with arbitrary, make-work "arts." Ironically, such profound world-weariness can only be alleviated through more images. For many people, visual images assuage a dearth of meaning and purpose. Most images take us into an external realm, as it were; images keep us from cultivating intimacy with ourselves. In this regard, let us take stock of the root meaning of the word ecstasy: to be totally outside ourselves.

2001: A SPACE ODYSSEY

Stanley Kubrick's majestic film, *2001: A Space Odyssey* has not only solidified its position as one of the best science fiction films of all time, but it is also one of the greatest examples of world cinema. *2001* is a superb visual articulation of profound human thought and exalted emotions. *2001* captures the sublime in ways that few cinematic works ever have.[2]

2001: A Space Odyssey is a marvelous combination of entertainment—this is the ultimate purpose of cinema—and an uplifting look at the human condition in relation to the intimidating vastness of space, time, and infinity. It is important to make a sound clarification: *2001: A Space Odyssey* was released in 1968 and was rated "G" for general audiences.

2001 speaks thunderous volumes through employing a minimum of dialogue. This may seem a curiosity to us, today, in an age saturated with visual imagery. This is also a testament to the ideas and emotions that *2001* conveys. Without utilizing the exaggerated, frantic, and breakneck editing that is so fashionable today, this film achieves a timeless cinematic beauty that places it on an artistic pedestal, where only few other films dwell.

Interestingly, *2001* is a film that comes across as employing a mythological form of storytelling, where ultimately the story is what matters, not the special effects or the popularity of the actors. Some critics of the film have referred to it as being abstract. Perhaps this is best characterized as reluctance to embrace and work within the demands that this intriguing work makes on the viewer. This is precisely the metaphysical/existential quality that drives *2001*.

What makes the metaphysical/existential aspect of *2001* so intriguing for many viewers is that it makes us work for its meaning. Few films are as demanding on viewers as *2001*. This is not a work that lazily telegraphs its punches, as it were. The idea that beauty and truth should make us work for their attainment has become anathema in our age.

At no time during this film are we given a cheap and transparent exposition of its direction. *2001* begins and ends in with philosophical speculation. *2001*, some critics suggest, is just too much for most audiences to figure out. This may be true. This is ironic, for *2001* is a science fiction film, and science fiction—at least in written form—demands a great deal of imagination from its readers. I will suggest that *2001* takes viewers on a metaphysical/existential tour of space, time, infinity, and immortality.

Stanley Kubrick said that he left the meaning of the film up to the viewer. Of course, this is his prerogative as a director. Yet *2001* is not deliberately made incomprehensible, as is often the case with a great number of avant-garde films. This does not preclude the possibility that several possible meanings inform the film, for *2001* is indeed a sophisticated picture that demands introspection from viewers.

A work of art, such as *2001*, may contain one unifying and several correlative meanings or interpretations. However, this does not mean that the director has not ascribed an overarching meaning. *2001* is a challenging film, both philosophically and as high entertainment, but no one can say that it is meaningless. The short story that partially inspired the making of *2001*, "The Sentinel," comes from the literary imagination of science-fiction author Arthur C. Clarke.

The immediate meaning of *2001* has to do with man's technological development, and how this has taken us from Earth to the stars. There are several clear indications of this. Stanley Kubrick's original title for the film was *Journey Beyond the Stars*. He referred to the film as being akin to "a space odyssey." He later changed the title, adding the *2001* portion.

There is some significance in the film being a kind of odyssey, for an odyssey is a long journey replete with difficulties that usually culminate in the discovery of human reality as transcending the immediacy of the lived experience. If we take Odysseus' odyssey as an example, we can attribute the idea of an odyssey in *2001* as the return of man to his original source—what in this case is a state of innocence and pure intelligence.

The film begins with a barren landscape that is inhabited by a species of apes. The words: "The Dawn of Man" appear as the viewer witnesses a moonlike landscape. The apes are seen coexisting with tapirs. One of the apes is then attacked by a leopard. The appearance of the large cat showcases the raw power of brawn. The apes are next seen squabbling with each other over a watering hole, but no physical confrontation ensues. The apes are later awakened from their sleep by the appearance of a black, rectangular monolith. They go up to it and reluctantly begin to touch it. This scene conveys a form of primaeval awe and wonder.

The monolith remains stationary. One of the apes curiously studies the remains of large animal bones. The ape develops a kind of curiosity that is easily identifiable by his smart countenance. Clearly, the ape is now confronted with a heightened awareness, a new perspective about the same bones that he had previously ignored. The animal learns to use the largest bone that it can find to attack and kill a tapir. The discovery of tools? The apes eat the tapir. These animals have discovered technology. Is it an external stimulus or internal awareness of essence that prompts the apes to discover technology?

When the next squabble for water takes place between the rival ape clans, the apes that possess tools attack the others. Why some apes receive higher intelligence from the monolith and not others remain an interesting question. One answer is that some of them touch the monolith while others do not. This is a valuable metaphor to ponder in terms of man's development, especially in light of the structure of essence that the apes discover.

Of major significance to the film is the next cut, when the large bone that the ape has launched into the air gives way to a shot of a large, elongated spaceship. After about 28 minutes, *2001* moves into the space age.

The transition from the ape's discovery of tools to the space age is a major component of the film's inherent meaning. Because the monolith resembles a form of intelligence, artificial or otherwise, we can surmise from this that we owe our technology to intelligence. Contact with the monolith takes place several times throughout the film.

But what exactly is the monolith? Is it intelligence, pure and simple? Is it a metaphysical/existential guiding principle for man? Apparently, all of these, for man's discovery of tools is directly tied to the appearance of the monolith. Some commentators have surmised that perhaps the monolith is representative of some alien intelligence. This is conceivable, but this interpretation is not readily supplied by the film. If one embraces this possibility, we are still left with the question of whom or what send it. The monolith may be of an intelligent design, but it certainly shows no signs of life, as we know it.

If the monolith is interpreted as some kind of alien intelligence, one can assume that intelligence may have something to convey to man. But what? The monolith only makes a humming sound. It is true that those who come in contact with the monolith are changed by it, as are the apes at the start of the film and Dave Bowman at the end. Yet these entities do not understand what has happened to them. Thus, to interpret the monolith as a form of alien intelligence leaves us with more questions than answers. Such an interpretation adds very little to the coherence of the film.

In addition, if we argue that the latter is the case, we also have to ask: What exactly is the point of sending this metallic envoy to appear before man? We cannot view communication with humans as a motive for the appearance of the monolith, because clearly that does not take place in the film. Given that the monolith does not communicate, what can the guiding reason for its mission, if any, be? It is perhaps more fruitful to assume that the monolith is either a God-like entity that is the cause of all things intelligent in the universe or that it is a symbol and metaphor for intelligence proper.

Either way, the monolith has a transformative power over the apes and, subsequently, the astronauts. This is evident at the end of the film, when the lone astronaut is transformed into an old man, before returning to childhood. Whatever the message that the monolith imparts to the astronauts, it enables them to have greater understanding. This alone makes the monolith a transcendent power that the astronauts pay heed to. We ought to be careful with hyper interpretations.

What is important in the sequence of appearances of the monolith before ape and man is not so much that the monolith appears to man, but that man (or ape) always finds itself where the monolith is: at the dawn of man, on the lunar base and beyond the orbit of Jupiter. This is not a coincidence, for technological man goes out of his way to investigate the monolith, on the moon and in the orbit of Jupiter.

2001: A Space Odyssey is a film about space exploration. This is a basic driving motive for making the film. Arthur C. Clarke and Stanley Kubrick convey this theme admirably. From the 1930s through the 1970s, space exploration was a dominant concern of science-fiction writers. The science fiction magazines of the time, and reaching into today's vast market, has kept the exploration of space, aliens and intelligent life forms a predominant concern.

Scientists, too, warmed up to the realistic possibility of near-space exploration, mainly of the moon, after Robert Goddard's successful launching of his liquid fuel rocket, and after World War II, with the advent of the V-2 rocket. Before that, literature had already entertained such a possibility in the works of Jules Verne and H. G. Wells.

Hence, a film about space exploration must undoubtedly have a human component, either in the form of unmanned or manned space vehicles. *2001* is part of that human drama. Of course, the film develops a rather unique and highly complex drama of its own. One of the plot components of the film is the drama of what we can expect to encounter in space; the passage of time, ageing, transcendence, the sublime, and immortality; all of these themes are metaphysical/existential concerns par excellence.

2001 also entertains a man-versus-machine theme in the form of the tenacious HAL 9000 computer. While the computer is said to fail, it only does so because of the instructions that it has received from its designers and programmers. If it feels that the mission will be compromised by the astronauts in any way, HAL, which has been programmed to have an emotional response, will act accordingly. The problem is that what it deems as rational behavior entails the "termination" of the hibernating astronauts and Bowman's partner, Frank Poole.

The drama that drives the film has everything to do with the human condition. Bowman and Poole embark on a journey that will take a very long time to complete, and one from which they may never return. This is a consideration that they must accept. How does this affect them as concrete persons?

Astronauts in the year 2001 must maintain a modicum of cool that keeps them distant from their loved ones. This is a mechanism that they must cultivate in order to safeguard themselves from too great an emotional connection to the people they leave behind on Earth.

When Bowman is called by his parents on the teleconference screen, he acts serene and unemotional, even though they are calling to wish him happy birthday. Bowman talks to his parents in the same sterile way that he talks to HAL. His intonation matches his cold and clinical surrounding on the ship. One can gather that the psychological make up of Dave Bowman must be this way in order to protect himself from the harsh conditions and distances that he must endure. When HAL begins to act up, Bowman remains calm and collected, as he has been trained to do. One wonders how he must truly feel to find himself in such a sterile environment and lived experience.

When I first watched *2001: A Space Odyssey* at age twelve, I was awed by the visual spectacle that the film presents us with. I was also moved by the sophisticated themes of the film. However, what I was most profoundly impacted by was the character portrayed by Dave Bowman. Viewers may wonder what Bowman feels and how he avoids losing all sense of reality. A metaphysical/existential approach to *2001* does not view Bowman as a mere astronaut who is sent into space by a space agency, but rather, Bowman totally alone and having to deal with his thoughts and emotions. This is an aspect of *2001* that very few writers comment on.

Dave Bowman's existential drama captivates the imagination of viewers because we can easily imagine ourselves in his situation. Lost in all the talk about computers, space travel, and the harsh violence of space on the human body and psyche, we can lose sight of the essential drama of the film: Dave Bowman's existential condition, as he stumbles into old age and is later transfigured once again into a child.

Space travel, no different than gardening, let us say, can only make sense to the subjects directly invested in it. The view of the world and himself that a Dave Bowman subscribes to is probably vastly different from those of most people. When we watch Bowman struggling to undermine HAL, we see a man who must exhaust his entire stock of ideas and emotions in order to safeguard his safety. What we don't realize is just how much existential energy he consumes to garner the success of the mission.

Voltaire's famous notion of "cultivating one's garden" requires a minimum modicum of existential self-awareness. One cannot cultivate one's garden without having conceived the idea that cultivating one's garden is a higher value, say, than forms of existential inauthenticity that keep us from cultivating the self.

Bowman tends to his ship like Candide does his garden. However, he does so from the understanding that he is in control of his choices. Thus, when HAL threatens to override Bowman's command and eventually take his life, this very practical, unassuming man must take action. If the latter action does not spring from an existential understanding of danger and survival, then Bowman would be turned into a HAL of flesh and blood. This is the interesting part of Bowman that we only see emerge under duress.

Bowman takes his mission seriously. He is seen going over technical details, exercising and relaxing. He knows that he will be on the ship for a long time. Perhaps he will die there. When the first signs that something is wrong onboard appear, he does not immediately come to suspect HAL, the master computer. This is an indication of the kind of trust that he and the others have placed on this machine, on technology. Though, knowing that HAL has his life in its control is not something that Bowman takes for granted. From the outset of the mission, Bowman demonstrates great respect for the computer.

Bowman is shrewder than he appears. When problems surface on the ship, he goes about trying to figure out what is taking place. Things only turn sinister when the hibernating astronauts are terminated—killed by HAL. Whatever working relationship Bowman has with HAL ends when the astronaut discovers just what it means to have human free will and agency controlled by a machine. HAL refuses to acknowledge that he has done anything wrong in terminating the lives of the hibernating astronauts. How could he? HAL does not possess a moral compass. Having been instructed to follow certain guidelines and operating logic, the computer can only respond accordingly.

We give away our freedom, or so it appears, to computers for a greater return on our overall freedom. This is the idea behind our desire for freedom in undertaking difficult tasks. Bowman's decision to go on the voyage to Jupiter is his initial choice. Astronauts work with highly sophisticated machines. This is the first rule of thumb for them. But this is only half of the equation, for astronauts place their lives at the mercy of machines that they themselves have to operate, regulate, and calibrate. This is an uneasy marriage that requires metaphysical/existential reflection at some level.

When HAL acts up, Bowman has no choice but to take over in a way that he never needed to before. The purpose of having HAL run the ship is so that the astronauts can save their energy for the important task of confronting the monolith. Bowman's capacity to take action against this computer never wavers. On the contrary, the so-called relationship that the astronauts have with HAL is predicated on the fact that it is merely a computer.

Critics who argue that HAL essentially creates a mutiny on the ship are right, but only to a certain extent. When HAL disconnects the hibernating astronauts, it does not do so from computer error, and certainly not from a sense of moral evil. The effect, of course, is the same. The idea of mutiny hardly passes muster. HAL acts, not from existential freedom, but from the opposite—an implanted command that he is determined to obey. By acting up, HAL forces Bowman to exercise his freedom. The latter is not theoretical, but lifesaving.

Much can be made of clichés like machines ruling over man and man becoming at a loss to enact any sense of control, etc. While some of these concerns may ring true, we must recognize that we have had over a century now to grapple with these questions. Technology, either in 1968, when *2001* was released, or today is not new to man. If we become tongue-tied by an inarticulate capacity to understand our circumstances, either collectively or as concrete persons, this is of our own doing. The proof of this is that man has lived with technology dating back to prehistory.

Bowman's condition on the spaceship resembles that of a metaphysical/existential proto first-man who encounters the world and human reality afresh every day. His scientific training can only deliver him so far. Whatever existential reservoir he has as a person will determine how he acts in any given situation.

The question of the inevitability of technology to take over the human person remains with us, even though, one suspects that it is more a tongue-in-cheek exercise than a genuine concern for most of the people who raise this question. We simply do not know how to live without technology of any kind. Technology may appear anathema to existential authenticity, but the technology that we enjoy has originated in the entrails of our existential longing. This is a paradox.

Bowman demonstrates his existential concerns once he finds himself alone and threatened by HAL. Throughout the "star gate" sequence, when he is traveling over strange and frightening terrain, we watch his face in amazement, as he fears what is yet to come. Bowman is a man alone. He is not alone in the sense that we speak of being alone on Earth, for here the possibilities of companionship are truly real. Bowman is alone, as perhaps no person in human history has ever been.

Through his encounters with space, time, and a malfunctioning computer, Bowman arrives at the realization that he has transformed himself into immediate old age. Finding himself old, Bowman comes face-to-face with his own mortality. He sits in bed in a lavishly decorated room, breathing hard and staring at the ceiling—or the stars—as he begins to die.

The end of *2001: A Space Odyssey* finds Dave Bowman reeling with amazement at what he has become. At the end of the film, Bowman is transfigured into a star child, or what is essentially a child once again. Bowman has found the ultimate meaning of human reality, as this has transformed him into a kind of being that has no need to continue searching. This is the kind of metaphysical/existential awe and wonder pertinent to the human condition that *2001* explores.

NOTES

1. See: Pedro Blas González. "Jacques Tati: Last Bastion of Innocence." *Senses of Cinema*. Issue No. 37, Oct.–Dec. 2006, 1–11.

2. Stanley Kubrick. *2001: A Space Odyssey*. MGM. 1968. Joseph D. Olander and Martin Harry Greenberg, editors. *Arthur C. Clarke*. New York: Taplinger, 1977.

Chapter Two

Andrei Tarkovsky

Truth Endorsed by Life

SOLARIS AND STALKER

Synopsis

Andrei Tarkosvky's films are some of the most reflective and metaphysical/existential films ever created. The Russian cineaste takes a poetic and impressionistic approach to human existence. Deliberately slow-paced, Tarkoysky's films explore the nature of the individual vis-à-vis a world of fleeting sensual impressions.

The Spanish philosopher José Ortega y Gasset refers to man as a "conscious cosmic phenomenon." What he means by this has everything to do with the fact that there is at least one cosmic entity that is capable of self-awareness in the universe: man. Ironically, Ortega recognized that this reality remains the most transparent truth that many people fail to recognize. Throughout his collected work Ortega argues that life and reason, that is, pure reason, are not compatible. He differentiates between pure reason and vital reason. What ought to matter most for man, he tells us, is the realm of the vital in human affairs. Vital reason, then, is the tool that is most appropriate for life. Ortega's work returns sobriety to philosophy. The task of the philosopher, Ortega argues—he does this eloquently and convincingly—is to reflect on human existence without simultaneously robbing it of its lived vitality. He writes in *The Dehumanization of Art*, a book that was published in 1925: "Perception of 'lived' reality and perception of artistic form, as I have said before, are essentially incompatible because they call for a different adjustment of our perceptive apparatus."[1]

SOLARIS

Like Ortega y Gasset, the Russian cineaste Andrei Tarkovsky's (1932–1986), vision of man as a spiritual entity who is embraced by spatial-temporal objectification is the guiding force behind his cinematic and written works. Tarkovsky made seven full feature films, beginning in 1958. Even though, I will mention his other films, this chapter focuses on *Solaris* (1972) and *Stalker* (1979).

Solaris is considered a science fiction film. This is a rather misleading understatement. To test this, we only have to look closely at the reaction of most science fiction fans, whose idea of this genre is based on the likes of *Star Wars*, *Alien*, and *Terminator*. Such moviegoers have an adverse reaction to films that do not move along at the speed of video games.

Solaris uses a fictional world in order to make sense of our own. The story essentially explores the power of memory, the sacredness of the passage of time, and how this dictates our past as well as the future. But make no mistake about it, as Tarkovsky says in his brilliant book *Sculpting in Time*, *Solaris* is only accidentally a science fiction film. He explains: "Unfortunately, the science fiction element in Solaris was nonetheless too prominent and became a distraction. The rockets and space stations required by Lem's novel—were interesting to construct; but it seems to me now that the idea of the film would have stood out more vividly and boldly had we managed to dispense with these things altogether."[2]

Tarkovsky was enthralled by Stanislaw Lem's novel *Solaris*. While the film is based on the novel, Tarkovsky does not fully develop the science fiction element of the book. Instead, Tarkovsky develops other themes, including love and the memories that are formed from this human emotion. Tarkovsky is clear and upfront about this: He writes in *Sculpting in Time*: "I have to say at the outset that not all prose can be transferred to the screen. Some works have a wholeness, and are endowed with a precise and original literary image; characters are drawn in unfathomable depths; the composition has an extraordinary capacity for enchantment, and the book is indivisible."[3]

The latter was a rather bitter point of contention for Lem after he viewed the finished film. Lem, too, has criticized most science fiction for its exaggerated plots and conventions. The film opens with a shot of a gently flowing stream and Chris Kelvin, the protagonist looking at falling rain. He then walks around the back of a country house. Two men walk up to the house. They come to tell Chris that "the Solaris crew is transmitting puzzling data." Chris is to go out to the station and confirm that this is truly the case. If this is proven to be the case, the station will then have to be shut down. This is interesting because the impression that the scientists have is that perhaps those aboard the station are suffering from fatigue. This is an optimistic account. What is actually occurring on the Solaris station cannot be solved by applying additional science. After hearing of the strange events taking place on the station, Chris decides to stay out in the rain, as if he might never get to experience it again. From the start, *Solaris* conveys a strong feeling of isolation. This emotion is powerfully conveyed by Chris Kelvin in his country home long before we witness the same emotion on the Solaris station. Tarkovsky's images and moods effectively depict a vital and lyrical poetry of life that is rooted in daily reality. Dr. Kelvin, who is a psychologist by training, as we come to see later in the film, is mourning the death of his wife.

The film that Chris is shown about what is taking place on the Solaris station and the planet that it orbits is shot in a sepia tinge. The color of the film resembles Tarkovsky's other science fiction film, *Stalker*. The brown look of the documentary film has a sense of unreality that Burton, the astronaut who filmed it, cannot truly reveal. This is the first time the viewer is offered the suggestion that the planet the station orbits is intelligent. The question is then brought up: "Is it possible that Burton was affected by the vital force of the ocean, which is thought to be a gigantic brain, a substance capable of thought?" The documentary film also shows a briefing of Burton that turns into a kind of hearing that attempts to confirm what he indeed witnessed. The tone of the briefing becomes condescending when a scientist argues that the problem lies in Burton and not with the planet. Some indication of Burton's resistance to the overbearing scientific scrutiny that he is exposed to is felt in his comment to Chris that, "Knowledge is truthful only if it's based in morality." Chris rebutes this by saying, "Moral or immoral, it's man who makes science." The latter is an early indication of Dr. Kelvin's training as a scientist. As the film progresses, Kelvin's respect for scientific materialism begins to wane. Not knowing if he will ever return, he proceeds to burn his papers before going into space. This is a powerful scene of anticipation and foreboding. The next scene shows Chris in space over Solaris. Once he enters the space station Dr. Snouth tells Dr. Kelvin that one of the three men onboard has committed suicide after the "trouble" began.

The initial scenes after Chris arrives on the station create a surreal drama of expectation and resolution. At that point in the film, we are confronted with a new level of metaphysical phenomena—strange occurrences and uncomfortable situations that force us to make sense of our human condition. Chris attempts to solve the enigma of the personality disorders that the others on the station are experiencing. Our initial thought, along with Chris, is that the desperation that those onboard suffer from is born of asphyxiating loneliness and disorientation that can only be solved by returning the astronauts to Earth. This is the scientific explanation that is called for. As we witness later, science was the last thing on Tarkovsky's mind at the time of filming *Solaris*. We are reminded of Nietzsche's notion of whether man truly wants to know ultimate truth. Tarkovsky adds:

> Solaris had been about people lost in the cosmos and obliged, whether they liked it or not, to acquire and master one more piece of knowledge. Man's unending quest for knowledge, given him gratuitously, is a source of great tension, for it brings with it constant anxiety, hardship, grief, and disappointment as the final truth can never be known.[4]

The latter is one of the dominant themes of the film. This quote captures the essence of the many exchanges that take place between Chris, Dr. Snouth, and Dr. Sartorius. This theme is developed alongside Chris's internal struggle to understand his wife's appearances. This is a key ingredient in Tarkovsky's films because his characters are developed according to their own internal struggles and not through outward action. The major contribution of cinema, according to Tarkovsky, is to represent interior reality through a visual medium. He writes:

> The prerogative of film, which has to do with what distinguishes its impact on his consciousness from that of literature or philosophy: namely the opportunity to live through what is happening on the screen as if it were his own, the experience imprinted in time upon the screen, relating his own life to what is being shown.[5]

When Chris enters the station and goes to Dr. Gibarian's room, he encounters the problem that is afflicting those on the station in a video made by someone who has already committed suicide. Gibarian addresses him:

> I have a little time and must tell you something and warn you. By now you know about me. If not, Sartorius or Snouth will tell you. What's happened to me is not important. Or rather, it's indescribable. I fear that this is just the beginning. I hate the idea but here it can probably happen to anyone. Only, don't think I've lost my mind. You know me well. If I have time, I'll tell you everything. If it happens to you, just know that it's not madness . . . That's the main thing. As for further research, I lean towards Sartorius's suggestion subjecting the ocean of radiation. That has been forbidden. But there's no other way. We . . . you . . . will only get bogged down. Radiation may get us out of deadlock. It is the only way to deal with this monster. No other way.[6]

After watching the video, Chris becomes baffled by Sartorius's suicide and the latter's contention that he is not insane. Chris walks around the space station disoriented, out of place, as if someone is hiding the truth from him. Gibarian believes there is little time to explain what has taken place on the station. The second important thing he alludes to is that what is taking place is indescribable. This seemingly epistemological breakdown is a fundamental theme of the film. What is more significant is the way in which Tarkovsky presents the question. If he presents the phenomenon that is taking place onboard the space station as a paradigm change, this will constitute yet another problem to be solved by science. Instead, Tarkovsky's wants to demonstrate that if truth could reveal itself to man in its totality, it would undermine our present worldview.

Tarkovsky presents the viewer with the possibility to entertain a new model of understanding. What is pressing about his method is that we are not introduced to beings from another world that possess new truth to enlighten us with. Tarkovsky does not entertain us with aliens and fright that originates in another dimension. Tarkovsky explores our relationship to ourselves, existentially and spiritually. What if, he seems to suggest, the understanding of human existence that we possess is not only limited but lacking in some fundamental clarity? What appears to be taking place on the Solaris station is the imprinting of human memories in a universal, cosmic mind. Fanciful? Perhaps. Tarkovsky suggests that perhaps we live superficially on the surface of human existence. Tarkovsky is not concerned with scientific exploration, rather nonrational aspects of the lived experience. What is the role of memory in our lives? Can we live without them? Must we relive our worst memories? Can we be selective? Chris's wife, Hari, dies again on the space station; Chris is forced to experience her death again.

As Chris walks around the station, he looks out onto the pulsating sea of the planet that Solaris orbits. He sees a woman walking past him. He follows her. Chris immediately comes to understand the indescribable anomaly that Gibarian mentions in his video. The woman is Hari, his wife. His understanding is verified by Snouth after Chris tells him, "I know you're not insane." Snouth replies, "Insane! Good God. Insane! That would be relief!" Truth that is too much to bear becomes a living hell for all onboard the station. The next time he sees her, Chris has just awakened and stares at a young woman who is sitting on a chair facing him. She comes and kisses him. After Chris asks her where she came from, she just utters. "How wonderful." After Chris asks her how she knew that he was there, she becomes confused and asks, "What do you mean?" Chris places Hari on a rocket and launches her into space. Chris is reacting to what he considers to be a hallucination. The decisive moment in this sequence of scenes takes place when Snouth reveals to Chris: "It's the materialization of your memory of her." Snouth explains that the problems began when "we finished the experiment, of beaming x-rays down at the ocean's surface. Apparently, the x-rays enabled the ocean to explore all the little islands of our memory."

Dr. Sartorius, too, offers a scientific answer to what they experience as a metaphysical conundrum. Sartorius figures that the hallucinations "consist of neutrinos, and not atoms like everywhere else." He explains that neutrino systems are supposed to be unstable, but Solaris' force field stabilizes them. This scientific explanation is a valid point. They are scientists. When faced with questions of an irresolute nature, the best route to take is the simplest: a scientific explanation that decodes aspects of our superficial understanding.

Even if the above-mentioned is true, Tarkovsky is concerned about how we experience reality, not so much what it is. A point in question in the film is the relationship between his memories and the hallucinatory, external experiences on the station. Chris plays a home movie of himself as a boy walking in the snow that juxtaposes the two. The home movie evokes true memories. The same cannot be said of the hallucinatory memories. While memories cannot exist of their own accord, they trigger a return to a real place and time. This is easily evidenced when Hari cannot remember or make sense of her past; she does not exist for herself, only for Chris. Hari arrives at the realization that she is not the real Hari, given that Hari was poisoned. She begins to view herself as a memory. This reminds us of Sartre's pour-soi and en-soi and Descartes' cogito ergo sum. This is also the case for the replicants in *Blade Runner*. Chris initiates a conversation with Hari that may be interpreted as being a conversation with himself, that is, with his memories. As this conversation ensues, Hari presses him to tell her what or who she really is. Hari is desperate to find the ontological basis to establish her own existence. Hari wants to know why the real Hari poisoned herself. Chris replies, "I suppose she felt that I didn't really love her."

A great deal of the film can be understood from the conversation that takes place in the library. Some critics who perhaps have not understood Tarkovsky's vision of cinema accuse his films of being dominated by conversation. Yet conversation in Tarkovsky's films is essential in broadening his visual storytelling. Tarkovsky writes in *Sculpting in Time*: "Pictures, visual images, are far better to achieve that end than any words, particularly now, when the world has lost all mystery and magic and speech has become mere chatter—empty of meaning."[7]

The pathos of his films explores man's capacity for feeling, not the intellect. Ironically, some people are under the impression that his films are "intellectual" in nature. A close look at his work demonstrates that all of the idle talk of some of his characters is always juxtaposed with profound silence that refutes all forms of overintellectualization. A significant scene has Chris and Hari reading a passage from one of Cervantes's works: "I only know Señor, that while I am sleeping I have neither fear nor hope, nor delight, nor glory. Sleep makes the shepherd equal to the king. It has only one fault . . . it looks like death."[8]

Sartorius offers a toast to science and Snouth,as if to curtail the effect of the reading of the text. But Snouth does not share in his respect for science. He says:

> Science? Nonsense! In this situation, mediocrity and genius are equally helpless. We don't want to conquer space at all. We want to expand Earth endlessly. We don't want other worlds; we want a mirror. We seek contact and will never achieve it. We are in the foolish position of a man striving for a goal he fears and doesn't want. Man needs man![9]

Hari enlightens the scientists by telling them that the "guests," as they are called, represent their conscience. "They are yourselves," she tells them. *Solaris* has a surreal quality that is reflective of man as an interior being who lives outwardly on borrowed time. It is interesting to speculate on the nature of a form of reality that projects our memories into the external world as materializations for all to speculate. In our cyber age, we find ourselves debating the nature of intellectual ownership, hyper public reality placing man's internal character up for review. What effect would a reality such as that on the Solaris station have on man, if our memories become public property? What tyrannical control would the public sphere have over our lives in such a world? Isn't it enough that we give the world a portion of ourselves through our actions, works of art, conversations, emotions, writing, and goodwill?

The reliving of memories on the Solaris station suggests a phenomenological reduction, whereby we would take time out to reflect or "relive" our past to the detriment of our present life. This form of reality might actually harbor a state of hell for us. Some people might become addicted to their past. This surreal sense of life is invoked in Bruegel's painting *Hunters in the Snow*. The painting is reflective of how the people and places in the painting are only real to us in the same degree that we are real to Solaris' overseeing ocean.

Hari, too, begins to have memories. She has a memory of herself in the snow. Tarkovsky brings those on the station back to their present state of being through the periodical thirty seconds of weightlessness that the station experiences. This oscillation between what is real and what is merely a memory creates a timeless, emotional buoyancy in the lives of those onboard. This compounds a phenomenological commentary on the film.

Chris is moved by what he feels for Hari and how his sensations are real regardless of their illusory nature. He contemplates staying on the space station in order to not let go of his memories of her. He believes that in doing so he will find new longevity for the reality that he values most: his love for Hari. Chris believes that we only love what we can lose. He says: "Maybe the very purpose of our existence is to perceive mankind as the reason for love. Shame! That's what will save mankind."[10] This same point is proposed by Rantes, the mysterious and spiritually gifted protagonist of *Man Facing Southeast (Hombre Mirando al Sudeste)*. In that film, Rantes, who shows up in an asylum, tells the head physiatrist that he does not understand how humans can bury their dead so easily. Rantes does not want to let go of his loved ones.

Staying on the station comes with a heavy price. Chris can be with Hari but he must witness her death again. Chris asks Dr. Snouth, "Snouth, why does he (the ocean) torture us?" Dr. Snouth answers: "We've lost our sense of the cosmic." Tarkovsky suggests that for those involved in the Solaris project, a sense of the cosmic returns only under dire and abnormal conditions. What makes this reality so surreal is that often what is most translucent, what is closest to us, is also what we neglect the most.

Snouth counters Chris's longing for understanding with the notion that we only ask ultimate questions when we are unhappy. He tells Chris, as if to play devil's advocate: "When a man is happy, the meaning of life and other eternal questions don't interest him. Those are questions to be asked at life's end." South's comment can be interpreted in several ways. He might not be aware of the passage of time like Chris, or he is afraid to confront such questions. Chris counters by telling him: "We don't know when the end will come, so we hurry." But Snouth is not prepared to drop the question. He tells Chris: "The happiest are those who never ask these damned questions." Dr. Snouth appears irritated by such questions. Chris's rebuttal is essentially the main point of the film: "Questioning means a desire to know. But to preserve basic truth, we need mysteries. The mysteries of happiness . . . death . . . love." The importance to the film of these few lines of dialogue cannot be undermined. On several occasions throughout the film, the subject of exploration and knowledge comes up as a central focus of the lives of those involved in the project. Back in Chris's home, at the start of the film, this appeared to be the main plot vehicle of the film. When they are watching the video of the conference, the viewer gets the impression that Chris will join the others on the station to solve a scientific problem. This is what scientist do and what most viewers expect of this genre. But *Solaris* is not a typical science fiction film. It will frustrate the viewer who expects high-flying special effects, alien beings, and exploration of a merely physical nature.

Tarkovsky's point in the aforementioned dialogue is not to come across as a skeptic or critic of science. When he says that knowledge safeguards a sense of mystery, he is suggesting a Socratic notion that to know is to know that reason has a limit. Either we can know all things, eventually, or we can know all things at once. The latter point is not the case. This leaves us with the possibility that we can attain knowledge in the future. The eventuality of knowledge is contingent on our desire to know. To want to know originates in our recognition of ignorance. Tarkovsky suggests that our ignorance has always been greater than the scope of our knowledge.

When Chris sees Hari upon first arriving on the station, he becomes confused. Progressively, this confusion leads to a sense of disorientation, that keeps him guessing whether Hari is even real. As he becomes more attached to her materialization, he is taken hold of by his emotions. Naturally, he finds her presence to be a gift. However, he decides to return to Earth. His decision is based on the understanding that his memories of Hari are real as long as he feels them, and not when they are the effect of a cosmic hallucination. Chris's decision to return to Earth is a sacrifice in the sense that he can easily remain on the station and use the ocean as a form of projector, where memories are conveyed in three dimensions. The ocean serves Tarkovsky much the same way that the murti-bing pill serves Witkiewicz in his novel *Insatiability:* as a narcotic that assuages the passage of time and the heaviness of human existence.[11]

The film ends as it begins, with scenes of flowing water and Chris walking around the woods by his father's house. His return home is more than just a physical return. In visiting the space station, Chris discovered a sense of cosmic mystery that he must retain in his worldly existence. This is the strongest suggestion that Tarkovsky makes at the end of the film. The water that surrounds his father's house is not only a symbol of nature, but also vital renewal. Tarkovsky's juxtaposes vital and immediate existence with the overtly intellectual. Solaris' ocean signifies a realm of pure thought, pure consciousness. At the end of the film, we are made to see how such a one-dimensional aspect of human existence necessitates an infusion of the concrete and vital. The profound irony in the film is that Tarkovsky makes use of what some have criticized as a too cerebral form of filmmaking to emphasize vital life.[12]

STALKER

Like *Solaris*, *Stalker* is a science fiction film that breaks with the traditional themes of this genre. *Stalker* begins with a quote from an interview that Professor Wallace, a Nobel Prize winner, gives to RAI press. The caption reads: "What was it? A meteorite that fell to Earth? Or a visitation from outer space? Whatever it was, there appeared in our small land a miracle of miracles: the ZONE. We sent in troops, none returned. Then we surrounded the ZONE with police cordons. We did right . . . although I'm not sure."[13]

What is significant about the quote is that a scientist should use the word miracle in describing aspects of the physical world. Also, the word itself depicts a zone of mystery that goes beyond physical devastation. As Stalker lies in bed with his wife and young daughter in a grungy room, the room begins to shake due to a passing train. They live in an industrial area. He goes to the kitchen in what is essentially a barren home. His wife follows him and asks a series of questions: "Why did you take my watch?" "Where are you going?" She is concerned that he will be killed going back to the ZONE. She tells him: "You promised me . . . I believed you. If you don't want to think about yourself, what about us? Think about your child. She's not even used to you yet and you're back to your old ways." She doesn't want him to return to the ZONE; he has already served five years in prison for taking people there.

Stalker's wife is concerned with the danger that he will encounter the state authorities that closed off the area. He welcomes the enchantment that the ZONE incites. Stalker essentially treats the ZONE as fertile moral ground for the initiated. When he takes people there, they are instructed to respect its internal principles. The ZONE demands a level of spiritual engagement from those who enter it. Tarkovsky's Stalker is a kind of Prometheus who disperses cosmic secrets to man. Unlike Prometheus, Stalker understands the inherent dangers of the knowledge that the ZONE dispenses. His fundamental problem is that he cannot guarantee the moral and spiritual integrity of those who enter with him.

Stalker meets the two people that he is to take into the ZONE in a small and unkempt café. They go by the simple description of writer and professor. As stalker approaches writer, who is talking to a woman who is dropping him off, he hears writer utter the following words to her: "The world is governed by cast-iron laws, and that is terribly boring. And don't know how to be broken. It was interesting to live in the Middle Ages, each house had a goblin, each church had a God."[14] Writer tells the professor that he is going into the ZONE because "I've lost my inspiration. I'm going to beg for some."[15] The little physical action that occurs in the film takes place in the opening sequences. Driving through the entrance to the ZONE, where armed guards are posted, is the epitome of action in *Stalker*. Physical danger does not concern Stalker in the least bit. Driving the professor's jeep up to the gate where the ZONE begins seems a mundane exercise for him. Driving through the entrance of the ZONE, they are shot at, but they are not pursued. Once inside the ZONE, they ride a railroad handcar closer to the center. When this episode comes to an end, the film takes on a sense of calmness that continues until the end. At this point, the film becomes colored, while before it was sepia color.

Stalker was taught everything he knows about the ZONE from a man who is referred to as "Porcupine" who brought people there for many years. This conversation about Porcupine is important because in telling the viewer that Stalker was imprisoned several times for stalking, we come to an understanding of what Stalker does and why. Who is Stalker stalking? He stalks no one. Why then do the authorities make it illegal for anyone to go to the

ZONE? After the meteorite hit the village and burned it down twenty years earlier, stories began to circulate that the center of the ZONE granted wishes that became true. The problem began, Stalker tells us, when the ZONE was "guarded by barbed wire, for who knows what wishes a person might have." This explains the government restrictions as well as his reticence to take just anyone there for fear of what they may find. The film's symbolism alludes to the notion that in order to attain truth, they must not go straight ahead—the shortest path always being the most dangerous.

When Writer walks away on his own, he makes Stalker nervous because he fears that he too will become affected by Writers' irrationality. Stalker cautions: "The ZONE's a maze of traps. All of them death traps." When Stalker lies down to rest, he hears a voice that tells him a story of how man can destroy himself due to his intemperance.

Stalker and *Solaris* contain many scenes of water. Water in Tarkovsky's films serves as a form of purity and renewal. The scene when they enter a tunnel and come out in another strange room that is filled with water signals a rite of passage for those who have completed the trek. Writer levels an unforgettable confession at anyone that is willing to listen.

"But what's the use of your knowledge? Whose conscience will be bothered by it? Mine? I have no conscience. Only nerves. Some rat will pain me; it leaves a wound. Another rat will praise me: it leaves another wound. You put your soul into it, your heart into. They'll devour your heart and your soul. Remove filth from your soul: they'll devour filth. Why, they are all literate! They suffer of sensory hunger. They keep crowding around: the editors, the critics, the endless dames. All of them clamoring for more! More! What kind of writer am I if I detest writing! If it's torture, a painful, shameful occupation, something akin to extruding pities."[16]

This is a significant conversation that signifies Tarkovsky's critique of the coldness of intellectualizing over vital emotions. What writer is describing is an impersonal world, where no one can retain the right to his or her personal vision. The problem with the wishing well at the center of the ZONE is that our wishes mean nothing when devoid of sweat and will. The import of Tarkovsky's point concerning human vision suggests that sincerity and purity are attained through suffering:

> I used to think that my books helped some to become better. Why, nobody needs me! I'll croak and in two days they'll be devouring somebody else. I had hoped to change them, but they changed me! To fit their own image! Once, the future was only a combination of the present. Its changes loomed beyond the horizon. But now the future's a part of the present. Are they prepared for this? They don't want to know anything, all they do is gabble![17]

Besides being visually stunning, *Stalker* manifests the truth contained in axioms. Tarkovsky is adamant about not talking his story through. Yet this is what seems most apparent to the casual viewer of his films. What appears to be a diatribe against editors and readers in Writer's commentary turns out to be a heartfelt look at the anatomy of disillusionment. Writer's disparaging comments on the nature of writing come as the result of placing a great degree of faith in the written word. His disappointment is metaphysical. Because we know very little about what constitutes his life, besides writing, we come to view his statements as universal examples of life itself. His level of disenchantment remains universal in the same measure that axioms achieve their desired goal: he speaks about principles and not particular oddities. He has the following to say about the wishing-room at the center of the ZONE: "But world supremacy? A just society? These aren't wishes, but an ideology, action, concepts. Subconscious compassion cannot yet be realized as a common, instructive wish."[18]

Writer's verbalizing of his knowledge is indicative of Tarkovsky's regard for the dichotomous rift that he views as central to human reality. The problem is the attainment and subsequent objectification of knowledge. Writer undergoes an internal dialectical settling about the truths inherent in human reality. He guides his actions with his understanding. His problem is to make his knowledge known. Stalker's conversation with Writer finds the latter man at a crossroad in his life. Writer comes on the trip in an attempt to reconcile himself to vital existence—that he has lost due to his cynicism. His attempt is sabotaged by the thing that he is trying to run away from: himself. He makes no progress as a consequence.

Writer and Professor are philosophical materialists performing an experiment. Professor has a past that he wants cleared. His motivation for going to the ZONE has to do with a vendetta. Stalker worries about the type of people that he takes to the ZONE, for the ZONE is a Pandora's Box, where good and evil are manifest. Stalker's idea of human life is summarized by the notion that we see and feel what we are capable of and no more. He tells the others: "Music: If it has anything at all to do with life its mechanical, lacking ideas or associations. But it goes right to your soul. What chord in us responds to its harmonies? What gives us such pleasure, and unites us, and stirs us so? In the long run, everything has a meaning and a season."[19]

After their return from the ZONE, Stalker appears to be the one who has suffered the most. While the other two appear to be merely entertained by the experiment, it is Stalker who returns home to his wife, disenchanted. He is disillusioned that he cannot improve the circumstances of the other two men. Stalker does not fashion arguments to debunk the overintellectualizing of Writer and Professor; he lives his emotions and is subsequently guided by them. Is there a dichotomy in human existence between the intellect and our emotions? When Stalker returns home, he talks to his wife in a different manner. He is shocked by the world of the men he has come into contact with. He tells her: "Some intellectuals, those writers and scientists. They don't believe in anything! They've lost their sense of hope! My God! What kind people are they?"[20]

His return home is the culmination of the story. If Tarkovsky had ended the film in the ZONE, the film would have remained a tale of adventure and self-discovery. Given Stalker's paralyzing disenchantment when he returns home, the story progresses into a broader scope than just the fulfillment of three people. This rounding effect to the film is best understood when Stalker's wife tells him: "It's not their fault. They should be pitied."[21] Her allusion is indicative of the split between life and the intellect that defines modern life.[22] Stalker, still reeling from his shock at the emptiness of the men that he has just spend some time with, adds:

> But their eyes are black! They keep worrying about getting their full share. Getting paid for every breath they take! They know they weren't born for nothing. Can their kind believe in anything? Nobody believes. It's not just these two. But the worst of it is that nobody needs this. Nobody needs the room.[23]

Once he returns to the simplicity of his room, his wife, and his handicapped young daughter, he puts into perspective the difference between his world and allegedly worldly and sophisticated intellectuals. Stalker is kept rooted in reality by his core beliefs. At the end of the film, we understand that the room at the center of the ZONE confronts people who enter it with a moment of truth, when we must make sense of reality based on our beliefs and convictions. The room confronts people with the limits of the knowable and what this means for human existence. Reflection has a transformative and cathartic power.

Tarkovsky elaborates on human existence and aesthetics in his book *Sculpting in Time*. Tarkovsky's cinematic vision transcends his films. His vision is made manifest by the reflective clarity of his spiritual embrace of reality. Tarkovsky's sense of reality is brilliantly transformed into a visual collage, a reflective aesthetic sense for the sublime.

NOTES

1. Ortega y Gasset, José. *The Dehumanization of Art*. Princeton: Princeton University Press, 1972, 25.

2. Tarkovsky, Andrei. *Sculpting in Time*. Translated from the Russian by Kitty Hunter Blair. Austin: University of Texas, 1986, 198.

3. Ibid., 15.

4. Ibid., 198.

5. Ibid., 183.

6. Andrei Tarkovsky. *Solaris*. New York: Fox Lorber Home Video, 1991

7. Ibid. *Solaris*.

8. Ibid. *Solaris*.

9. *Sculpting in Time*, 228.

10. *Solaris*.

11. Stanislaw Ignacy Witkiewicz. *Insatiability*. Witkiewicz's novel is perhaps the greatest example of the brave new world that man seeks; like small children, their sole responsibility being to play in make-believe worlds. His narrator says: "That they were living, thinking, sentient creatures seems indisputable, whereas the existence of inorganic matter, of the sort physics would like to posit on the basis of data derived from its own mundane vision of the world, would seem highly problematic, unless one assumes the existence of a mundane dualism, a mundane 'pre-conceived order,' and that people have altogether ceased to think in a mundane way—so there! The 'collapsing' of time was un en-dur-able. Life teetered on an arête like a seesaw. On one side were sunny valleys of normality and great numbers of cozy little retreats; on the other loomed the murky gorges and chasm of madness, smoking with thick gases and glowing with molten lava –valle inferno, kingdom of eternal remorse and unbearable guilt," 400.

12. In *Sculpting in Time* Tarkovsky develops a spiritual aesthetics that cannot be separated from man's vital responsibility for his own existence. He writes: "I am convinced that any attempt to restore harmony in the world can only rest on the renewal of personal responsibility," 235.

13. Andrei Tarkovsky. *Stalker*. New York: Fox Lorber Home Video, 1993.

14. *Stalker*.

15. *Stalker*.

16. *Stalker*.

17. *Stalker*.

18. *Stalker*.

19. *Stalker*.

20. *Stalker*.

21. *Stalker*.

22. Allusions to this dualism are in evidence throughout *Sculpting in Time*.

23. *Stalker*.

Chapter Three

Fahrenheit 451
A Brave New World for the New Man

FAHRENHEIT 451

Synopsis

Fahrenheit 451 is French cineaste, François Truffaut's only English-language film. It is a film adaptation of Ray Bradbury's book of the same name; a dystopia of totalitarian world order, where books are outlawed and consequently burned. Beyond book burning, *Fahrenheit 451* is about the annihilation of the individual by a brutal totalitarian dictatorship. This film is a fine example of why a reflective metaphysical/existential approach to human existence makes for a higher existence that does not owe allegiance to day-to-day sensuality.

Truffaut's *Fahrenheit 451* begins with a striking narration of the film's credits. The premise is simple: talk becomes the natural medium in an illiterate state. When the firemen, that is, the book burners, arrive at a high-rise with orders to burn books, we are immediately struck by the stark and vulgar aesthetics of the buildings that are so typical in totalitarian countries—globs of spiritless, unimaginative, state-commissioned modernism.

This drab and socially engineered reality is contrasted with the imaginative ways in which readers hide their books: one book is hidden in a ceiling lamp, more are found in a hollowed-out television set, and others in the tight confines of a heater. It is difficult to imagine greater realism than this depiction of the double morality—the duplicity forced on its citizens by totalitarian systems.[1]

Fahrenheit 451 is more than an allegory of the future and the dangers that lurk for modern man in the totalitarian state. In many respects, the film as well as the novel are studies of a type of human temperament that prides itself in tyranny and destruction.

The twentieth century ushered in the creation of institutionalized mass control in the twin murderous ideologies that are: communism and Nazism. In terms of the moral double-dealing that these systems of physical and psychological terror thrive on, consider what Arkady Shevchenko, United Nations under-secretary-general and former advisor to Soviet Foreign Minister Andrei Gromyko, wrote after his much-publicized defection to the United States in 1978:

> So, I had become part of the stratum that tried to portray itself as fighting what it coveted. While criticizing the bourgeois way of life, its only passion was to possess it; while condemning consumerism as a manifestation of philistine psychology, a result of poisonous Western influence, the privileged valued above all else the consumer goods and comforts of the West. I was not immune. The gulf between what was said and what was done was oppressive, but more oppressive still was what I had to do to widen the gap. I tried to remember everything I ever said, and what others had told me, because my survival and success depended greatly upon that. I pretended to believe what I did not, and to place the interests of the Party and the state above my own, when in fact I did just the opposite. After I had lived that kind of life for years, I began to see Dorian Gray's real picture in my shaving mirror.[2]

The confusion that has been propagated by many commentators of Ray Bradbury's *Fahrenheit 451* neglect that Bradbury wrote the novel in 1950, as a vivid commentary on Stalin's communist Soviet Union. A striking example of Bradbury's purpose in writing *Fahrenheit 451* is Shevchenko's description of his discovery of bookstores in one of his diplomatic forays to New York: "But for me, the crown, the jewel, of the great city was its bookstores. If I had been allowed, I would have spent all my time in them. The variety of titles, including Russian-language books by Soviet émigrés and defectors, was seductive, almost overpowering."[3] His appraisal is an honest discovery of someone who is privileged member of a totalitarian state. Many critics have wasted a vast number of pages describing fantastical future worlds and future book burners without acknowledging the essence of the novel or the film.[4]

Fahrenheit 451 is more complicated than just a mere look at some future horror story that has the state as its protagonist. Both, the novel and the film, are a study of what the seminal twentieth-century thinker Karl Popper has called the "tribal instinct" in his book *The Open Society and its Enemies*. Popper views democracy as a system of values that is diametrically opposed to collectivism, a movement of individual autonomy that moves away from a deeply seated collective tribal longing of man. Popper's anthropological description goes a long way in explaining the motives of the fire chief in

Fahrenheit 451. For instance, Popper argues that what has traditionally been the lure of some intellectuals toward the totalitarian impulse is merely the longing to return to a more primitive, tribal, and communistic social set-up. This serves as a significant analysis of the plight of democracy as a historical process, given Popper's notion that the open society is a perpetual attempt at humanizing the social-political process. This is an important point to consider in the film, especially as we get to know the chief.

High school and college students are often confronted with "what if" and "in the future" scenarios of governments that could potentially threaten our civil liberties. Myopic critics remind us of sinister plots by secret and mysterious people and organizations that operate in the shadows of civility. Yet this all goes very much against the grain of Bradbury's purpose in writing the book in the first place. Most of the aforementioned commentators seem to be awaiting a future world where the events, cynicism, and mood of *Fahrenheit 451* will be put on display. The problem with this naive historical sense is that the time line of the future that such commentators envision is one that simultaneously moves along with our present time. In other words, to assume that the future is always a time to come is tantamount to practicing a fundamentally flawed logic. People who promote dystopias like *Fahrenheit 451* and *1984* are guided by dangerous passions. If the future offers us a frightening face, it is not because it is the future, but because such events can come true. If a given form of future is possible, it arises our curiosity because we deem it possible. The future concerns us because we understand that regardless of our desire to waddle in a static-present condition, some form of future will eventually manifest itself as a yet-to-arrive present. This is not conjecture, rather mere understanding of the passage of time. The question then becomes, "which of these future horrors have already come to pass?"

The artistic value of *Fahrenheit 451*, the novel and the film, is twofold: to recognize that the artist is depicting a present existing condition through a fictional medium that was once only a future possibility, and that the future is a potential reality—if it is to exist at all. The obvious fact in all of this is simply that the future cannot exist merely as a projection of a sophomoric imagination. Isn't this why we plan ahead and anticipate problems and dilemmas that can arise?

Regardless of our inability or desire to recognize institutionalized evil, the book burners in both the novel and Truffaut's film already have had and continue to have their day. These book burners have already burned, defamed, distorted, and rewritten history. The problem is that this continues to happen while the very elements responsible for doing so continue to direct our attention to a future science-fiction world. The illiterates that Bradbury comments on are not the simple firemen but the masterminds who commission a deeply held hatred of truth. Bradbury makes this point clear in an interview that he gave Robert Couteau in 1991. When asked how the fall of the Berlin Wall would affect science fiction, Bradbury said:

> I don't think it will affect it much. Because we've always talked about freedom, we've always talked about totalitarian governments. After all, *Fahrenheit 451* is all about Russia, and all about China, isn't it? And all about the totalitarians everywhere, either left or right, doesn't matter where they are, they're book burners, all of them. And so *Fahrenheit 451* will continue to be a read book, by people all over the world, 'cause there are still totalitarian governments.[5]

What is it about books—that is, those that purport to tell the truth—that brings out the censorial, collective impulse in people of a totalitarian temperament? While censors ultimately arrive at a cul-de-sac when attempting to silence individuals, this same task becomes simplified when dealing with entire classes of people. Part of the reason for this has to do with envy and resentment. Historically, we have witnessed that it is more efficient for totalitarianism to attack goodwill and truth by allowing its apparatus of disenfranchisement operate through collective measures. This enables the totalitarian temperament of the would-be leaders of such a state to flourish. An example of this is the rapid response brigades for the defense of the state that are so integral a part of the totalitarian state. In the film, we see this same resentment in Fabian, Montag's colleague.

Another artistic quality of *Fahrenheit 451* is its ability to portray the manner in which totalitarian praxis erodes our ability to decipher reality. After they burn a huge bag of books that they have confiscated, Montag (Oskar Werner) is called over by the chief and asked what kind of books he just burned. The question is neither innocent or spontaneous. Instead, it is an example of the machinations of the terror state probing to qualify what it determines to be thought crimes. Montag naively answers that he does not really know: "I don't know, I was not paying attention." Then the chief asks: "What does Montag do on his day off duty?" We cannot help but notice the artificial distance created between the apparatchiks in control and their subjects. Montag answers: "Mow the lawn." The chief's duplicity and suspicion is not easily abetted. He continues: "And what if the laws forbid that?" Montag has no choice but to continue to answer in a manner that has been inculcated in him: "Watch it grow sir." The chief then smiles with relief, a definite sign that Pavlov's dog is behaving as programmed. What is so important about the chief's level of suspicion is the insistence of subjecting human beings to a barrage of theoretical hypothesis, each which has been designed to illicit fear in the person being questioned. The intent is to remind the person in question that he must remain abreast of the moral, intellectual, cultural, and political mandates of mother state. These dictates include an ever-expanding catalog of crimes of intent or what amount to thought crimes. He then says to Montag: "Good. Montag might be hearing some important news in a day or two." A promotion is what the chief has in store for him, but first comes the obligatory stamp of submission to the state.

On his trip home on the monorail Montag is approached by a young woman who tells him that they make the same trip every day and that they should talk. This juxtaposition is a stroke of genius on Truffaut's behalf. While the chief is cynical and sinister, as the state demands of its subjects, the young woman is spontaneous, sincere, and genuinely interested in exchanging ideas. She asks if he does not mind talking—already a sign of a coerced existence—Montag answers, nervously: "No, no. Go ahead talk. I can't promise to think of anything to answer, though." In an open society, Montag's awkward admission to the young woman on the train would merely qualify him as socially inept, someone that lacks all social graces. But because he is an automaton regulated by a suffocating state, his response, "I can't promise to think of anything to answer, though," takes on a gravity that can only be described as pitiful. It is important to realize that he does not say, "I don't have anything to say" now, at this moment, but rather "I can't promise to think." Given the all-engulfing political climate in which he lives, not thinking becomes a natural response for him.

When they get off the monorail and begin to walk, she looks at his firemen outfit and asks him what the inscription "Fahrenheit 451" that he has on his collar means. After he tells her that the number signifies the temperature at which paper catches fire and begins to burn, she then asks him if it is true that a long time ago firemen actually put out fires and not burn books. His response is genuine, even though pitiful: "Put fires out? Who told you that? What a strange idea. The young woman's natural curiosity does not faze Montag. He is stunned to hear that there are people who think as she does. She then asks him: "Why do you burn books?" His answer could not be more nonchalant: "A job like any other? We burn them to ashes and then burn the ashes. That's our motto." The state has trained him to do his work well and be proud. He tells her that people read books "precisely because it is forbidden. Books make people unhappy. Books disturb people. They make them antisocial." What he means by this is that reading books is a form of leisure; leisure is the great sin in a totalitarian state. Life in a totalitarian state must always be on the move: marching, demonstrating, picketing, attending Party meetings, communicating private thoughts and emotions with Party officials who are best adept at determining one's mental and emotional standing.

If one way to measure the power of science fiction films is through their power of persuasion and appeal to memory, then *Fahrenheit 451* remains at the top of the list. The measure of its value is not strictly historical acuity, but aesthetics. The brilliance of Truffaut's direction is his masterful integration of realism with a visionary stance on the nature of man, time and human existence. His adaptation of the novel pays serious respect to Bradbury's novel, even though it is more realistic than the novel, at least as a visual medium. That was not an easy task for Truffaut. He writes in a letter dated from January 14, 1963: "I think that, after *Fahrenheit*, I'll give up adaptations in favor of original screenplays, which are unquestionably easier to do."[6]

It is a strong compliment to Bradbury and Truffaut that the film version of *Fahrenheit 451* remains one of the most realistic science fiction films of all time. *Fahrenheit 451*'s great contribution to humanism and cinema is its indictment of totalitarianism in our time. Few science fiction films create a sophisticated aesthetic, through narrative clarity and visuals, and remain grounded in the reality depicted.

FAHRENHEIT 451 AND OTHER "WHAT IF . . . " SCENARIOS

When compared with other prominent science fiction films, *Fahrenheit 451* is undeniably a unique work of cinema. Robert Wise's 1951 *The Day the Earth Stood Still* is an interesting film that paints man's human reality in a provincial light vis-à-vis cosmic visitors. This is not a story of a de facto visitor, but one of possibilities. *Enemy From Space*, following much the same angle of *The Day the Earth Stood Still*, is the initial entry of director Val Guest's trilogy, which was followed by *The Creeping Unknown* and *Five Years to Earth*. In *Enemy From Space*, aliens take over the governments of the world, as is also the case in Don Siegel's (1956) *Invasion of the Body Snatchers*.

Films that deal with apocalyptic themes like, *Last Man on Earth* (1964) and its remake, *The Omega Man* (1971) are provocative in their appeal to demonstrate that the last human is always essentially a proto first man. These two films deal with the search for a serum that will cure a plague epidemic. These are chilling portrayals of "what-if" scenarios. Also similar to *Fahrenheit 451*'s social science theme is Michael Anderson's 1976 film *Logan's Run*. This film is about a society where the mandatory age/life limit is 30. Even more radical is the premise of *Soylent Green* (1973), a tale of New York City in the year 2022, when food has become so scarce that the government is forced to create a new food source called soylent green. *Soylent Green* is an imaginative reminder of primitive cannibalism in the form of recycled humans. Directors have treated the world of the future in some very interesting ways; the 1936 adaptation of H.G. Wells book *Things to Come* and the time travel scenario offered in George Pal's *The Time Machine*, in 1960.

The Twilight Zone television series offered a clinic of metaphysical themes that ennobled us with its literary flair and lucid writing. Suffice it to say that even though *2021* explores several key themes, one that receives the least attention is the malfunction of its HAL 9000 computer. In the late 1960s computers where still mammoth machines whose performance was all but a mystery to the general public. To suggest that a master computer could malfunction and in doing so jeopardize an entire space mission and the lives of its crew was only a possibility for engineers. This theme takes on more relevance today given our reliance on computers.

Another fascinating film that explores the future of technology is *Colossus: The Forbin Project*. Colossus is a supercomputer that is used by the defense department, until the electronic beast has a plan of its own for world domination. The computer is given free rein to control the national defense of the United States. Technologically speaking, this makes sense given its memory capacity and the speed at which it can decipher problems. But when Colossus begins to communicate with a similar Soviet supercomputer, its human counterparts are left out of the equation. The two computers create a language of their own and refuse to take any orders from their respective programmers. At the end of the film, Charles Forbin, the engineer who designed and operates Colossus, is literally held hostage by the computer. The philosophical implications of such films abound with daunting examples of recent technological developments.

Westworld also has much to say about a world that demands gadgets for our ever-expanding recreational needs. Are we so bored that we demand infinite varieties of entertainment? Are we so morally, spiritually, and existentially empty that we must constantly seek external stimuli to fulfill our incessant catalog of pleasures? How much has the vital will to live deteriorated for people in hyper-democratic societies, where drug use is encouraged, while simultaneously lamenting its abuse? How can we accurately measure the spiritual implications of a society that craves elective aesthetic surgery for self-gratification? The reality behind this phenomenon suggests a deeper level of spiritual malaise. In John Frankenheimer's 1966 film, *Seconds*, a middle-aged man who is bored with his status quo decides to receive a new identity, one that begins with the reconstruction of his face. His prior state of boredom pales in comparison with his newly found level of horror and regret.

Another interesting aspect of *Fahrenheit 451* is that Montag's eventual curiosity about books is indirectly inspired by his wife, Linda (Julie Christie). The contrast between burning books and the daily televised state sermons serves as the pivoting point for Montag's eventual turnaround. Montag's quest becomes to counter the behaviorist's dream of a totally engineered society. Montag awakens to the reality that surrounds him because his curiosity can no longer be suppressed. His effort to reconstitute himself is a heroic act, when he leaves behind a primitive collective and embarks on a voyage of self-discovery. Now, his sense of wonder must work for understanding.

The Greek word for truth, Alētheia, demonstrates an objective intransigence that readily surprises the casual observer. Perpetually dovetailing, Alētheia teases the seeker of truth with its revealing un-revealing nature. When Montag begins to discover that reality is more expansive than the mandates of a totalitarian council, only then does he realize how much work his newfound loneliness entails. Alfred North Whitehead makes this point clear in *Modes of Thought*: "In other words, reaction to the environment is not in proportion to clarity of sensory experience. Any such doctrine would sweep away the whole of modern physical science as being expressed in terms of irrelevancies. Reaction does not depend upon sense experiences for its initiation."[7]

When Montag goes home, he finds his zombie wife watching television—again. The program is bombastic and propagandistic. She greets him by telling him about the importance of acquiring another wall unit. The wall unit is a huge television. Montag is not taken in by the stupidity that he witnesses coming from the daily broadcasts. The commentator has the following to say about the enemies of the public peace: "Today's figure for operations in urban areas alone account for the elimination of a total of 2,750 pounds of conventional editions; 826 first editions, and 17 pounds of manuscripts were also destroyed. 23 antisocial elements were detained pending reeducation."[8]

The antisocial elements in question are the book readers. The pseudo news broadcasts are important to the film early on because they eventually force Montag to seek the truth on his own. It is interesting to note that these same antisocial book readers are currently being arrested in communist Cuba, for attempting to organize public libraries that operate out of private homes.[9] As for the reeducation part of the broadcast, this is a staple of socialpolitical control and humiliation in totalitarian nations.

The only time that Montag's wife is seen animated is when she plays an alleged part in a televised play, where the audience is asked to say how good it feels to be part of the collective family that is the state. Montag shocks her naive sensibility when he tells her that the state probably put 200,000 Linda's in the play. She tells him that this cannot be true, "and even if it were, you didn't have to tell me. That was very mean." Her response has everything to do with her state-induced, feel-good, excessive tolerance that has turned her into an automaton. After this exchange she takes more nerve-calming pills while Montag sits in bed reading a wordless newspaper.

The next day we witness Montag back at work. Montag teaches the technique of book searching inside homes, because "to learn to find, we must first learn how to hide." Montag is summoned to the chief's office and told he is being considered for a promotion. There we see the cynical chief asking Montag personal questions that have no bearing on his qualifications. The chief primes Montag as to the nature of being a fireman. In a revealing scene, the chief tells Montag: "Keep them busy and you keep them happy. That's what matters." After asking Montag more questions, he tells him: "Montag has one quality that I appreciate greatly, he says very little."

When Montag arrives home that evening, he finds his wife Linda on the floor. She has overdosed on a variety of mood-enhancing pills. He calls rescue and they ask what kind of pills she takes. This is an admission that a great number of the population is taking such pills. When the medics enter the house, they are ready to pump her stomach. Their matter-of-fact manner and jokes are impersonal. They inform Montag that they handle over fifty overdose cases per day.

Montag gradually awakes to the reality that he is a book burner. One day after work Montag arrives home and takes out a copy of Dickens *The Personal History of David Copperfield*. He can barely read. Upon opening a book, he does not discriminate between the title and publisher information. He reads aloud and very slowly, like a child who is learning to read. This scene is of fundamental importance to the film because for the first time we see Montag engaged in a genuinely private moment. His eyes glide through the page with great anticipation. He is thrilled by his discovery of books and the written word.

Montag undergoes a transformation that removes him intellectually, culturally, and morally from the Platonic cave that the state keeps him in. He experiences existential awakening. Gabriel Marcel argues that the toil of daily life in a modern, open society, and more so in the stale air of totalitarian oppression stymies self-reflection. He explains in *Tragic Wisdom and Beyond*:

> Many of us know from experience how one can come to grips with himself in calm and solitude. But that happens only if one enjoys a certain inner permanence, and present conditions of life, the influence of radio and television especially, tend to obliterate any performance of this kind, as Max Picard has seen so clearly, replace it with a discontinuity to which one may at first merely submit but which one ends up demanding. Why? Because above all each of us wants to be distracted. We want our attention diverted. From what? To say from ourselves would probably be wrong. I would rather say it is from a certain emptiness experienced in an agonizing way as an anticipation of death.[10]

As Montag reads *David Copperfield*, there is a cut to a scene of the firemen raiding a park and searching elderly women and babies. The juxtaposition of Montag's innocence while reading and the chief's aggressiveness in searching a baby goes a long way in explaining Montag's growing discomfort with his job. Innocence is further explored when Clarisse, the young woman Montag meets on the train, follows him to work to inform him that she has been fired from her job as a teacher. Montag can't believe this has happened. He accompanies her to the school to talk to the principal. When they are walking through the school hall, two small children run away upon seeing her—a clear indication that her superiors have poisoned the well. Seeing her distraught state, he confides to her that he has read a book.

At this point in the film Montag begins to live the same duplicitous life that all readers must live in order to survive. At this juncture in the film, it is interesting to speculate how events will turn out, given that he is in danger. When night falls, Linda comes out of the bedroom to discover Montag sitting at the kitchen table reading a book. She rummages through a closet and finds the rest of the books that Montag has hidden. She confronts him: "I don't want these things in the house. They frighten me," she tells him. He responds: "You spend your whole life with your 'family' on the wall. These books are my family."

Montag's complete turnaround does not take place until the firemen go to an elderly woman's house that holds an entire library. This is one of the most memorable scenes of the film. In the woman, we witness a level of conviction and autonomy that is not shared by any other character up to that point in the film. When the chief discovers the woman's library, he gasps with sinister excitement. He tells Montag that that is a rare moment in the life of a fireman. Here we see the worst of human nature bobbling up to the surface of life: calumny, spite, envy; clearly defined herd instinct. The chief tells Montag, "Go on, Montag. All this philosophy. Let's get rid of it. It's even worse than the novels. Thinkers, philosophers, all of them saying exactly the same thing, only I am right, the others all idiots. One section they tell you that man's destiny is predetermined, the next says that he has freedom of choice. It's just a matter of fashion, that's all. Just like short dresses this year, long dresses next year."

Montag's superior is a fine example of what Ortega y Gasset refers to as mass man in *The Revolt of the Masses*—one who does not want to create, but who keeps others from doing so.[11] The chief continues to demonstrate his shallow, tyrannical nature: "It's no good, Montag. We've all got to be alike. The only way to be happy is for everyone to be equal. So, we must burn the books." The chief serves the role of anti-thinker, a hater of liberty and free will, either by training or temperament. Collectivism of this kind converts everything serious and sublime into spurious cynicism, fashion, cliché, and political propaganda. On the other hand, Montag is a burgeoning idealist who is beginning to discover the intricacies and possibilities of human reality.

Of the many Soviet poets whom were critical of Soviet totalitarianism, we must mention Yevgeny Yevtushenko, Andrei Voznesenky, and Nicolay

Klyuyev; Soviet philosophers, most who started out as Marxists, with the notable exception of Ayn Rand, we must mention Nikolai Berdyaev, Bulgakov, Frank, and P. B. Struve. These thinkers were persecuted by Soviet apparatchiks and labeled idealists. In this regard, idealism simply means, as Lenin dictated, anti-materialist. They were accused of being metaphysicians—this philosophical position, as Engels understood it, merely means to be anti-dialectic. Lastly, we must mention the tragic fate of Osip Mandelstam, who was arrested and later died en route to one of the many Soviet gulags. His wife, the writer Nadezhda Mandelstam, and writer of *Hope Against Hope* ended her days living in poverty and destitution. Vladimir Solovyov, in his insightful work *The Crisis of Western Philosophy* illuminate us, when he writes in reference to the political disposition that lies at the heart of all collective movements:

> Philosophical knowledge is expressly an activity of the personal reason or the separate person in all the clarity of this person's individual consciousness. The subject of philosophy is preeminently the singular I as a knower . . . philosophy is a separate world-view of separate individuals. The common world-view of nations and tribes always has a religious, not a philosophical character.[12]

Montag's expression becomes one of horror when he cannot believe that the woman who owns the books will not leave her house and is willing to die with her books. Furthermore, he can't believe that the woman is murdered by the firemen for the simple reason that she owns books. Montag's mounting frustration finally boils over when he comes home and finds his wife and three of her friends mesmerized by the television. He goes up to them and tells them: "You're just zombies. You're not living, you're just killing time." He then storms over to the television set and turns it off. He can no longer allow himself to be oppressed by pseudo reality. He returns to the living room and tells the women: "When an old woman chooses to be burned with her books rather than be separated from them." When one of the women has the audacity to tell him, "Don't be silly, Montag. Things like that don't happen," he rebutes by telling them, "You mean you don't hear about it. I saw it." Yet his words do not stir up a response, rather disbelief. Linda asks him if he is alright.

Once again, we witness Montag's newly discovered naivete in his zest to read the books smuggles home. He tells Linda, "I've got to read. To catch up with remembrance of the past." Remembrance, he quickly finds out, is the best antidote to state reeducation.

Truffaut infuses *Fahrenheit 451* with literary and cultural astuteness. The film reveals a world of tomorrow that is strange to people who are ignorant of recent history. In Montag, we witness a young man coming of age. Truffaut depicts a social-political claustrophobic world. Missing from the film are people out on the street, gardeners in their yards, and panoramic shots that showcase open vistas.

Montag's new sense of reality finally unravels when Linda asks him: "What about the promotion?" He answers, "My promotion? That was before." Montag goes to Clarisse's house, after he has a nightmare about her. Her house has become condemned. A neighbor tells him that she has been taken away because she was different; the neighbor points at all the homes with television antennas.

A central theme of the film is the power that the state has to brainwash people into making fanatical decisions. Linda places the demands of the state over the love of her husband and household. She turns Montag in to the fire chief. In 1942 Hitler appointed Alfred Rosenberg, born in 1893, as head of political education and the indoctrination of the German people. Rosenberg's fanciful dream included the founding of a mythic Nordic Christianity that would show no residue of Semitic, Etruscan, or Roman influence. Rosenberg's spirited notion of a religious component to National Socialism was offered mainly to strengthen the ideological basis necessary for the formation of a totalitarian government. Rosenberg was found guilty of war crimes by the Nuremberg War Crimes Tribunal and hanged on October 16, 1946. More recently, Gao Xingjian, the 2000 Nobel Prize winner in literature is another case in point of totalitarian oppression. Mr. Xingjian was awarded the Nobel Prize by the Swedish academy for "the bitter insights and linguistic ingenuity in his writing about the struggle for individuality in mass culture." Xingjian, like many other faceless, nameless writers, had to burn his writing during Mao Tse-Tung's 1966–1976 Cultural Revolution due to their content, which was critical of the regime. About his books, which have not been available in China after his expulsion from the country, Xingjian writes: "In China, I could not trust anyone, not even my family. The atmosphere was so poisoned, people were so brainwashed that even someone from your own family could turn you in."[13]

Linda's fanaticism and masochistic devotion to the impersonal power of the state is countered by Clarisse's trust in Montag. She never doubts Montag's ability to see the truth, even though she must wait for his complete break with the state. When she takes him back to her condemned house, she tells him to help her look for a list of collaborators and their hiding places.

The end of the film is a study in disenchantment. When Montag tells the Chief that he is resigning, he is told to go on just one more mission. It turns out that the house the Chief takes Montag to is Montag's home. Montag greets Linda at the door as she leaves with her bags. She merely tells him, "I couldn't bear it. I just couldn't bear it." This is an easy move on her part given that Linda never intimated any notion of love or tenderness toward Montag. As the Chief burns Montag's books, he asks him cynically, "What did Montag hope to get out of all this print, happiness?" Truffaut's close-up shots of the books burning is a marvel of filmmaking that would paralyze any bibliophile in disbelief. As the pages peel away into ashes, we begin to realize the utter evil of having to live in a totalitarian state. That a person should be arrested—their lives destroyed because they read books and have strong convictions is nothing less than institutionalized evil.

Montag burns the Chief in a moment of self-defense and flees into the countryside to meet up with the "book people" that Clarisse has told him about. Montag's fleeing is essentially an act of defection. In one of the most telling examples of totalitarian realism, one of the book people shows Montag's presumed capture on television. The arrest that is shown on television is meant for mass consumption to demonstrate that the state always wins. Of course, the person that they shoot down is not Montag. However, he will have to do. This is a closed society where the state has rewritten history and has the final word about what is real.

NOTES

1. *Fahrenheit 451* is a fine exposition of the double-speak propaganda technique that is the heart and soul of the totalitarian state. Other great dystopias of our time include: Yevgeny Zamyatin's *We*; George Orwell's *Animal Farm* and *1984*, and Aldous Huxley's *Brave New World*. In these works, the written word is stripped of its metaphysical significance. Destruction of meaning, as this is communicated through language has served as the main vehicle for attaining control of reality in totalitarian states, even if this means the murder of those that just cannot "get it." Have these works served as the inspiration for our current barrage of fashionable theories, Methods, and deconstruction of the vital nature of common sense itself? In *We, Animal Farm, Brave New World*, and to a great extent Witkiewicz's *Insatiability*, nothing means what it formerly meant, simply because the project that is the formation of a new man cannot afford this. The new man—a zombie imbued with an intellectual, spiritual, and cultural monstrous dimension—must be cradled through life and watched so that his reeducation does not become contaminated by the sting of reality proper. Zamyatin makes this most clear when he writes in *We*: "If they will not understand that we are bringing them a mathematically infallible happiness, we shall be obliged to force them to be happy. But before taking up arms, we shall try what words can do." See: Yevgeny Zamyatin. *We*. New York: Penguin Books, 1993, 3. Bradbury's *Fahrenheit 451* demonstrates that language, too, is no longer necessary precisely because the dichotomous and often ambiguous nature of reality has now been leveled to what is politically expedient—what is politically correct.

2. Arkady N. Shevchenko. *Breaking with Moscow*. New York: Alfred A. Knopf, 1985, 17. Shevchenko continues: "I smiled and played the hypocrite not only in public, at Party meetings, at meetings with acquaintances, but even in my family and to myself," 17.

3. Ibid., 90.

4. Ray Bradbury. *Fahrenheit 451*. New York: Ballantine Books, 1996. Concerning the origin of *Fahrenheit 451*, Bradbury tells us: "In the spring of 1950 it cost me nine dollars and eighty cents in dimes to write and finish the first draft of *The Fire Man* which later became Fahrenheit 451," 167.

5. Robert Couteau. "The Romance of Places: An Interview with Ray Bradbury." Quantum: Science Fiction & Fantasy Review. (Gaithersburg, Maryland: Thrust Publications). Spring 1991, 1.

6. François Truffaut. *Correspondence 1945–1984*. Edited by Gilles Jacob and Claude de Givray. New York: Cooper Square 3 Press, 2000, 205.

7. Alfred North Whitehead. *Modes of Thought*. New York: The Free Press, 1968, 113.

8. *Fahrenheit 451*. François Truffaut. Universal Studios, 1966.

9. The independent library movement in Cuba was started in 1998, in Las Tunas. The idea was simple: to provide an avenue for people to read books and documents that the government prohibits. Running such libraries is what the Cuban government calls "foreign-funded counterrevolutionary" strategy to destabilize the government. All newspapers, the media, television, as well as radio are controlled by the government. See: "Call to Conscience: Library Group is Shamefully Silent on Cuba" Union-Tribune, January 9, 2004. In Cuba, the role of the intellectual is often played out in secrecy, through sheer survival instinct, much the same as in the Eastern bloc and other Soviet satellite regimes. It is a well-documented fact that the Cuban Dirección General de Inteligencia (DGI) was set up and controlled by the Soviets under the direction of general Viktor Simenov. In Cuba, the Bulgarian Darjavna Sugurnost (DS), one of the most adept terror organizations in the world, as well as the East German secret police, the infamous Stasi, played an instrumental role in training the Cuban secret police. The intellectual in Cuba serves as a puppet of the central committee for the defense of the revolution. In other words, whoever opposes the official government line is committed to a life of endless suffering in the form of harassment, unemployment, imprisonment, or firing squad. Reinaldo Arenas, the emerging Cuban writer had to come to the United States in 1980 to tell us this old and appalling tale. Arenas, writer of *Celestino antes del alba*, (*Celestino Before Dawn*) a novel written in 1967 that is critical of the Castro regime and *Persecución* (*Persecution*), was placed in a reeducation camp and later imprisoned and had his work banned. His novel *Antes Que Anochesca* (*Before Night Falls*) was made into a motion picture in 2000.

10. Gabriel Marcel. *Tragic Wisdom and Beyond.* Translated by Stephen Jolin and Peter McCormick. Evanston: Northwestern University Press, 1973, 151.

11. José Ortega y Gasset. *The Revolt of the Masses*. New York: W.W. Norton, 1960, 63. Ortega writes: "Contrary to what is usually thought, it is the man of excellence, and not the common man who lives in essential servitude. Life has a savior for him unless he makes it consist in service to something transcendental."

12. Vladimir Solovyov. *Crisis of Western Philosophy*, 13.

13. M. August. Associated Press. October 13, 2000.

Chapter Four

Citizen Kane
Biography and the Unfinished Sentence

CITIZEN KANE

Synopsis

Considered by many critics the greatest film ever made, *Citizen Kane* is undoubtedly Orson Welles's masterpiece. A man who owns many newspapers and can sway public opinion, Charles Foster Kane lacks what he deserves most: to have enjoyed a normal childhood. Kane is both shrewd and innocent, a man of the world, and a man holding on to lost childhood. A dominant theme of this film addresses the question whether people can be truly understood by others.

Citizen Kane is essentially a tale told in the hope of answering the question: What is the essence of the being called man? More importantly, the story is about the life of one individual. *Citizen Kane* unfolds around an enigmatic character named Charles Foster Kane. When Kane's life finally expires, his associates and friends are contacted and urged to say what they know about the enigmatic newspaper magnate. In the opening sequence we are treated to a glimpse into the world of Charles Foster Kane's mansion—his castle—as some call it. The camera stands outside a black cast-iron gate that has a large letter K affixed at the top. The night is dark and foggy, this, perhaps intimating or foreshadowing a mystery that is about to unravel. *Citizen Kane* is most definitely a suspense yarn that surprises us with its metaphysical/existential complexity.

In some respects, the film is truly a supreme portrayal of childhood. The theme of the film hinges on the understanding or lack thereof that Charles Foster Kane's friends, colleagues, and the media have of this puzzling man.

While the film suggests that the life of public individuals can never remain private, we are also to believe that the inner life of private individuals can never be made truly explicit. Part of the reason for this is that if we understand individuality to mean an autonomous, self-reflective form of contemplation, Kane's individualism, is his stamp of originality. Kane is a complicated and multifaceted man. In this respect, he is a genuine character and not just a caricature or cardboard entity. Kane already displays his personality and idealism as a young man.

The great irony that surrounds Charles Foster Kane is that he is everyman. He is a composite sketch of many men. His struggle is characterized by the anonymity imposed on individuality and an autonomous sense of interiority by the contingencies of the objective world. Kane knows what he wants; he is a public figure who possesses a singular mind. These two components of Kane's circumstances distract us from coming to terms with Kane's identity and not just with what he does as a public persona. *Citizen Kane* is an existential tale portrayed in words and pictures.

Guillermo Cabrera Infante, Cuban writer and acute observer of cinema, makes the point that the two themes that inspire the film are the degradation of privacy of public persons and the crushing weight of philosophical materialism. Cabrera Infante makes the poignant argument that the former is expressed verbally, while the latter theme is visual. This is a strong case of counterpoint.[1] The essential ingredient that makes *Citizen Kane* a tale of existential significance is the collage of different characters from Kane's past that offer testimonies about his life. The firsthand account of these people creates a vital reality to the story yet cannot penetrate into the essence of Charles Foster Kane—the man.

Do these testimonies succeed? How well do these people know Kane? After we have dispensed with the outright malicious will of those who have an ax to grind, the limitations placed on us by time and memory, romantic exaggerations, and simple forgetting of details, we arrive at bare-naked reality. It is a privilege having so many people who are willing to make known their memories of him. The strength of their insights depends on the moral quality of his acquaintances and friends. Depending on their ability to articulate what they know about him and their goodwill, will Kane's essential qualities become known. This process also involves a case of good fortune. If we are moved by the truism that the dead tell no tales, what are we left with? The answer is one's legacy, essence, and work, as these can only be rounded off by people who knew Kane. This is a case of justice.

Citizen Kane explores existential autonomy by juxtaposing the virtues of human essence with the exigencies of the objective world. We can contrast this dualistic approach, where the main emphasis is the internal, with one of Orson Welles's last films—*F for Fake*, a film that also seeks to uncover the difference between appearance and reality. *F for Fake* focuses on the daily lives of several people and their chic, incessant chatter. *F for Fake* tries to answer the question: What is reality? In the latter film, Orson Welles is back to his old cinematic tricks, the very staple of imagination that brought him notoriety, beginning with his radio broadcast of H. G. Well's novel *War of the Worlds.*

The story connects the life of Elmyr D'Hory, perhaps the greatest art forger of the twentieth century, with Clifford Irving's fake biography of the reclusive Howard Hughes, and one of Pablo Picasso's love affairs—a fake one at that—we learn at the end of the film. Welles displays his ability for cinematic deception. He titillates, teases, and goes fishing for suitable and gullible suitors who are quick to accept the fashionable and kitsch in the contemporary world. *F for Fake* is a romp through appearance, ambiguity, and pretense. As much as Welles is credited with brilliant writing and direction, it is his cinematography, as is the case in *Citizen Kane*, that steals the moment.

The existentially subjective aspect of Kane, who serves as the central focus of the film, is neither blatant nor conspicuous. The film is literate and thus it demands—like all higher art—a level of sensibility and engagement from the viewer that determines its appeal. This existentially subjective angle can be easily compared with the explicitly surreal quality of Resnais's *Last Year at Marienbad*, for instance.

Where *Citizen Kane* solicits our understanding through the linear and temporal narrative of Kane's associates, *Last Year at Marienbad* is ruled by a deliberate negation of temporal succession. When the female protagonist tells a male character, "You're like a shadow visiting for me to come closer," we hear distinct echoes of Leland, Kane's associate, describing Kane as being "disappointed with the world, so he built one of his own," or a reporter who says, "a word can't explain a man's life." *Citizen Kane*, like *Last Year at Marienbad* and *F for Fake,* is a film characterized by shadows—the shadows that time casts on an autonomous, vital will.

Kane is a man who is moved by a vision of transcendence, of remembrance. The end of his life, however, is nothing less than tragic. As we witness strangers rummaging through his personal belongings, one cannot help but witness the futility of his vision. But this tragic temporal sterility is only one component of the equation. Given that a portion of the story is told in retrospect by those who did or merely profess to know him, one must not forget that Kane counters or reassures his critics by showing his greater than life vitality in person.

The question comes to mind in *Citizen Kane* of how much people actually listen to each other in conversation. This is suggested by the clamor that Welles portrays so powerfully in the diverging paths, origins, and destination of the simultaneous and overlapping speakers in the film. Again, we can cite *Last Year at Marienbad,* when the narrator says of the surreal silence that engulfs the character: "Conversation flowed in a void apparently meaningless . . . or, at any rate, not meant to mean anything. A phrase hung in midair, as though frozen . . . though doubtless taken up again later." Just how much our conversations flow in an unreceptive void remains a point for speculation. What is certain is that we always leave many notices of our being posted throughout, as examples of our personal essence.

It is interesting to figure out how many of Kane's unofficial biographers are up to the task of the existential vision that he created for himself. Kane's circumstances are perhaps nowhere more clearly described than in what the Spanish essayist Salvador de Madariaga notices about the solitude that engulfs Hamlet. Madariaga writes, "Vague and unexplained to the mind, real and concrete to the instinct, known before he is understood as are persons and their affairs in life."[2]

Madaraiga's comment is insightful in two respects: existentially, and also in the objective and external manner that some people consider "to know someone." Kane is known as a newspaperman and a collector of antiques, but he is not known for who he truly is. The film opens in a mood indicative of mystery. On first viewing the film one can get the misimpression that *Citizen Kane* is a mystery or suspense tale. It turns out that this is one of a select few viable interpretations of *Citizen Kane*. Yet this is the case for all the wrong reasons. The opening scene is of Kane's castle, Xanadu, shrouded in fog. The place is abandoned. Then . . . Kane utters "Rosebud" as he dies, dropping a crystal ball. The scenes that follow are of "news on the march," a newsreel describing the grandeur of Xanadu, his home. The newsreel shows how difficult it is to attain the truth of a public person. The mystery aspect has to do with the notion of seeking firm ground in understanding how Charles Foster Kane viewed himself. Suspense is a central staple of the film. We want to know more about this mysterious man who drops the crystal ball at the start of the film. And . . . of course, the great suspense has to do with uncovering the meaning of Rosebud.

The objective understanding that the press and the public seek is paradoxical because it seeks to dispense with Kane's anonymity by knowing more about his private life, not about him as a person. The more objective tidbits that the public is fed, the more it thinks it knows him. A genuine subjective and existential knowledge of the man's essence is not what the press seeks. More often than not, such understanding would just prove to be a bore. One reporter who edits a newsreel is heard saying, "It's not enough to know what a man did, but to know who he was." What afflicts Kane as a private/public entity is similar to everyone else, except that the expectations of the public are magnified in regard to public figures.

In some respects, what qualifies a person as a public persona is often very much governed by capricious and arbitrary rules. If a bank clerk commits an indiscreet act away from his workplace, only the press can propel this person into the maelstrom of public scrutiny. In such a case, there is no immediate need to know more about this person.

Kane is such a victim. He is also a public entity with a great deal of panache and flair for public affairs. He gets into squabbles, financial brawls, and spirited arguments with many people who, as we have witnessed in Socrates's case, are in a position to hurt him. Kane lives his life on a grand scale, laughing, carousing with people, and displaying himself for all to see. In his form of living, as is true of any other, we disclose contradictions that are not easy to reconcile. Such is the human person. Kane wants to show people the truth but in doing so he also creates tabloids that achieve just the opposite. He builds a castle for himself; he is barely home to enjoy it. Contradictions loom large in most peoples' lives. Ortega y Gasset has this in mind when he writes. "The beliefs that coexist in any human life, sustaining, impelling and directing it, are on occasion incongruous contradictory, at the least confused."[3]

At least some of Kane's contradictions spring from an unbridled idealism. At age twenty-five Kane set out to run a newspaper "for fun" and to help the working man. When he first takes up *The Inquirer*, he says, "If the headline is big enough, then the news is big enough." The tension that exists between the public and private Kane is filmed brilliantly by Welles in his use of deep focus. Deep focus shots allow the viewer an almost omniscient look at the relationship of the characters without interfering with the action. The deep-focus shot, unlike a conventional shot spreads the arena of man's relationship in what is essentially a quasi-three-dimensional cinematic look at the human world. Now, what is most important is not necessarily what lies at the surface of life. For instance, a fine example of this is the shot of the reporter in the telephone booth, while the maître d' is framed by the door, as Kane's second wife, who does not want to talk to the press, is seen in the background. This is the view that an alert viewer would have of the world. The greater significance of deep focus is its portrayal of simultaneous depth—the multilayered foundation of human reality. One philosophical implication of this technique is that it affords for different moods to flow out of any given scene. In *Citizen Kane* this is manifested in the transcendence of narrative into an almost real-time perception of the passage of time. These different moods are captured in isolation, but also in relation to their prescribed position in the scene. Welles has essentially transferred the main line of action and dialogue from one of a given fixed place in the screen and spreads it in every direction. Now, the camera captures the entire field of view.

Citizen Kane remains an interesting film on many fronts. One of these is the great deal of attention that is paid to the William Randolph Hearst connection.

How much Welles's inspiration or motivation for the film owes allegiance to the former newspaper magnate remains a question. Welles proved to be a showman who knew the public's collective psychology. However, there is no doubt that the film stands alone very well on its own merits without the help of historical invective. In fact, most viewers of *Citizen Kane* are not privy to this information on their initial viewing. What remains important in this film is that it focuses on some jarring universal notions: subjective autonomy, loyalty to one's convictions, the misunderstanding of others, friendship, and the passage of time.

Concerning the latter point, one can argue that the film is a compressed drama of time itself. Beginning with a boy in a desolate Colorado farmhouse in the grip of winter, the story follows the trajectory of this young boy until his death as an old man. This alone is just cause to create a compelling story. And yet, of all the themes of the film this one seems the most neglected. This is partly due because the mundane lack of appeal of this theme. Another reason is because so many critics have concentrated either on the technical merits of the film, e.g., deep focus, the overlapping soundtrack, floor-level camera angles, and the film's alleged political angle, e.g., capitalism, etc., that so many other aspects of the film are neglected.

At a philosophical level, Kane intrigues and even teases the audience with snippets of his inner world. What goes largely unnoticed in *Citizen Kane* is that the biographical narrative that ensues right up to the time of his death is Kane's own life, his acceptance or failure thereof to understand this phenomenon as such. *Citizen Kane* is a visual biography. How would our own biography play out in public? The biographical component in *Citizen Kane* takes control of the film in several respects. First, because of the cinematic genre itself: a two-dimensional illusory visual collage depicting four-dimensional vitality. Secondly, a great portion of his story is framed, for good or worse, by the contingencies of other people. What seems such a captivating aspect of the film is the question of just what Kane would have expected from his many biographers.

Ortega y Gasset, a thinker who has taken great strides in reflecting on the nature of biography, articulates the question in the following manner: "Nothing seen from within has form. Form is always the external appearance which a reality offers to the eye when the eye con-templates it from outside, making it a mere object."[4]

To interpret Kane's life as formless, to use Ortega y Gasset's word, is a little misleading. His life is not formless in the sense that it lacks a definite center that guides his actions. This remains far from the truth. His life, as a biographical entity in space and time, is wholly transparent to itself. This is essentially a problem of our proximity to ourselves. Ortega y Gasset argues that human life is transparent to itself, and thus forgets itself. To focus the transparency of life upon itself becomes the essential existential project of every life, Ortega argues. Kane's biographers reduce the internal vitality of the man to that of a mere biological being; one more material entity to dissect. Kane's life is spent in avoiding precisely that form of objectification that is so easily confused with happiness. He attempts to transcend this by contemplating on the order of time itself.

Welles's treatment of the fullness of human life is achieved in a very convincing notion of real time through the confines of cinema. Kane's biographers are characters that work well as cinematic conventions because they are testaments to the passage of time. First, and most obvious is the fact that they outlive Kane. Secondly, they are sought out in their respective stage of life and circumstances to comment on Kane. Once we have taken in the importance of dismantling Kane's castle—the rough-and-ready manner in which his precious household items are thrown about—compare this to the early images of the young Kane playing in the snow—we begin to understand how effective Welles's treatment of time truly is.

Part of the meaning of biography in *Citizen Kane* is already answered when we consider that the investigation into his life—the reward of finding out who he was—is initiated by a reporter who has become intrigued by the word Rosebud. This comes as the recognition that Kane's life, as is perhaps also true of other's, is often motivated and inspired by a singular motive. Rosebud is a mystery; the reporters will not grant this public persona that privilege. Why should the passion that fueled Kane's life become important at all? Isn't this need also an admission of just how little we know of others whose life's trajectory has become part of our circumstance? That none of his friends and acquaintances know what Rosebud means is a further testament to the inner complexity of human beings.

Attempting to decipher the meaning of Rosebud becomes essential to the film because it would give his biographers, they believe, added understanding of how Kane conducted his life. However, it is not entirely clear what this new clarity would be. One way of viewing this is to suggest that knowing the meaning of "Rosebud" would give his critics additional power over Kane, especially after he has died. Why did Kane keep this childhood memory alive and quiet for so long? Or did he mention it to someone but that person or persons did not pay attention to him? What remains clear is that Rosebud was immensely important to him given his memory at the end of his life.

Welles's treatment of the passage of time and the changing world is again marvelously undertaken in *The Magnificent Ambersons*, his follow-up film to *Citizen Kane*. Unlike *Citizen Kane*, however, which was solely Welles's project, *The Magnificent Ambersons*, according to Welles, had about forty-five minutes cut out. Welles says, "The whole heart of the picture really."[5]

The Ambersons endure a familial saga that pins an aristocratic Indianapolis family against the demands of the industrial age.

Citizen Kane is a saga, but a personal one at that. The first thirteen minutes of the film is a retrospective documentary that is in the process of being put together by newsmen in a dark screening room. The film's opening sequence is a shot that looks in through a gate into Kane's castle. At the top of the iron gate is a large letter K. The beginning of *Citizen Kane* is replete with drama and mystery. For instance, what country could this mansion be in that has two monkeys on the premises? To compound this early oddness, we also see two gondolas, gently floating.

This is further complicated in the subsequent scenes, when we realize that Kane's castle is located in America. Welles's editing mastery is evident when we hear some time later that Kane created his own world out of disappointment with the real one. Things begin to make sense. We are convincingly awed by the scale and splendor of Kane's world. As the camera moves stealthily through the fog, we get the impression that the place is abandoned. High in a corner of the castle, a light is seen in a room. Soon after, the light goes out, signifying Kane's death. This is the point in the story when Kane utters "Rosebud" as he drops the glass ball. This scene is significant not only because this is the rallying point—Rosebud—on which the film is anchored, but also because of the symbolism of the crystal ball. The ball is a self-contained world of a small cottage that is covered in snow. Because the introduction of Rosebud and the crystal ball take place before the actual scenes that they allude to, the viewer tends to forget their importance as the film progresses. *Citizen Kane* is one of those films that do not give away its secrets on first viewing it. The crystal ball is important to Kane because it is a rendition of his early years in Colorado. As the glass ball drops to the floor, the scene turns to that of a fisheye shot of a nurse entering the room to cover Kane's body.

The next scene is one of "news on the march": "In Xanadu did Kubla Khan a stately pleasure dome decree"—the comparison is to Coleridge's poem *Kubla Khan*. The newsreel shows who Charles Foster Kane was, as scenes of Kane's castle follow: "A collection of everything so big it could never be cataloged or appraised. Enough for ten museums, the loot of the world." At the end of Kane's life his uncataloged and unapprised antiques create a problem for those responsible for his estate. Kane did not purchase his pieces for profit or even as a collector. To Kane, whatever he bought, he did so because he liked the object. It is interesting that the narrator, as an outsider, should view Kane's castle with such derision. In a prophetic statement, the narrator adds: "Xanadu's landlord leaves many stones to make his grave."

Kane's vexing ways run the gamut from admiration to hate. He is considered a communist by some, a fascist by others, while Kane simply says about himself, "I am, have been, and will be only one thing—an American." As the newsreel runs through Kane's life, we begin to imagine this distant, unapproachable man. We learn that he married twice and divorced the same number of times. His first wife died in 1918 in an automobile accident along with their son. His second wife, Susan Alexander, was a singer. He even built her an opera house, but to no avail, her talent just wouldn't do. As an old, balding Kane is wheeled around through his gardens, the narrator continues: "Alone in his never finished, already decaying pleasure palace, aloof, seldom visited, never photographed."

All of these descriptions of Kane are external vignettes that probably convey very little about the man. Is he a loner or aloof because he stays out of the limelight? How can we be sure that he is never visited if the press is not allowed to photograph him? At this point, the newsreel ends. The newsmen turn on the light and begin to discuss the best approach to take in their documentary. One of the reporters says, "seventy years is a lot to try to fit into a newsreel."

Another gets an idea, "what we need is an angle." This might all be very appealing to the audience, but does it have anything to do with Kane—the man—not just what he did or represented?

Some of the reporters think that Rosebud was a girlfriend, or an "it," or even a horse that he once bet on. The melodrama of the Walter Parks Thatcher library scene is exquisite—the light streaming down on the table, the safe with a guard standing nearby. Thatcher's manuscript about Mr. Kane reads: "I first encountered Mr. Kane in 1871 . . ." the story then begins with the young boy playing in the snow outside of Mrs. Kane's boardinghouse in Colorado. The rest of the story is about Kane living his life.

NOTES

1. Guillermo Cabrera Infante. *Arcadia Todas Las Noches. Bogota*: Editorial La Oveja Negra, Ltda, 1987, 19. Notable Cabrera Infante's works, include: *Three Trapped Tigers, Mea Culpa, Holy Smoke, Cine o Sardina, Infante's Inferno,* and *View of the Tropics*. Cabrera Infante has written screenplays, including that for Richard D. Sarafian's 1971 film, *Vanishing Point*.

2. Salvador de Madariaga. *Don Quixote*: *An Introductory Essay in Psychology*. London: Oxford University Press, 1961.

3. José Ortega y Gasset. *History as a System*. New York: W.W. Norton, 1961, 167.

4. José Ortega y Gasset. *The Dehumanization of Art and Other Essays on Art, Culture, and Literature*. New Jersey: Princeton University Press, 145.

5. Peter Cowie. *Seventy Years of Cinema*. New York: Castle Books, 1969, 14.

Chapter 5

Treasure of the Sierra Madre
Socrates in the Desert

TREASURE OF THE SIERRA MADRE

Synopsis

John Huston's *Treasure of the Sierra Madre* is a film with several redeeming qualities. It is a moral tale of men who are tested by nature and human contingency. The film is animated by a Socrates-like figure who serves as a mirror to the others around him, who become consumed by avarice.

On first encountering Howard, the old prospector (Walter Huston), in *Treasure of the Sierra Madre*, our immediate impression is one of sheer delectation. Howard is wisdom personified. He is also a fine example of the Socratic dictum, "know thyself."

Howard represents that rare form of contentment that is more readily found in literature than is often exercised by people in real life. He guides the viewer through a meticulous rendering of how avarice debilitates its victims. Avarice employs treachery and craftiness. Howard reminds us of what Havelock Ellis has to say about morals in *The Dance of Life*: "There is no separating pain and pleasure without making the first meaningless for all vital ends and the second turn to ashes. To exalt the meaning of pain; and we cannot understand the meaning of pain unless we understand the place of pleasure in the art of life."[1]

Treasure of the Sierra Madre displays universal themes that throw light on human nature. The moralizing that takes place in the film is ruled by a spirited, categorical ought that demonstrate how intemperance breeds the seed of its own destruction. John Huston doesn't so much depict particular examples of avarice, but avarice itself. Avarice—a universal human character trait—is the major theme of the film. The powerful appeal of the film is that Huston allows Dobbs (Humphrey Bogart) to destroy himself without having to resort to anything more than universally recognized values.

Along with avarice, Huston also explores envy, and perhaps most importantly, temperance, a character trait that is the central topic of discussion in Plato's *Charmides*.[2] One of the reasons that the film has enjoyed such great success is that these topics are not treated in isolation, as if existing in a vacuum.

For instance, temperance plays a direct role in the outcome of all the characters in the film. We witness this not only in those who are intemperate, but also in the effects that this has in the lives of others. The vital interplay of the characters in the film, as they would interact in real life, is a refreshing cinematic perspective that ends with cathartic resolution. Huston grounds the drama in a fine understanding of human reality. Real life situations serve as the foundation of the behavior that we witness in the film.

Treasure of the Sierra Madre is a two-dimensional, visual fable of human existence. Fables are an essential source of understanding because they confront us with fundamental truths. Also, fables remind us that our actions and their consequences are the result of our perspective or the lack thereof. While the focus of the film might be Dobbs's self-destruction, the essential motivation for his destruction retains universal appeal and validity.

Dobbs's potential salvation remains an open question. To this we must add that avarice cannot exist without the interaction of some key players, events, and circumstances. Hence, the overriding effect of the film is to demonstrate the correlation between wisdom and temperance. Again, the relationship of these two human traits makes us wonder if Dobbs can be saved under any circumstance. When confronted by wisdom, Fred C. Dobbs antagonizes Howard in the only manner that a fool can: he struggles against himself.

Perhaps the most effective way to make sense of the impact of this film is to view it as a fable. While it remains true that fables often make use of animals to demonstrate a lesson, this is only the case because the fable is designed to teach young people a valuable moral lesson. In the absence of personified animals, Huston instead utilizes men, a mountain, some bandits, and the passage of time. Huston, I believe, employs the very same staples of the fable, except that adults often make for very bad students when learning fundamental truths.

Allegory is a powerful teaching tool that removes us from the myopia that often comes about through the immediacy of the human condition. Man's proximity to himself can be his greatest nemesis. The beauty of *Treasure of the Sierra Madre* is its ability to showcase how wisdom is often shunned for the rewards of instant pleasures or simply because it is met by deaf ears. Howard is a teacher. Lessons are not made any truer because the teacher initiates them, rather because the teacher acts as intermediary between the pupil and truth. Ideally, the best pupil is the one that seeks the teacher. Consider what Karl Jaspers writes about Socrates. This can easily be applied to Howard:

> Socrates does not hand down wisdom but makes the other find it. The other thinks he knows, but Socrates makes him aware of his ignorance, so leading him to find authentic knowledge in himself. From miraculous depths this man raises up what he already knew, but without knowing that he knew it. This means that each man must find knowledge in himself; it is not a commodity that can be passed from hand to hand, but can only be awakened.[3]

Fables often make use of the supernatural. At the end of *Treasure of the Sierra Madre*, the mountain reclaims the gold in a sudden burst of wind. Intemperance, which is left to its own devices, the mountain appears to suggest, is always corrected by its own unforeseen effects. Dobbs's fate is sealed by his actions. What remains to be seen is how his life will play out. Fate plays a central role in the film.

Treasure of the Sierra Madre is a colossal tragedy. There is at least one additional observer of human reality—beside the omniscient one that seems to hover over the tale—namely Howard, who is cognizant of Dobbs's downfall. The story also has great bearing on the destiny that Howard assumes for himself. The viewer is invited to witness a common human folly from a distance.

At the end of the film Howard is rewarded for his wisdom in several ways. He earns the respect of the village Indians for saving a young boy. Howard is offered a secure set of circumstances that he can enjoy for what he calls "the rest of my natural life." He also earns Curtin's respect and friendship. The tragedy is intensified in the manner that their lives and destinies become intertwined. Curtin does not appear to gain much from the adventure that he is thrust into. Actually, he almost dies when he is shot twice by a delusional Dobbs. His reward is a sober perspective on life. He admits that he is no worse off at the end of the journey than when he began.

The film ends on a note of hope that perhaps Curtin will find happiness, if not contentment, in delivering the closure that Cody's widow will be searching for. Cody's death also contributes to the story. His struggle to create a better life for his wife and small child results in disaster. Fate does not always supply happy endings.

Treasure of the Sierra Madre is a moral tale that is told from the perspective of a quasi-omniscient and detached observer of cosmic human follies who takes in the action prima facie. The impact of the story on the viewer's imagination depends, as is the case with other artistic forms, on the viewer.

This is a story told from the perspective of time and the ironic constitution of the former, as this relates to human existence. What is so daunting about Dobbs's fate does not seem important, that is, until we attempt to make sense of it. How does Dobbs's story play out in actual human existence? Because cinema employs a closed-ended logic, that is, a resolution, the viewer is afforded a propaedeutic for future action.

Huston achieves a beautiful demonstration of the power of fate in a condensed format. The essential problem of wisdom, as is equally that of truth, is that human reality is often antagonistic to these. Instead, their validity and worth as guides for human life are always proven in time, or what is the passage of time. The same thing occurs when Spencer Tracy tries to impart a moral lesson to a young Robert Wagner in *The Mountain*, as the latter helps himself to the valuables of the victims of an airplane crash.

Treasure of the Sierra Madre begins with Fred C. Dobbs asking passersby for some spare change. He is down and out in the small Mexican town of Tampico—an American ex-patriot looking for a friendly face and a break. This scene is compelling because in light of what is to follow, one wonders, at the end of the film, whether his indigent condition has made him avaricious or if he has always suffered from this character flaw.

Early on in the film Dobbs elicits the viewer's sympathy, while later, only our pity. However, despite what we know of Dobbs, early in the film we remain curious about his personality. He is an engaging character. The world contains many Fred C. Dobbses.

From the opening segment of the film, when we see Dobbs begging for money from a wealthy passerby played by John Huston, we question whether Dobbs is avaricious, lazy, or merely wallowing in his misery. He buys a box of cigarettes with the money the stranger gives him. However, after the two men have met a third time on the street, Huston tells him, "From now on you're going to have to make your way through life without me."[4] Dobbs then gets a haircut and shave with the money he receives from the stranger.

In the next significant scene we find Dobbs in a tavern and a small boy persuading him to buy a lottery ticket. Dobbs is not interested. He has just ripped up the last lottery ticket he bought. He eventually buys a ticket from the boy.

The turning point in the film comes about when Dobbs finds temporary work. When he asks a man in a bar for money the man is quick to answer, "I won't give you a red cent. If you wonna make some money I'll give you a job."

While working for Pat McCormick building a derrick, Dobbs meets a fellow drifter named Bob Curtin (Tim Holt). After about two weeks of working for this man, they are brought back to the mainland on a ferry. McCormick tells them that he can't pay them because he has no money. He tells them that he will pay them later. One day, as they sit in a town square they see

McCormick, well dressed, with a lady in his arm. They confront him, and McCormick invites them to a bar to buy them a drink. There, a fight ensues, and McCormick comes out the loser. In an honest gesture, they only take the three hundred dollars they are owed and return McCormick his wallet, leaving the rest of the man's money.

The action/adventure sequences in the film explore the internal condition of the characters: how they think, how they view the world and their emotional and spiritual state. No scene serves a gratuitous purpose. The fight scene with McCormick is a precursor to the avarice that we witness in Dobbs later on in the film. The cathartic importance of these scenes is not that people can harden with unfavorable circumstances, but that Dobbs does not know how to internalize these events. Curtin, who accompanies Dobbs throughout most of the film, reacts differently. In addition, consideration must also be given to Cody's fate. Cody, a loner engaged in the stringent pursue of a better life for his family, moves in the shadow of murderers. His fate is tied to the fate of the others.

Dobbs and Curtin rent a cot for fifty cents per night, where they meet Howard, a fast-talking old prospector who delivers a powerful monologue on the value of gold and human nature. Howard tells them that they can get $5,000 worth of gold from the nearby mountains. He explains: "The price of gold is worth what it is because of the human labor that went into getting it." This dialogue, which is essentially a monologue in its intensity, can easily rival Hamlet's "to be or not to be" soliloquy because of its multifaceted probing of human reality. It is almost as if Howard is talking to himself, and the other two characters are privy to his thoughts.

Howard warns them that they will want more gold than they can carry down from the mountain. Howard tells them: "As long as there's no find the noble brotherhood will last, but when the piles of gold begin to grow, that's when the trouble starts." The two men are mesmerized by the possibilities. This exchange is significant because it foreshadows the direction of the drama that is to follow. More importantly, it serves as the beginning of a lesson, a moral of the story.

This is the point in the film when we realize that Howard is entertaining a wager with the viewer as to the nature of man. He is not interested in the gold per se, but rather in witnessing the transformation that some men undergo. John Huston's direction in effect employs what the ancient Greeks referred to as a prolepsis, that is, an innate anticipation of events that takes place without rational effort on behalf of the subject. Howard tells the two future prospectors, "I've never known a prospector who died rich. That's what gold does to a man's soul." Howard challenges the two men to disclose their genuine selves. At first, Dobbs and Curtin don't think too much of the old guy.

Interestingly, while Howard tries to tell them about the inherent weaknesses in human nature, the two men only manage to hear how much gold they can get. Howard goes on with his tease, "Prospecting is only good when you have a partner, but a partner can cause you to get killed. Alone is best, but you have to have a stomach for loneliness. Men are friends until they find the gold." Are you two up to the task? he seems to ask them. This scene encapsulates the overall theme and meaning of the film. Howard is not avaricious, yet he has been a prospector for a very long time. He does not personally care for gold but is willing to guide the other two to the mountain.

Howard's incessant talk about gold reverberates in Curtin's and Dobbs's heads. This leads to a prophetic conversation between the two:

Dobbs: "Do you believe what that old man that was doing all the talking at the Oso Negro said the other day night about gold changing a man's soul so he ain't the same kind of a guy that he was before finding it?"

Curtin: "I guess that depends on the man."

Dobbs: "That's exactly what I say. Gold doesn't carry any curse with it. It depends if the guy that finds it is the right guy. Gold can be as much of a blessing as a curse."

The trek up the mountain embodies a moral cleansing for Howard. What are we to make of this simple yet wise character who appears on the scene out of nowhere? Surely, he is atypical of one who seeks riches. In Howard, we have the key to the meaning of the story. He embodies the perennial point and purpose of all Aesopian tales: No matter how much advice one offers, fools will still rush into things. Howard's character acts out the part of a wager, a jest. He seems to be betting on the judgment that his wisdom is sound and thus wants to prove it. Howard acts as a sort of neutral narrator of the tale; he is certain of what is going take place, but he is not capable of stopping it. In the subsequent scenes of avarice, infighting, mistrust, and cynicism we witness Howard intently looking on, as vindicating his wisdom all along. From the look on his face, he enjoys the other two jostling for the gold. Howard's countenance and well-placed words are indicative of his anticipation of a total moral collapse in Dobbs's and Curtin's makeshift friendship.

Three weeks after purchasing his ticket, Dobbs wins the lottery. The three men pool their money together and buy the equipment needed for the trek and set out for the mountain. When they shake hands in a show of partnership, the old man looks on in curious anticipation. This is significant. Howard tells them that prospecting costs a lot of money. Howard explains that gold can't just be ripped out of the mountain with one's own hands. He tells them that they need equipment. This equipment will cost them money. Dobbs and his companion are young men, but they are nowhere as tough as the old man, who is constantly seen climbing ahead of them. The old man's toughness is mental, not necessarily physical. This is John Huston's manner of stating that wisdom is more valuable than youth and physical strength.

Howard's mental and spiritual resources allow him to endure the many difficulties that the other two men can hardly accommodate. Given the disparity between Howard's age and that of Dobbs and Curtin, these scenes of physical travail can only be interpreted as a spiritual prowess that Howard possesses. Dobbs and Curtin are surprised by Howard's stamina. "The old man is tough. He's part goat, part camel," they utter, but Dobbs never stops to think what makes the old man so tough. As they ascend the mountain, Dobbs is vexed by Howard's stamina. He says: "Hey, if there was gold in those mountains how long would it have been there? Millions and millions of years. What's our hurry? A couple days more or less ain't going to make any difference." This is merely a roundabout way of not admitting that he is fatigued. Also significant in the action scenes is the moral condition of the two men. This is especially exaggerated in Dobbs's character. Dobbs's will is defined by exhorting minimum effort to achieve the greatest gain.

Treasure of the Sierra Madre interweaves the clash of physical exertion and a strong will in a manner that goes a long way to point out the importance of character on our actions. Bernard Travern (1882–1969) wrote *Treasure of the Sierra Madre* in 1948. The novel, like most of his other works: *Rebellion of the Hanged* (1954), *Ship of the Dead* (1959), and *Bridge in the Jungle* (1971) are essentially action/adventure tales.

When a sandstorm paralyzes their progress, Howard is the only one that has any clear understanding of what is taking place. A northern, Howard informs them. Dobbs's violence begins when he becomes exhausted and attempts to hit Howard with a rock. "Leave him alone," Curtin tells Dobbs. "Can't you see the old man's nuts?" Howard rebutes, "Nuts. Nuts, am I? Let me tell you something, my two fine bedfellows. You're so dumb there's nothing to compare you with. You're dumber than the dumbest jackass." Howard then breaks out into a mocking dance, as he continues, "You're so dumb you don't even see the riches you're standing on with your own feet." They finally find gold.

Part of Howard's charm as a character is his ability to tell the truth while not moralizing. In a very prophetic moment, Howard tells Dobbs some essential truths while they talk about gold. Howard says: "You know, gold ain't like stone in a riverbed; it don't cry out until you pick it up." This could easily apply to truth and wisdom. He continues: "You're learning. Pretty soon I won't be able to tell you a thing," after he tells Dobbs how they are going to hide the gold from each other. Dobbs objects, "What a dirty, filthy mind you have." Howard seems to be way ahead of the game; he answers: "Oh, no. Not dirty. Not dirty, baby. Only I know what kind of idea even supposedly decent people get when gold is at stake." Howard is quick to cite the differences between being trustworthy and honest. He considers himself trustworthy because he is old and slow and can't easily run away from the two younger men. Whether Howard knows more than he is letting on is a matter for speculation, but in telling them this, he is suggesting that he understands just how they think.

The problems begin shortly after the initial elation of finding gold has subsided. Dobbs, out of mistrust, wants to split the proceeds. At this point the old man gives them a speech about honesty and what gold does to people. This is the second major turning point in the story, given that now we begin to see that the old man is right. When asked how he will spend his money, the old man offers an unassuming reply: "I'm going to spend my time reading comic books and adventure stories." Dobbs goes out in the middle of the night to check on his gold. Dobbs's mistrust becomes pathological when Howard asks him to go down the mountain to the village to buy some materials. He objects.

Next, we see Dobbs's paranoia manifesting itself as Curtin stumbles into his gold while looking for a Gila monster under a rock. Dobbs points his gun at his partner. It is Curtin who goes to the village to buy provisions, instead. There he meets another American who also wants to dig for gold. The man follows Curtin back to the camp, where he is not welcomed. Dobbs is the first one to let the man know this. The stranger wants a percentage of the gold. But when they are about to "bump off" the stranger, a band of bandits is seen riding up the mountain toward their camp. Cody, the stranger, helps them ward off the bandits in the gun battle that ensues. Cody is killed. As they look through his pockets to find out who he is, they find a letter from his wife telling him that she and their son miss him dearly.

The three men decide to leave the mountain after they have secured about $35,000 worth of gold each. At this point, Howard, in a mystical vein, tells them that it will take about another week to "break down the mine and put the mountain back in shape." Dobbs finds this idea startling and asks, "Do what to the mountain?" Howard then gives them a lecture on the nature of gratitude: "Make her appear as she was before we came. We wounded this mountain, and it's our duty to close that wound. It's the least we could do to show our gratitude for all the wealth she's shown us. If you guys don't want to help me, I'll do it alone." Again, the scope of Howard's understanding transcends what he lets the other two men know. His decision to clean up the site of their digging for gold can be viewed as simple superstition. But this would be an oversimplification, given Howard's character and the scenes of respect and veneration that he receives from the Indians for saving the child. Howard reminds us of Charmides telling Socrates, "For I would almost say that self-knowledge is the very essence of temperance, and in this I agree with him who dedicated the inscription 'know thyself!' at Delphi."[5]

When they are about to leave, some Indians come from the village to seek help for a dying boy. This can be explained as coincidence, but it is also consistent with the idea that goodwill is repaid in very vexing and unexpected ways. Howard says at one point: "You start out to tell yourself you'll be satisfied with twenty-five thousand handsome smackers worth of it. After months of sweatin' yourself dizzy and growing short on provisions and finding nothing, you finally come down fifteen thousand and then ten, finally you say, 'Lord, let me just find five thousand dollars' worth and never ask for anything more the rest of my life." After the old man saves the boy's life, the Indians return and make Howard their guest of honor. The child's father feels that he must pay his debt; otherwise, all of the sacred spirits will become upset. This is consistent with Howard's loyalty to the mountain. Dobbs, on the other hand, cannot make more out of this episode than to tell Howard, "Remember this next time you try to do a good deed," as Howard goes away with the Indians. They promise to meet the old man two weeks later in Durango. Dobbs becomes suspicious and paranoid of his partner as they head to Durango alone without the old man.

A powerful scene ensues when Curtin has to constantly watch Dobbs. Dobbs's paranoia becomes pronounced on their first night alone, when he attempts to kill Curtin. Dobbs shoots Curtin during the second night, off camera. When he goes to sleep, leaving Curtin for dead, he begins to reflect on the nature of conscience. "Conscience?" he questions. "What is it anyway? If we don't have a conscience, I won't worry." Dobbs prescribes to the view that ignorance is bliss. The next morning, when he is going to bury Curtin, he breaks out into a monologue about the dead man's eyes being open. He begins to blame the dead man for bringing about his own demise.

Dobbs's eyes become the central attraction of the scenes that follow. He sweats, walks around aimlessly, and talks to himself like a man who needs convincing. His eyes tell a tale of repentance, of understanding what he can't will himself to do. This is the first time in the film that we witness conscience eating away at Dobbs, like a tormented soul.

Dobbs goes into his venerable conscience soliloquy, "What if his eyes are open, looking at me?" John Huston does a marvelous job of bringing the viewer into Dobbs's head, as it were. The soliloquy is a particularly effective device in this instance for its nondramatic, personal, and claustrophobic qualities. What we get instead is qualified, rationalized behavior that struggles to attain genuine justification for its motives. He goes back in the morning to bury Curtin, but Curtin is not there. Dobbs searches for the wounded man in the surrounding area. Then he gets a brilliant idea. He convinces himself that perhaps a tiger (mountain lion) took the dead man: "I got it. A tiger. Ah, yeah, that's it. A tiger must have dragged him off to his land," he tells himself. And then, in the manner characteristic of people who shy away from personal responsibility at all cost, he goes on, "Pretty soon not even the bones will be left to tell his story. Done as if by order." He is happy to see that nature is on his side, thus assuaging the weight of his heavy conscience.

Howard is seen enjoying himself in a kind of Shangri-La promised land of rest, food, drink, and women in the Indian village. He is revered as a medicine man for saving the life of the boy. The Indians inform him that Curtin has been found half dead. Howard and some Indians go out to find Dobbs, but poetic justice has already taken care of him.

The rest of the film involves a search for Dobbs on behalf of Howard, Curtin, and several Indians who saved him. Retribution is the call of the day now, as some bandits kill Dobbs and steal his gold. They store the gold in some ruins outside of town, only to be captured by the townspeople while trying to sell Dobbs's mules. Later the three bandits are executed.

The last sequence of the film entertains what appears to be the perspective of the mountain itself. Howard and Curtin go to retrieve the bags of gold. As the search party arrives on the site where the gold has been hidden, a sudden windstorm develops, blowing all the gold out of the bags and back into the mountain.

Treasure of the Sierra Madre is a brazen look at human life that avoids a trite climax. The film captures the essence of avarice without making a political statement of any sort. The film is a metaphysical rendering of human destructiveness and how this manifests itself in the physical world. I suppose that what John Huston portrays is akin to Luigi Pirandello's *Six Characters in Search of an Author*. In other words, Huston has, in my estimation, avarice itself searching for a manner to tell a story.

The final episode has Howard breaking out into frantic laughter. He says, "Laugh, Curtin, old boy. This is a great joke played on us by the Lord, fate, nature, or whatever you prefer. But who or whatever played it had a sense of humor. The gold has gone back to where we found it." The fable as allegory comes full circle when those involved reach the understanding that human existence possesses an underlying structure that must be respected and appropriated.

John Huston's direction does a marvelous job of effacing any sense of strenuous moralizing. Cinema achieves this best when it becomes so transparent that it does not become bogged down by its own medium. Cinema always places us in a given arena that, depending on our sensibility, we can incorporate its meaning in our own lives. Ernst Cassirer reminds us of this in *An Essay on Man*: "Every work of art has an intuitive structure, and that means a character of rationality. Every single element must be felt as part of a comprehensive whole."[6]

NOTES

1. Havelock Ellis. *The Dance of Life*. New York: Random House, 1929, 265.
2. *The Collected Dialogues of Plato*. Edith Hamilton and Huntington Cairns. Editors. Princeton: Princeton University Press, 1985, 99. Benjamin Jowett, who translated the *Charmides* in this edition, writes about the Greek word Sophrosyne in relation to arrogance: "Sophrosyne was the exact opposite. It meant accepting the bounds which excellence lays down for human nature, restraining impulses to unrestricted freedom, to all excess, obeying the inner laws of harmony and proportion."
3. Karl Jaspers. *Socrates, Buddha, Confucius, Jesus: The Paradigmatic Individuals*. Translated by Ralph Manheim. San Diego: Harcourt Brace & Company, 1990, 8.
4. John Huston. *Treasure of the Sierra Madre*. Hollywood: Warner Brothers, 1948.
5. *The Collected Dialogues of Plato*, 110.
6. Ernst Cassirer. *An Essay on Man: An Introduction to a Philosophy of Human Culture*. New Haven: Yale University Press, 1972, 167.

Chapter 6

Jean-Pierre Melville
Encounters with Conscience

BOB LE FLAMBEUR, LE SAMURAI, LE CERCLE ROUGE AND UN FLIC

Synopsis

Often cited as the spiritual father of the French New Wave, Jean-Pierre Melville wrote and directed films about rugged individuals, loners who delved into human reality with trimmed illusions. A fan of American film noir, Melville took the genre to stylish new heights that contrast sensual experience with the inner life of his characters.

BOB LE FLAMBEUR

Paris takes a momentary respite from the clamor of its citizens. The city is quiet. Dawn pins man against himself. Missing are the aggravated and intemperate intentions of some of its inhabitants—at least this is true of the Pigalle district. The relative absence of others—who often only serve as resistance, speaking the same language without communicating—forces a reflective glance for Bob the gambler.

Bob (Roger Duchesne) walks out in the early dawn from a gambling joint and finds himself staring into a storefront mirror and uttering: "A good looker." This is merely a consolation. Bob has just exited a losing round of craps. Bob is used to losing. He is going home to sleep, and he tells an attendant. As customary, he never retires to bed before 6:00 a.m., his dignified anonymity intact.

Bob Le Flambeur is an explicitly introspective yarn. More so than Melville's later films, *Bob Le Flambeur* invites the viewer to live along Bob and enter into his world. The film sets this introspective mood from the very beginning. We are quickly allowed into Bob's world through an omniscient and friendly narration, an exquisite luxury that is rarely granted to most mortals who surround him.

Bob, the local legend, even though a scammer, always concocting a new angle to help him pass the time, is also a gentle soul to those who know him. The exception is fate, given that destiny never knows the inside of a man: "As told in Montmartre, here is the strange tale of . . . Bob Le Flambeur." As a sentimental jazz score plays, the narration continues: "The story begins in those moments between night and day, by the dawn's early light. Montmartre is both heaven and hell." At this point, the camera moves to a descending sky car. The friendly and omniscient narrator goes on, as it will do throughout the film: "The signs are going out. Strangers pass one another. Workers, like this charwoman who's very late . . . wanderers like this young girl who has bloomed early for her age. But let's get to Bob. Bob the gambler, an old young man, legend of the recent past."[1]

Bob walks alone through the deserted dawn streets. He looks at himself in a storefront mirror, as if to reaffirm his solitude. But this gesture has nothing to do with vanity, for Bob is at the crossroads of self-effacement and hubris. Everybody seems to know him, the taxi drivers, the newsstand man; police detectives give him a lift in their squad car. They drop him off at another gambling house. Meanwhile, the musical score sets a somber and melancholic mood. After he is dropped off at his destination, one policeman asks another if Bob is an informer. He answers that that is absolutely not the case. He explains that Bob shoved him aside once when a guy named Ficel shot at him some time back. Unlike the squalid morality of so many postmodern men, Bob has earned his loyalty.

Bob Le Flambeur exhibits the characteristically Melvillian respect for why people act as they do, when psychoanalysis and psychobabble won't do. Melville, much like Georges Simenon in his *romans policiers*, is more concerned with people's motives than with solving crimes. As they drive off, the policemen begin a discussion of Bob's moral makeup. They offer an interesting expose of Bob's life that goes a long way in describing fundamental traits of his character that frame his life in a broad perspective.

Melville's characters often appear to exist in an existential vacuum. We learn from the policemen in *Bob Le Flambeur* that he robbed the Rimbaud bank twenty years earlier. They believe that he is wiser now. Of all of Melville's characters, Bob seems the most human and interesting. He has a tastefully furnished apartment, where Costello in *Le Samourai* lives in a dungy, drearily discolored prison-cell-type room. Where Bob has works of art and books, Costello has a lonely bird that is kept in a cage in the middle of the room. Bob stands out as likeable, spirited, approachable. His demeanor is jovial. This seems to come as a result of having lost his freedom while incarcerated. Like Maurice Faugel in Melville's next film, *Le Doulos* (1961), Bob is also an ex-felon who knows the law of the street and who has no fear, ever entertaining the opportunity of another caper.

More interesting than their plot construction, Melville's films can be viewed as living, vital axioms that become manifest through his characters. They can also be described as visual poetry. Gambling is acceptable and jewel heists are seen as mere jobs that require a sophisticated level of difficulty and willful engagement. So is life. Melville treats the affairs of daily life as vital sketches. Implicit in Melville's treatment of unsavory characters is always a slice-of-life attitude that asks: How do some men pass their lives? What are the trajectories of any given life? Bob is not as mysterious as Costello in *Le Samourai* and Corey in *Le Cercle Rouge*. *Bob Le Flambeur* is less interested in portraying a gambler than in showcasing the intricate and complex interactions between free will and fate. This question is poignant in Melville's work. Despite the metaphysical mechanism at work in human reality, destiny is cast from the relationship between free beings.

Bob's code of morality, what amounts to conscience, cannot be explained through theoretical moral abstractions. When a small-time crook named Mark comes to his apartment to ask Bob for money and to hide out for some time, Bob is ready to comply. When he discovers that Mark has beaten a prostitute who works for him named Lydia, he throws him out. Bob doesn't like pimps. This singular incident will prove to be the decisive reason for Bob's next incarceration. Bob's conscience is unwavering. He is loyal to his friends. Consistent with his dislike for pimps, Bob is the protector of a young orphan girl who he doesn't want walking the streets. He takes the young orphan to his apartment to live. Ironically, it is Bob's goodwill that sidetracks his life at the end of the film. The orphan becomes romantically involved with a young man, the son of Bob's deceased friend, who Bob also looks after. Ironically, the getaway that Bob and others plan for their next jewel heist is foiled when the young man tells the young woman the plan in an unguarded moment of bravado.

Another clear indication of Bob's past and upbringing takes place when Bob and the young woman go for a ride to the part of the city where he grew up. He admits to her that he left home at age fourteen. He tells her that his mother scrubbed floors until the day she died. No further social commentary is needed. This is Melville's genius at work. The linear plot of *Bob Le Flambeur* corresponds with the time-conscious reflection of the protagonist. Bob eventually arrives at the realization that most of his life has been lived with internal turmoil. He hopes for a definitive caper that will round out his existence. His days, like the bourgeois men he passes in the street, are spent in pursuit of a future-promise. The daily having-to-do of human reality transform into life a long series of events and emotions that, in the absence of a unifying vision, makes life a mere heap of days. A succession of days is not a substitute for quality of life. There is something to be said for the heroism of people who attack daily life with zest, for life does not come with a manual.

A parallel can be drawn between *Le Samourai* and Eric Ambler's *A Coffin for Dimitrios.* In the former, Jef Costello, unlike Bob, lives mostly in his own head, expressionless, loveless, and careless. Ambler's Dimitrios is created on the same principle of anonymity. Clearly, Costello has a past. Someone must know him. Bob lives in a neighborhood where he has several friends and many acquaintances. This is not so for Costello, who lives in a kind of existential suspended reality; the world only exists as the unfortunate container of his being. Costello appears to be waiting for life to begin.

Le Samurai tries to make sense of the daily travails of a loser. At the end of the film, we are left thinking that perhaps Costello had a way out of his predicament. We almost come to believe that we can help this man. This affected moral superiority on our part is the fingerprint of postmodern faux-pas values, Melville appears to suggest. Costello dies due to his honor, not out of any extraneous environmental contingency. His death is defined by his code of honor—of his own doing.

The world is large and complex, human reality too slippery and fleeting, thus we conjure up endless institutions and yellow ideologies that are bent on creating a new man—a mechanical man who must cover all angles, at all times. Life proper cannot be lived without an angle. Costello lives and dies—like so many others before and after him. What bothers us most about his death? That he has apparently taken his own life? Is it his oppressive anonymity that haunts us? Yet a dignified anonymity is a core characteristic of existential freedom. The concrete beauty and effectiveness of Melville's work leaves such questions to reflective viewers. The driving force behind Melville's cinematic conventions is imagination.

It is philosophically interesting to extrapolate where the existence of an onscreen Costello begins and ends. This is the cinematic treatment that Carol Reed offers his villain Harry Lime in *The Third Man*. While Harry Lime is hiding in the half-light and confusion of World War II, his old friend Martins, the writer, is innocently seeking his company through the rubble-laden Viennese streets. As in *A Coffin for Dimitrios*, most of *The Third Man* is spent building the suspense of a mystery man who may already be dead.

Bob the gambler is not as sinister a character as Costello, Dimitrios, or Harry Lime. Bob is an amicable character who we forget is a criminal for great stretches of the film. For the most part, we encounter Bob in his role as senior neighborhood gambler. He is even funny. Bob is a man with a pressing sense of the passage of time. It is not until the end of the film that Bob and his accomplices take arms against the police, during the casino heist, that we regard him as a criminal. Before the casino heist plot is unveiled and rehearsed, Bob is just a lovable loser. His love of horses exposes his wretched history at the track. For Bob, losing is consistent with living. To win would be a bonus. He says: "Fortune smiles on the bold." When he does win at the horse track, he and his friend Roger go to a casino, from where they emerge broke. The vault at the Deauville Casino holds 800 million francs. Bob begins thinking seriously about the job. He says: "800 big ones. The job of my life!"

Melville's main characters exhibit a stoic and cavalier attitude toward life. In Bob's case, he appears to be content. Bob's character is an example of ataraxia, what is better expressed as a subdued sense of contentment. The Spanish philosopher Julian Marias illustrates this state of being as:

> In other words, ataraxia consists in a state of alertness, which is serenely and foresight directed toward action. Courage in the midst of dangers, and above all in the midst of sudden, unexpected, and unforeseeable dangers, is an attitude. Composed of serenity, of acutely perceptive calmness, that allows one to act promptly and with certainty, even without prior preparation.[2]

Bob's resolute calm springs from an awareness that crime is only one aspect of human life. While Jef in *Le Samourai* and Corey in *Le Cercle Rouge* may not know better, Bob does, but waits for fate to smile upon him. Unlike these other men, Bob exhibits a great sense of control. His world is colored by contemplation of his fate. One of the more interesting aspects of Bob's character is his sense of time—that is, of time slipping away. Like the Professor in *Seven Thieves* who merely wants one more opportunity to "make the world gasp" (see page 85), Bob is possessed by an awareness of time. However, Melville does not convey this inner reality through conventions associated with outer action. Instead, we find that Bob's serenity is one aspect of his inquietude. One can argue that Bob is the maker of his own possibilities. What can his attention to detail and meticulousness sense of timing signify, if not the exercise of free will? One can liken Bob's world to that of the inner world of an artist, often living by the dictate of his voice.

Consider Pierre Assouline's insightful description of writer Georges Simenon's ritual of thought and writing in his book *Simenon: A Biography*:

> Simenon described the creative procedure as ritual: a walk, a trigger of inspiration, a state of grace, material preparation, manila envelope, search for names in the telephone directory, isolation, rising at six in the morning and writing from 6:30 to 8:30, more walking, lunch, a nap, television, children, walking

again, reading newspapers but no books, early to bed. Eight or nine chapters in as many days.³

Let us compare this to Bob's attention to dress, his well-ordered apartment, never going to bed before 6:00 a.m., and loyalty to friends, including the memory of the dead. Always unwavering in his ways, Bob recognizes himself as a gambler. His equanimity is a natural driving force that must not be overintellectualized, especially by adherents of pop psychology, where the emphasis is placed squarely on the shoulders of environmental forces. Bob craves his environment, even when negating the existence of the likes of prostitutes, pimps, and police informers. Assouline writes about Simenon:

> He would take longer walks than usual, always alone. This was an early sign that withdrawal was imminent, but also a way of attaining what he called the "state of grace," a condition in which he felt a void within himself that would soon be filled by his characters. The walks would get longer as he sought to elicit "the trance" he needed in order to enter "novel mode."⁴

Like Simenon, *Bob Le Flambeur* also depicts a controlled world, where most scenes are close-cropped to entice the viewer to wonder what takes place outside each frame. Melville's cinematic world is consumed with what happens in the life of his characters. This larger philosophical view is neatly portrayed in the day-to-day experiences of the characters. This perspective works for any type: businessman, politician, ballplayer, and portrait painter. However, because Melville's characters are more detached from most people's immediate experience, they become flamboyant anomalies that capture the imagination.

When Lon, the lawyer in *The Asphalt Jungle*, returns to his bedroom after being interrogated by the police in his living room, his wife says to him: "Oh, Lon when I think of all those awful people you come in contact with, downright criminals. I get scared." Lon, who proves to be a not so-stoic-character, answers: "After all, crime is only a left-handed form of human endeavor." This is the kind of talk that inspired Melville in his treatment of film noir themes. Melville credits *The Asphalt Jungle* as inspiration for his work. While Lon and Paul in *Un Flic* only see the immediate gains in a life of crime, both who incidentally end up by committing suicide, Bob knows the price of his gambles. Bob, like Doc Erwin Riedenschneider in *The Asphalt Jungle* is a competent and disciplined character who does not fool himself about the perils of his chosen life.

Melville's work is not as amoral as some critics suggest. The bond that is forged between equals is the driving force behind most of his characters. Bob and Roger are best friends who respect and trust each other. Bob's friendship and allegiance to the female restaurant owner is reciprocated with genuine care for his well-being. Once the casino heist plan is put in place, the nine men who embody it become a close-nit unit. It is difficult to argue for amorality in Melville's characters given their devotion and respect for each other as equals. Perhaps the profound message that can be drawn from Melville's work is the unmasking of false moralizers.

Undoubtedly, Melville's experience in the resistance movement during World War II France is made felt in his regard for loyalty. Post–World War II French society has been marred by a dubious cynicism that springs from the political expediency of collaborators with the Nazis and the Soviet Union. This political expediency is repudiated in Melville's work in the moral flexibility of police informers.

Examples of self-respect are plentiful in Melville's films. When Simon in *Un Flic* is asked to stop by Inspector Coleman, but instead goes for a weapon, Coleman has no choice but to shoot him. Simon knows this perfectly well. When he is searched, no weapons are found on his lifeless body, suggesting that he was ready to die. Corey's end is also met in the same manner. In Melville one finds a strong suspicion that perhaps his criminals are more loyal to each other than in the practical nihilism and degeneracy of the bourgeois world. A telling example of this is the rampant cynicism of the inspector general in *Le Cercle Rouge*; his conviction that all men are born good but are eventually corrupted. Is this a reflection of himself as an instance of all men or is he excluding himself from this dubious category? Schopenhauer can best illuminate us. He writes in *Counsels and Maxims* that:

> A man bears the weight of his own body without knowing it, but he soon feels the weight of any other, if he tries to move it: in the same way, a man can see other people's shortcomings and vices, but he is blind to his own. This arrangement has one advantage: it turns other people into a kind of mirror, in which a man can see clearly everything that is vicious, faulty, ill-bred and loathsome in his own nature; only, it is generally the old story of the dog barking at its own image; it is himself that he sees and not another dog, as he fancies.[5]

Statements such as the inspector general's are never issued by the criminals. In fact, the inspector general's comment is sharply refuted by Santi, the nightclub owner in *Le Cercle Rouge*. Mattei goes to the club to get information from Santi, but the latter does not cooperate. Mattei then decides to arrest him and coerce information out of him. Santi counters by reminding him: "You said even if I haven't an informer's nature, you'd force me to help you. You've got your psychology all wrong." Santi's contention is that nothing can change a man's basic nature. Melville does not concern himself with abstract and impersonal moral codes, rather with conscience.

This serves as a fine example of cinema reflecting life. But this mirror image, even when it is a realistic and accurate portrayal, can only cover a given perspective. Cinema is perspectival by nature, if not solely by intent. Through its basic limitation, the camera can only offer a rendition of what appears directly in its field of view. This is no different than what occurs in life. Edmund Husserl's phenomenological contention that consciousness serves as a container of the limited reality that it entertains can be applied to cinema. Cinema offers us a limited, often phantomlike world that we do not recognize as our own. The essential point to keep in mind is that cinema allows us the luxury to view the immediacy of human reality as taking place in suspended reality. Cinema works as a kind of frozen immediacy that forever captures the essence of time in a manner that is impossible in life.

This approach works best for historical, dramatic, and realistic subjects. What can this perspectival rendition of cinema offer films that fall squarely into the science fiction and horror genres, for instance? What do films like Don Siegel's *Invasion of the Body Snatchers*, the dreamlike quality of *Last Year at Marienbad*, and the purely fantastic *Burn Witch, Burn* have anything necessarily to do with the human condition? The works of Wilkie Collins and Edgar Allan Poe, and the quasi-mystical Sherlock Holmes speak to a genuine, but fragmented form of human existence that bring together rogue aspects of the human condition. Granted, this attempt at cohesion takes liberties that violate our sense of reality. Because this is portrayed in a timeless, literary form, we are able to decipher some aspects of our world.

The narration element of *Bob Le Flambeur* exhibits a sense that perhaps Bob's story is retrospective of a life from long ago. Before undertaking a practice run of the casino heist, the narrator says, "Here's how Bob planned it to happen." At the start of the film, Bob walks in and out of shadows. Bob's life is lived in the twilight. The line, "Bob the gambler already a legend of the recent past" infuses this surreal quality that cannot be fully appreciated until the film's closing narration. At the end of the film, Bob goes to the casino as planned in the heist but he becomes distracted and begins to gamble. The narrator explains: "This is Bob Montagne the gambler as nature made him. Lady Luck, his old mistress, made him forget why he was there." This takes place as the young man is shot and killed by the police. Bob holds the dying man. Bob is then arrested as two casino workers bring huge stacks of money that was to be "the job of a lifetime." The formality of referring to Bob as Bob Montagne suggests the closing of a life and not just another chapter of Bob's escapades.

LE SAMOURAI

Unlike Bob's cheerfulness, Jef Costello's seemingly joyless life can be said to be lived entirely within his own head. What the two men have in common is the necessary fortitude that allows them to live a solitary existence. This is the pillar that supports *Le Samourai*. Melville's storied and profound cinematic output can be credited in part to his overarching vision as an artist. Even though the epithet of artist is an abused word today, it does describe Melville's vocation as writer/director. With the exception of his fourth film, *Quand Tu Liras Cette Lettre* (1953), Melville directed and wrote the script to all of his films. This general level of control is enviable today. Much is made today of collaboration. This constraining and often asphyxiating mentality comes about for several reasons: Either it is a recognition of the limitation of the aesthetic vocation, a self-survival mechanism—where true vision is lacking—or serves a social-political purpose. The timeless reality is that art bears the individual and subjective mark of an autonomous artist.

The confidence that Melville must possess in his vision and ability, the sheer direction that every project must have from its inception in order to assuage future difficulties, these are all objectifications of his visionary prowess. This aesthetic conviction is passed on to Costello in his stoic attitude toward life and fortitude. Costello's character is a study in solitude. Melville admits to this himself in an interview.[6] But the solitude that Melville has in mind and which he depicts is the precondition that goes into the makeup of the kind of person that embraces solitude. In other words, Melville's notion of solitude is not commensurate with that of the antisocial loner who goes off to live in the mountains. On the contrary, Costello's solitude is indicative of a particular strength of character that does not know or care for social interaction. Part of Melville's notion of the social world embodies a total rejection of affectation, hypocrisy, and the double morality that is embraced by some people for self-promotion. Costello appears content with his solitary condition. When a beautiful young woman looks and smiles at him from an adjacent car, he gazes at her and continues on his way. Costello never deviates from his task. This level of solitude is best described by Montaigne: "What you must seek is no longer that the world should speak of you, but how you should speak to yourself. Retire into yourself, but first prepare to receive yourself there; it would be madness to trust in yourself if you do not know how to govern yourself."[7]

Montaigne soundly demonstrates that indiscretion is not only reserved for our relations with others. In Costello's character we witness no subsequent emotional breakdown, whining, blaming, and the subterfuge of hiding in the ways of other men. Costello is his own man, so much so that to appreciate his solitude Melville suggests the viewer to come into his world. Montaigne adds: "There are ways to fail in solitude as well as in company. Until you have made yourself such that you dare not trip up in your own presence, and until you are self-respecting and ashamed."[8]

Le Samourai opens with a scene of Costello's small apartment. An open curtain, a gentle rain is falling outside the dirty window. A bird softly chirps in a cage that is placed in the center of the room, as traffic is heard outside in the wet street. Like *Le Cercle Rouge*, *Le Samourai* also begins with a quote. This time the saying comes from *The Book of Bushido*. It reads, "There is no greater solitude than the Samourai's . . . unless perhaps it is that of the tiger in the jungle."

The comparison between the Samourai's solitude and the tiger is interesting in that the tiger is a hunter, but it is also hunted by man. The Bushido—"way of the warrior"—was a way of life for the warrior who, like the tiger, is both hunter and hunted through its own sense of self-sacrifice and discipline. Costello's dingy studio apartment is in keeping with the values of the Samourai: The austere and frugal condition of the room. His demeanor is consistent with his physical appearance and stoic morality. In the opening sequence, Costello is seen lying in bed smoking a cigarette, the smoke rising slowly on the right side of the screen. He then puts on his coat and his fedora and looks in the mirror in a Melvillian moment of self-consciousness before exiting his small apartment. The stillness of the room, gentle rain, and set design are early indications of the inner serenity of Jef Costello. A striking example of Melville's attention to detail, we see the shadow of a passing automobile reflected in the ceiling. The opening scenes of *Le Samourai* are comparable to the early suspense that Fritz Lang establishes at the start of *Ministry of Fear*, when Stephen Neale (Ray Milland) sits anticipating the moment when the clock strikes midnight and he can begin to put the two years that he has spent at Lembridge Asylum behind him.

Costello is next seen on the sidewalk looking around. He gets into a parked Citroen and begins to try out keys that he keeps on a long ring of keys. He succeeds in starting the vehicle and drives off through the Parisian streets in the rain. He drives the stolen car to a garage, where an attendant changes the license plates, Costello patiently looking on. The man gives him some papers; Costello motions to him to hand him a gun. Costello then pays him. This entire sequence of scenes takes place without a word being uttered.

In a testament to Melville's economy of words and narrative structure, Costello goes about creating an alibi for himself. There are no wasted words or awkward movements that would detract from Costello's focus. He first goes to an apartment building to see a woman. She tells him, "I like it when you come around, because you need me," but he doesn't answer her. Then he goes to another apartment building, where some men are playing cards. He his solitude Melville suggests the viewer to come into his world. Montaigne adds: "There are ways to fail in solitude as well as in company. Until you have made yourself such that you dare not trip up in your own presence, and until you are self-respecting and ashamed."[8]

Le Samourai opens with a scene of Costello's small apartment. An open curtain, a gentle rain is falling outside the dirty window. A bird softly chirps in a cage that is placed in the center of the room, as traffic is heard outside in the wet street. Like *Le Cercle Rouge*, *Le Samourai* also begins with a quote. This time the saying comes from *The Book of Bushido*. It reads, "There is no greater solitude than the Samourai's . . . unless perhaps it is that of the tiger in the jungle."

The comparison between the Samourai's solitude and the tiger is interesting in that the tiger is a hunter, but it is also hunted by man. The Bushido—"way of the warrior"—was a way of life for the warrior who, like the tiger, is both hunter and hunted through its own sense of self-sacrifice and discipline. Costello's dingy studio apartment is in keeping with the values of the Samourai: The austere and frugal condition of the room. His demeanor is consistent with his physical appearance and stoic morality. In the opening sequence, Costello is seen lying in bed smoking a cigarette, the smoke rising slowly on the right side of the screen. He then puts on his coat and his fedora and looks in the mirror in a Melvillian moment of self-consciousness before exiting his small apartment. The stillness of the room, gentle rain, and set design are early indications of the inner serenity of Jef Costello. A striking example of Melville's attention to detail, we see the shadow of a passing automobile reflected in the ceiling. The opening scenes of *Le Samourai* are comparable to the early suspense that Fritz Lang establishes at the start of *Ministry of Fear*, when Stephen Neale (Ray Milland) sits anticipating the moment when the clock strikes midnight and he can begin to put the two years that he has spent at Lembridge Asylum behind him.

Costello is next seen on the sidewalk looking around. He gets into a parked Citroen and begins to try out keys that he keeps on a long ring of keys. He succeeds in starting the vehicle and drives off through the Parisian streets in the rain. He drives the stolen car to a garage, where an attendant changes the license plates, Costello patiently looking on. The man gives him some papers; Costello motions to him to hand him a gun. Costello then pays him. This entire sequence of scenes takes place without a word being uttered.

In a testament to Melville's economy of words and narrative structure, Costello goes about creating an alibi for himself. There are no wasted words or awkward movements that would detract from Costello's focus. He first goes to an apartment building to see a woman. She tells him, "I like it when you come around, because you need me," but he doesn't answer her. Then he goes to another apartment building, where some men are playing cards. He

LE SAMOURAI

Unlike Bob's cheerfulness, Jef Costello's seemingly joyless life can be said to be lived entirely within his own head. What the two men have in common is the necessary fortitude that allows them to live a solitary existence. This is the pillar that supports *Le Samourai*. Melville's storied and profound cinematic output can be credited in part to his overarching vision as an artist. Even though the epithet of artist is an abused word today, it does describe Melville's vocation as writer/director. With the exception of his fourth film, *Quand Tu Liras Cette Lettre* (1953), Melville directed and wrote the script to all of his films. This general level of control is enviable today. Much is made today of collaboration. This constraining and often asphyxiating mentality comes about for several reasons: Either it is a recognition of the limitation of the aesthetic vocation, a self-survival mechanism—where true vision is lacking—or serves a social-political purpose. The timeless reality is that art bears the individual and subjective mark of an autonomous artist.

The confidence that Melville must possess in his vision and ability, the sheer direction that every project must have from its inception in order to assuage future difficulties, these are all objectifications of his visionary prowess. This aesthetic conviction is passed on to Costello in his stoic attitude toward life and fortitude. Costello's character is a study in solitude. Melville admits to this himself in an interview.[6] But the solitude that Melville has in mind and which he depicts is the precondition that goes into the makeup of the kind of person that embraces solitude. In other words, Melville's notion of solitude is not commensurate with that of the antisocial loner who goes off to live in the mountains. On the contrary, Costello's solitude is indicative of a particular strength of character that does not know or care for social interaction. Part of Melville's notion of the social world embodies a total rejection of affectation, hypocrisy, and the double morality that is embraced by some people for self-promotion. Costello appears content with his solitary condition. When a beautiful young woman looks and smiles at him from an adjacent car, he gazes at her and continues on his way. Costello never deviates from his task. This level of solitude is best described by Montaigne: "What you must seek is no longer that the world should speak of you, but how you should speak to yourself. Retire into yourself, but first prepare to receive yourself there; it would be madness to trust in yourself if you do not know how to govern yourself."[7]

Montaigne soundly demonstrates that indiscretion is not only reserved for our relations with others. In Costello's character we witness no subsequent emotional breakdown, whining, blaming, and the subterfuge of hiding in the ways of other men. Costello is his own man, so much so that to appreciate asks, "How long will you be here?" One man answers, "We have the room all night," to which Costello answers, "Count me in from two o'clock." Then the man tells him, "Bring your money, in case you lose." In an affirmation of self-confidence, Costello assures the man: "Never lose. Not ever" and walks out. Costello goes to a nightclub to kill its owner. The club has a jazz trio playing; there are a lot of patrons present. Costello has no fear of being seen. Upon entering the club owner's office, the man asks Costello, "Who are you?" Costello simply answers, "It doesn't matter," to which the man asks, "What do you want?" "To kill you."

The calculated series of events at the beginning of *Le Samourai* is a staple of film noir. Costello does not belong to any organized crime ring. Even though he has been paid to kill the nightclub owner, the contract has been negotiated through a middleman. When Costello is arrested at the gambling house, none of the other men present protest or appear concerned. In this society of equals there is an agreement not to ask or repudiate others for their activities. At the police station identification lineup, he is presented as: "Jef Costello; age 30; no criminal record; not carrying a gun."

Le Samourai's pace is indicative of psychological passage of time and how this affects the protagonist. With the exception of being shot, the events of the film do not faze Costello. When he is shot, or to be exact, grazed by a bullet, he goes home and tries to bandage his wound. This is the only instance of emotion that he exhibits. The significance of this is that while everyone is afflicted with physical pain, not everyone is equally susceptible to emotional and psychological pain. Costello views the daily world of men as a kind of spectacle that he is merely passing through.

Perhaps Costello has a side to him that we are not privy to. In the absence of such information, we are left with many questions as to his daily life. One intriguing question is the fact that he does not have a previous criminal record. Why is he entrusted with a complex job given his background as a criminal novice? Is his solitary life an attraction for the people who hire him? It turns out that he, too, has a contract on his head.

At the police station his stoic demeanor is unchanged during the interrogation. He is released due to insufficient evidence, but the police begin to trail him. Several scenes later, three men discuss the pros and cons of leaving him out on the street without having to kill him. They think that he is really good because he fulfilled his contract. One of the three men is a bartender at the club where the owner was killed. In another scene, policemen talk about how he is different. They discuss how to break his alibi, including by bugging his home telephone. These scenes give the viewer respite from the film's narrative and force us to think about Costello's interior constitution. Melville says in an interview that he does not write his film scripts with a moral angle in mind. He does say that often a moral is present after the fact. This enables

Melville to showcase Costello's existential condition. Costello returns to the club and waits outside for the young female piano player to leave. The following exchange is the only time that Costello is seen engaged in anything remotely resembling social interaction:

Costello: "Why say you didn't recognize me?"

Girl: "Why kill Martey?"

Costello: "I was to be paid."

Girl: "What had he done to you?"

Costello: "Not a thing. I didn't know him. I met him for the first and last time twenty-four hours ago."

Girl: "What sort of man are you?"

Costello pays attention to detail. For instance, when he returns home, he finds his bird agitated and missing half its tail feathers. He realizes something is amiss. He realizes that someone has been in his apartment. He looks around and discovers the hidden bugging device. Paying attention to detail pays off. When Costello returns from making a telephone call from a drugstore across the street, he is assaulted by the same man who shot him on the overpass. The man points a gun at Costello and demands that he undertake another job. Costello refuses and the man says, "Is that a principle? Costello answers, "No, it's a habit." This suggests, as Ortega y Gasset argues in his book *Ideas and Beliefs*—habits are things that we embody.[9]

The implication is that there comes a point when principles are no longer conscious notions but rather become a manner of life. Costello then tells the man to tell him who sent him. The man tells him, "You don't know him. He's not in our league." The man's name is Olivier Rey. The admonition, "not in our league" is all that Costello needs to go on the offensive. He takes the gun away and walks out leaving the man tied up in his apartment. Costello takes the man's comment as an insult. He does not agree with the man's assessment of himself.

Confronted with a character like Jef Costello, the average analytic critic's monstrous mania for dissecting reality until there is nothing left, finds himself reaching for the Freudian bag of tricks: Is Costello a misanthrope? Is he a manic depressive? Or, is he merely arrogant? One can go on and empty the coffer of all the up to date, fashionable psychological categories, and the reality remains the same: Costello is a man of honor. Once someone finds sufficient reasons (proofs) to convince himself, only conscience, whenever this is present, can interfere. The two-sided blade of reason can cut both ways if misused. This brings to mind Cocteau's notion of what he refers to as "the collective hypnosis" where the desire for silence, stillness, and the calm observance of the mundane has been squandered along with so many lives that ignore it. Cocteau writes in an introduction to André Bazin's book *Orson Welles: A Critical View*:

> In fact, neither Welles nor I enjoy speaking about our work. The spectacle of life prevents us. We might remain a long time without moving and watch the hotel stir around us. Our immobility would demoralize busy businessmen and frantic specialists of cinematography. It resembled the ordeal of a gondola when busy businessmen and frantic specialists have to climb in and submit to its rhythm. Very soon we were receiving menacing looks. Our stillness had us taken for spies. Our silence caused fright and was charged with explosives. If we happened to laugh, it was frightful. I would see solemn gentlemen pass at top speed in front of us for fear of being tripped up. We were accused of lese-festival, of keeping to ourselves.[10]

The plot and drama of *Le Samourai* is Costello's story. The film is a study of solitude. Melville conveys a formal and stylistic unity that elevates even the most meager subject matter into an existential exploration of his character. Costello's life is a meditation on solitude. Costello's zest for moral clarity is stronger than his desire to flee danger. These qualities make Costello's drama more an introspective exposition of self than a mere rendition of cops and robbers. We witness an example of this when Costello returns to the piano player's apartment to find out if she is in with the people who commissioned the murder of Martey, the nightclub owner. He encounters the man who ordered the job and shoots him.

At this juncture in the film, it becomes clear that loyalty and sincerity are much more important to Costello than simple survival. Later he goes back to the nightclub. He puts on his white gloves and goes up to and begins to stare at the piano player as she plays. In a defensive move, she asks him, "Why, Jef?" He answers, "I've been paid." She understands that he knows just who ordered the killing and why, and that he knows she is in on it. A more conventional ending that could place *Le Samourai* at the mercy of some viewers never takes place. At this point, the police burst into the club and shoot Costello. When they check his gun, they discover that it is unloaded. Costello effectively commits suicide and honors the samurai theme. *Le Samourai* is a tale of solitude and deception. What makes this a fresh film is that Costello is portrayed as undergoing disenchantment and disappointment. What makes *Le Samourai* a tragedy in the classical sense is not that he got what he deserved—that would be a case of simple justice—but that he consciously lives out his destiny.

Chapter 6

LE CERCLE ROUGE

What can we learn today from Melville's 1971 film *Le Cercle Rouge*? His films possess a rare poetic quality that enlighten even the most bare and mundane subjects. Melville's cinematic control over conventions of space and time, set design, pacing and the interweaving of the idiosyncrasies and nuances of his characters make him a master of the mise-en-scène. The precise positioning of a hat, the stationary camera allowing the actors to perform their craft, the long intervals of silence—these are all fine examples of Melville's meticulous mind at work. An exemplary rendition of this technique is evidenced in the train sequence at the start of the film, when Mattei (André Bourvil) and Vogel (Gian-Maria Volonté) are beginning to settle into their compartment. Mattei is a policeman who is escorting Vogel from Marseille to Paris on the overnight train. He handcuffs Vogel to the upper bunk bed. Vogel is shown with his head on the pillow while simultaneously a similar shot of Corey (Alain Delon), who we see for the first time, has the future ringleader of the jewelry heist sleeping in his prison cell. This fine juxtaposition of one man who is on his way to prison, while the other is about to be released the next morning is an early indication of knitting the "red circle" theme. As Mattei opens the window shade, the camera slowly zooms out of the train, first showing the entire window, then the window flanked by other windows, then the length of three train cars. As this takes place, the window where Mattei is seen is always kept in the middle of the screen. Next, we see the entire train bisecting the French countryside. This shot offers a broader perspective of how significant this early encounter is for both parties.

Melville's cinematic themes are timeless and universal: loyalty, perseverance, a life of self-regulating discipline, and a cavalier and stoic attitude toward life. But classical philosophical motifs in a French policier, some cynics will cry out? In a *Midi* Magazine interview from May 27, 1970, Melville takes on this particular point when asked why his fascination with the policier. He explains: "I think the police thriller is the only modern form of tragedy possible. A protagonist doles out a sudden death or is himself killed. There's no doubt that the police thriller is a very practical vehicle for the adventure film in France." Melville then goes on to explain that because France does not have the vast open spaces found in the United States, action films there must conform to a lot "of twists and turns."

The twists and turns in a Melville film do not convey the same gratuitous and disjointed sense of physical action that some people have come to expect from this genre. Action for Melville denotes an overstatement. Much like George Simenon's novels, Melville's work is framed not by the action performed by his characters, but by the interior world that defines them. This is so much the case that Melville, like Hitchcock, did not enjoy the filming process because he found this to be merely the mechanical transcription of a personal vision.

Of the thirteen films that Melville made from 1947 to 1972, *Le Cercle Rouge* is without a doubt his greatest artistic and commercial success. The other Melville policier films are: *Bob Le Flambeur* (1956); *Le Doulos* (1963); *Le Deuxieme souffle* (1966); *Le Samouraï* (1967), and his final film, *Un Flic* (1972). *Le Cercle Rouge* is a tale of an "encounter" as Melville himself describes this work. The plot revolves around the break-in of a famous and well-protected jewelry shop on the Place Vendôme. This alone makes this film one of the great heist films of all time along with *The Asphalt Jungle*, *Rififi*, and *Topkapi*. A recently released felon, Corey, brings together a team of men to undertake this difficult job. The group includes a criminal on the lam named Vogel and an ex-policeman sharpshooter, Jansen (Yves Montand), who has been taken over by "the beast," as he refers to alcohol. While the heist scene itself remains a masterful example of filmmaking, the scrupulous and patient execution of this caper takes just twenty-five minutes. It is the preceding and subsequent scenes that give the film its balanced and intelligently sustained suspense.

What makes the heist so intriguing is the way that the characters are brought together. While all three men accept the job for various private motives, their destinies become intertwined in such a way that preclude the interference of mere luck. The film begins with an epigram taken from Siddhartha Gautama, the Buddha, that describes how the sage "drew a circle with a piece of red chalk and said: 'When men, even unknowingly, are to meet one day, whatever may befall each, whatever their diverging paths, on the said day, they will inevitably come together in the red circle.'"

Melville's task in *Le Cercle Rouge* is to show how this can occur. The outcome is a painstakingly elegant and flawless clinic on how to engage in cinematic art. What one does not find in a Melville film is the dizzying and nauseating effects provided by shoulder-mounted camera work that achieve nothing short of self-mockery, gratuitous violence, and vulgarity, sophomoric special effects, superfluous and pointless chatter, and the endemic lack of direction that characterizes a large percentage of post late-1970s films. Also absent is the ideological proselytizing of "committed" directors who have sacrificed cinematic art to the whims of cinema as bread and circus.

Instead, Melville creates suspense by allowing great lengths of time to take place between segments of dialogue and action. The responsibility is shifted to the viewer to tune in to the characters and their circumstances. Nothing comes cheap in Melville's films. Melville, like Tarkovsky, is a director gifted with a vision of how a story is to unfold, of which the filming process is merely the physical manifestation.

Chapter 6

One particularly interesting anecdote about *Le Cercle Rouge* is Rui Nogueira's, writer of *Melville on Melville*, conversation he had with Melville. The director told him: "You're one of those intellectuals for whom a filmmaker, once he's successful, no longer holds any interest. So, since *Le Cercle Rouge* is a great success, one of the most successful films in French cinema, I'm sure your intellectual side is stronger than the rest of you. And even if you don't have the courage to tell me, you think it's less important than the other films."

In an inescapably interesting paradox, the guard who tells Corey that he is the best man for the jewel heist, tells him that he wants out of his job, while Corey says that he doesn't want to return to prison. The sequence of events after his release from prison establishes a poetic regard for solitude—one of Melville's repeating themes. We see Corey eating at a diner as dawn is transformed into morning. Next, he goes to the apartment of an old acquaintance named Rico who betrayed him during his court hearing. There he finds his ex-girlfriend. He takes several thousand franks and a gun from Rico's safe. He then places a picture of his girlfriend in the man's safe as a reminder of a double betrayal. This is his encounter with the world outside of prison and it will eventually prove to be a costly one. Corey is next seen walking the streets at 7:30 a.m. before he enters a pool hall and begins to play alone, until two of Rico's men come in and attempt to shoot him. This is an important series of events. Even though he has not broken any laws at this point, this encounter with Rico will prove instrumental in the police investigation of the Jewry heist. This early series of engrossing events is indicative of a greater widening of the red circle theme.

Corey buys an American car. He is seen driving and listening to a jazzy score. Thereafter, the red circle comes into play once again when Corey stops at a police roadblock that is intended for Vogel, the escaped prisoner. There is no way for Corey to know; he assumes the search is for him because of the man that he shot at the pool hall. Melville essentially tells two tales in *Le Cercle Rouge*, Vogel's escape and Corey's freedom, which include Rico's wrath and the jewelry heist. Corey's fate is sealed when Vogel gets into the unlocked trunk of Corey's Plymouth Fury III while he eats in the diner. Corey's side-glance does not miss this, and he drives to a muddy field and tells the man to come out. Vogel comes out of the trunk with Corey's gun and tells him to put up his hands.

Corey: "Fine way to thank me."

Vogel: "You see me climb in?"

Corey: "Sure. Or I wouldn't suggest you get some air."

Vogel: "Why run the risk like that?"

Corey shows Vogel his prison release paper. Vogel then asks, "This morning? That's unbelievable." Corey then shows his character when Vogel asks him if he was not afraid of being found in his car. To which Corey nonchalantly answers, "Of what?" and then throws Vogel a cigarette box. Corey doesn't explain why he helped him.

The characteristics of the red circle theme are illuminating and suggestive of a deeper connection between the characters. What makes this deterministic and even fatal theme so vitally important is that it ties the dual thematic lines of narrative together. Might greater reflection on this theme not logically deliver us to Leibniz's monistic idea that to change one thing is tantamount to changing everything? Corey and Vogel remain together due to the prison guard having told Corey of the jewelry heist. If not for this central tenet of the film, they would both part ways after their initial meeting in the field. Human reality does not readily present itself as a polished moral tale, but rather incondite fragments.

The circumstances that surround Mattei, Santi, the nightclub owner who refuses to turn police informer, and Corey's girlfriend, who holds the same sense of loyalty, are indicative of the red circle theme. What would happen to Corey after he is trailed down a deserted country road by two of Rico's men in a Chevrolet Impala, if not for Vogel who comes out of the trunk right before they shoot Corey? This signals the beginning of their bond. This question is relevant because the encounter with Rico's men is an episode that, up to that juncture, belongs solely to Corey's experience. As more of these situations take place, we are granted the right to question whether these events are mere coincidence.

Equally true is Mattei's having to justify his beliefs to the pathologically cynical inspector general's. Mattei is a fine policeman? The chief inspector scolds him:

Chief inspector: "Mr. Mattei. Didn't you know that a suspect must be considered guilty?"

Mattei: "Not for me, sir. I've dealt with so many suspects who were innocent."

Chief inspector: "You must be joking! No one is innocent, all men are guilty. They're born innocent but it doesn't last."

Mattei: "Sir, my chief just told you that only chance can catch Vogel now. Chance and myself, actually."

Chief inspector: "Mr. Mattei, I don't doubt your goodwill, but allow me to doubt your efficiency in arresting culprits."

We get to know Corey better when he returns to his apartment for the first time since leaving prison. He looks around but shows no emotion, until he throws a picture of his ex-girlfriend into a trash can. This domestic scene depicts Corey, as we also witness in *Bob Le Flambeur*, as a man who possesses a sense of refinement. We are left wondering why Corey ended up in prison in the first place.

No less interesting is a biographical profile of Jansen, the ex-policeman. A biographical profile is important because it counters the chief inspector's disregard for individuality and autonomy. If it is true, as Ortega y Gasset asserts that, "Every life is a point of view directed upon the universe" then we see that Jansen has very powerful private reasons for entering into a partnership with Corey and Vogel.[11] Like the professor in *Seven Thieves*, Jansen's motive for taking part in the jewel heist is not the desire for money. Jansen uses the opportunity to confront his greatest fears, not the least which is his weakness for the bottle. Biography is important in Melville's film's because his characters are examples of subjective entities that refuse objectification in one way or other. Melville's films go a long way in depicting a valuation of life over the all-consuming objectifying superstructures of postmodernity. Ortega suggests:

> Every individual, whether person, nation or epoch, is an organ, for which there can be no substitute, constructed for the apprehension of truth. This is how the latter, which is in itself of a nature alien from historical variation, acquires a vital dimension.[12]

While the natural processes of life, illness, fate, chance, just to mention a few, regulate themselves—all that man can do is contemplate this reality. Jansen gives up drinking because the job requires a steady, expert hand. The preparation for the heist is a classic Melville exposition of patience, intrigue, and suspense. Corey and Vogel go through a maze of alleys, buildings, and rooftops until they enter the jewelry store through a small bathroom window. This scene is intense and intelligent, without unnecessary bravado and brutality. The reason that Jansen needs a sure hand is twofold: First, he makes a "soft" bullet out of lead, antimony, and tin that will turn off the electronic control that regulates the alarm system without destroying the mechanism. Secondly, Jansen has to be at his best to shoot the control device from about twenty yards away.

The post-heist scenes in *Le Cercle Rouge* concentrate on the problem of how to dispose of the jewels. This is not a matter of irony as is the case in *Seven Thieves* and the gold being claimed by the mountain at the end of *Treasure of the Sierra Madre*, rather human treachery. At the end of *Le Cercle Rouge*, Corey and Vogel become trapped by Mattei when they attempt to sell him the jewelry. Someone has already alerted the police. Jansen, who does not want the money to begin with, survives and gives up his vice. The circle is closed.

UN FLIC

Un Flic opens with a memorable scene of a storm in a deserted French coastal town. Four men drive slowly and park their car a short distance from a small bank, the only business open in the area. The inclement weather and the boarded-up isolation of the town make for a perfect bank robbery. The scene changes, and in parallel editing, we are introduced to police captain Eduard Coleman (Alain Delon) riding with three other policemen through the busy dusk Parisian traffic. Coleman narrates: "Every afternoon, at the same time I started my cruise by the Champs-Élysées. I was on duty just before nightfall. But it was only when the town was asleep that I could really work. My name's Eduard Coleman." Two aspects of Coleman's character are immediately felt—Delon is not playing a gangster, but a police detective this time. The other is that, in addition to being a detective, he is also a loner.

The scene of the bank robbery is a long and patient ordeal that is not intended for the fans of roller-coaster ride, gratuitous action, and cardboard character films. These scenes are intelligent and well crafted. The four bank robbers disappear into the mist and rain. They bury the money in a field and drive one of the men who was shot to a hospital. Coleman, too, is seen driving in the dark night. Simultaneous action, and the fact that the number of bank robbers and policemen is four, suggest the interconnection between people's destinies. This is confirmed when Coleman stops at a club to see Cathy (Catherine Deneuve). Also present at the club is Simon (Richard Crenna), the leader of the bank robbers.

Un Flic is Melville's last film; he died a short time later at age fifty-three. At the time of its release the film received legions of ire from Melville's detractors. While *Un Flic* lacks some of the tight scripting and suspense of *Le Samourai* and *Le Cercle Rouge*, its greatest contempt does not spring from aesthetic motives. *Le Cercle Rouge* was released in October 1971 and sold over four million tickets. This commercial success alone is reason enough in some ideological circles to disqualify and envy its director. Melville was a promoter of individual autonomy, American films, and automobiles and was hated by French communists. The outrageous personal attacks that were leveled at *Un Flic* bear out the pettiness of ideological criticism. The danger in this game is twofold—defamation of the artist personally, and more importantly, the deconstruction of the film for unsuspecting future viewers. Most of the criticism that has been brought to bear on *Un Flic* has come from the heretofore mentioned unfair critics.

The relationship of the bank robbers is strained when the three remaining gangsters pick up Schmidt at the hospital, who they left there after the heist suffering with a gunshot wound. They dress up as ambulance drivers, but they can't move him, because he is comatose. Instead, they have Cathy enter the room and give him a shot to kill him in order to keep him from talking.

The strongest ambiguity that the film establishes is the question of whether Inspector Coleman and Simon know each other. We know that both men are intimate with Cathy. What is not clear is whether Coleman knows of Simon's activities and to what extent. If so, does Coleman look the other way? The film is plotted in such a way as to suggest that Coleman does not know about the bank robbery. He certainly does not know about the second heist—the interception of drugs on the train—because he hears about it from an informer. Before the three hoodlums come together to discuss their second and more daring heist—stealing drugs from a Paris-Lisbon train—Coleman, Cathy, and Simon have a drink together. While the second heist is particularly fanciful, this alone is not sufficient reason to dismiss the film. This aspect of the film is in keeping with the adventure angle of the plot.

Lowering Simon onto the moving train from a helicopter utilizes Melville's staple techniques: silence, laconic dialogues, meticulous planning, and superb scene crafting. Melville's films are philosophically interesting because they depict a slice-of-life realism.

Melville's work contains great reverence for irony. What is a more fundamental tenet of the human condition than irony? However, irony often escapes us because of the temporal proximity of reality to our lives. The advantage of cinema over reality is the level of control that the viewer retains. Cinema serves as a container of life that enables discerning viewers the luxury to piece together fragmented reality. In effect, Melville's work is a pastiche or vignette of daily existence. Again, what is so important about Melville's films philosophically is their vital grounding in reality itself.

The ending of *Bob Le Flambeur*, *Le Samourai*, *Le Cercle Rouge* and *Un Flic* all convey a sense of time winding down. The ending of these films are: imprisonment for *Bob Le Flambeur*, reluctant suicide in *Le Samourai*, killed by police in *Le Cercle Rouge*, and another reluctant suicide in *Un Flic*. The final sequences of these four films offer a sense of tired characters who have become disillusioned and disenchanted, their vitality squeezed out of them—men who are destroyed by the loss of willpower.

NOTES

1. *Bob Le Flambeur* (1955).

2. Marías, Julián. *Philosophy as Dramatic Theory*. University Park: The Pennsylvania State University Press, 1971, 237.

3. Assouline, Pierre. *Simenon*. New York: Alfred A. Knopf, 1997, 340.

4. Ibid., 340.

5. Schopenhauer, Arthur. *The Wisdom of Life* and *Counsels and Maxims*. New York: Prometheus Books, 1995.

6. *Le Cercle Rouge*. The Criterion Collection. Booklet. Walter J. Black, 107.

7. Montaigne, Michel de. *Selected Essays*. Roslyn, N.Y.: Walter J. Black, 1943, 107.

8. Ibid., 107.

9. Ortega y Gasset, José. *Ideas y Creencias*. Colección Austral. Espasa-Calpe, S.A., 1976.

10. Bazin, Andre. *Orson Welles: A Critical View*. Los Angeles: Acrobat Books, 1991, 31.

11. Ortega y Gasset. *The Modern Theme*. New York: Harper Torchbooks, 1961, 91.

12. Ibid.

Chapter 7

Seven Thieves
Making the World Gasp

SEVEN THIEVES

Synopsis

Seven Thieves is a casino heist film. On closer inspection, Henry Hathaway's film employs the imaginative use of irony. The characters of this caper bring to life a blend of classic moral, Aesop-like vignettes that showcase the clash of appearance and reality, and how life is ultimately defined by personal choices. The main two characters have a lease on life, as they bargain to cheat Lady Luck and human contingency for a final time.

Henry Hathaway's 1960 film *Seven Thieves* falls in the heist category. The setting is Monte Carlo. In the opening scene we find the professor, Theo Wilkins (Edward G. Robinson), on the beach, conversing with two small children about the nature of seashell collecting—an innocuous beginning, to be sure. When a voice is heard in the background, the professor turns to greet Paul (Rod Steiger), an old friend. The two men go to a small café to talk about the job that the professor has in mind. The feisty Paul has just spent three years in prison and is reluctant to even consider another experiment, as the professor calls his plan. The latest caper that the professor has in mind is no other than breaking into the vault of the casino, what the professor calls the temple of Midas, on the night of the Governor's Ball. The professor's hope is that during an event like that, when people divert their energy to mingling, few will notice them. One of the major themes of *Seven Thieves* has to do with the consequences of neglecting the minutiae of everyday experience.

Seven Thieves allows us to rediscover or reenact the order of what Edmund Husserl has referred to as the lifeworld of experience. Theo's world-weariness is an indication of an incomplete life. We find him troubling himself with what is to be the last and definitive attempt to round out his existence. Theo's plan is not as one dimensional as the plot, that is, the surface structure of the film, may suggest. We gradually come to realize this as we get to know him throughout the film.

What is important about the idea of the everyday world as the ground of human existence? Why place so much emphasis on the fleeting and stubborn condition of daily experience? *Seven Thieves* brings together a motley crew of characters who do not depart too drastically from the lives of actual men and women. They are a cornucopia or slice of life of the human condition. None of them alone may paint a picture of most people, but when viewed as composites of human strengths and frailties, they manage to enlighten us with a good representation of human experience. A few of these characters live in a fog of suspended animation, where the only thing that moves them is reaping the monetary reward of the heist. Others, Melanie (Joan Collins) and Raymond (Alexander Scourby) use the heist to correct their moral deficiencies. Melanie's greatest wish is to find respectability, while Raymond aims for the exploration of carnal pleasure. Paul and Theo, on the other hand, have loftier goals than the mere attainment of money.

Theo and Paul respect the order of everyday life. In both men, we witness the same respect for detail in everyday life that we find in Jean-Pierre Melville's films. Theo and Paul exhibit a vitality that is not easily quenched with sensual rewards. Theo's hope is that he will be remembered whenever people think about the casino heist, when no explanation is found for the disappearance of the money. His strongest motivation stems from a contrarian, Volterian regard for laughter. "How did they do it? Who was it that accomplished such a feat?" This, he hopes, is what people will ask. Granted, Theo's answer to his existential crisis may appear extreme, but given the conventions of the film, one is to accept that the casino heist can actually stand for most any other human project. Cinema must allow for a degree of sensual magic that reminds us that we are engaged in fiction. Cinema is not life, rather a mere representation of life's essences. Cinematic visual magic corresponds to our personal level of imagination. For readers, film allows for a comparison of the virtues of the written word with the exigencies of the latter's visual manifestation. Some writers and readers refuse this on the grounds that visual representation of stories strip their vision of the fictitious quality of written works. Cinema and reading are not mutually exclusive activities. Nonreaders, delight in the control that film offers them in terms of imaginative possibilities. It is for this latter group that film has the best justification for being. For reflective and contemplative persons, cinema can be enjoyed as a kind of body double, where we can venture out of ourselves, away from our vital circumstance, as it were, and view aspects of our lives as they stand still before us. This is the greatest cultural contribution that moving pictures can offer. Cinema, as Tarkovsky suggests, is essentially the capturing of time.

Despite imaginative aesthetic conventions, human reality remains the anchor of how much we can actually reap from imagination—our inherent regulator of possibility. Cinema, as is the case in literature, ought not merely purport to demonstrate cases or modes of the believable—for that matter, we often find reality to be much stranger than fiction—but to serve as a silhouette or map of the human condition. In addition, we cannot neglect to appreciate the playful and often unserious nature of film as a propaedeutic of human experience.

It happens that the professor is a scientist, a chemist who lost his job a while back due to some academic imbroglio. The fine details of the professor's past are not made known, thus creating the impression of a more sophisticated character than one would normally expect in this genre, and perhaps also, in the academic world. The strength of Theo's character is that he is multidimensional. He is a man of culture who finds himself outside of his comfort zone. Yet he is also worldly, practical and innovative. He would never be able to manage the different personalities that he brings together and with the level of control that he retains, if not for the latter two qualities. We find the professor surprising us throughout the film. Theo understands that his choices cast a light on both, his inner self as well as in external conditions that transcend him. As a chemist, he is concerned with the nature of experimentation. We hear him mentioning this several times throughout the film. This notion of experimentation surpasses his regard for the scientific method, once he is no longer employed as a scientist. What does he mean by experiment, temperature, ingredients? He has incubated the idea of the casino heist for over a year. His experiment has essentially turned into an existential project. While scientists try to remain outside their experiments, as objective observers, Theo becomes his own project. He does so for posterity. When asked by Paul in his characteristic matter of fact manner why he wants to undertake this job, the professor responds, "I want to make the world gasp a little, Paul." This, he intimates, is his final testament to a world that, he believes, has wronged him.

The beginning of *Seven Thieves* showcases an existential zest in Theo and Paul that sets the mood for the rest of the film. These two characters are highly stylized and represent an individualized and personal direction to the casino heist plot. There is nothing stereotypical about them. They are not mindless criminals. Theirs is not a world ruled by greed or quick sensual satisfaction. This is evident in Paul's restrained composure in dealing with Melanie. Neither are they portrayed as territorial strongmen wielding weapons. Their manner is cordial and likeable. As they sit on a bench that overlooks the beach, Paul asks Theo why he sent him the airline ticket. Theo responds: "I thought you might enjoy a change, rest." Theo does not know how to break his latest idea to Paul. The professor's reticence stems from a recent failure that resulted in Paul going to prison. Paul answers in his characteristic wry manner, "I've been resting for the last three years, remember?" This is Paul's subdued way of admitting regret for a past that he does not allow himself to dwell on. Theo responds, "I have very few friends. Nobody closer than you." This line of dialogue proves to be prophetic, as we come to realize at the end of the film. Paul doesn't buy this and forces Theo to utter, "What's happened to you?" You used to have those treasured gifts: patience, silence." Paul answers, sarcastically, "I lost them resting." Paul is nobody's fool. Early in the film, Paul comes across as restless, an irascibility born of too many failed aspirations and illusions. Only later do we begin to see this jagged disposition as an overtly cautious and measured perspective.

The early scenes by the beach establish Theo as an idealist romantic who is coping with the events of his past. Paul is pragmatic and methodical, always cutting to the chase. Both Theo and Paul are concerned with time: Theo does not have much left, while Paul has an aversion to wasting it. Theo, trying to put his life in perspective, admits: "Me? A disowned Einstein. A man kicked out of the seat of higher learning and into the gutter." Theo views his future as thwarted. Paul, on the other hand, responds by shrugging off the past. He merely says, "Well, let's not indulge ourselves." Putting bygones to rest may be Paul's manner of dealing with his past—with the passage of time itself. He remains practical in disposition, not bitter.

Theo's unfettered idealism and optimism is best manifested when he tells Paul that, "Luck grows like apples on trees. If your reach is long enough it's there to be plucked." This is an indication of Theo's reticence. Judging by his immense enthusiasm for the new project, we realize Theo is motivated by renewal. Several times throughout the film Theo manages to offer glimpses of his wisdom, much as Howard, the wise prospector in John Huston's *Treasure of the Sierra Madre*. Theo's preoccupation suggests the question: What does it all mean? They go into the casino to have a drink. Theo tells him, "Look around you, Paul. You're in the temple of Midas. The holy of holiest. See all the worshipers of the golden calf." Paul agrees. Bringing the drink to his mouth, he then answers, "Everybody's rich but they want to get richer." Theo capitulates on this mutual perspective, turning philosophical: "Just think of it, Paul. Whose money is it? Where does it all come from? Tax-deductible expenses, excess dividends, rents paid to absentee landlords, or money of men who never got a fingernail dirty, who become rich on the sweat of . . ." at which point Paul interrupts him by reminding him that nobody forces then to gamble. Paul is not interested in self-pitying and ideological fodder that merely serves as justification for their actions.

This sequence of dialogue effectively establishes the confidence that the two men responsible for setting up the heist are equal to their task. The start of the film convinces viewers early on that Paul and Theo are not reckless and irrational criminals. If they were reckless, they would never successfully plan the heist or pull it off.

For the heist genre to work effectively a cinematic convention must be established that reproduces the essence and techniques used in real world capers. The exploits of Henri "Papillion" Charriere, the—"butterfly"—who allegedly escaped from Devil's Island in the 1940s; the twenty members of the great train robbery of 1963 in Cheddington, Buckinghamshire quickly come to mind as real-life examples of this kind of calculated daring. Many more real-life capers can be mentioned, but as Somerset Maugham asserts, reality makes for boring storytelling. Part of the reason for this is that imagination must be cultivated and allowed free reign for it to suggest something of substantial worth for most people. This process takes time and patience. This may explain the qualitative differences between imaginative heists as the above mentioned and examples of brutal and deadly hold ups.

Expediency is the main problem that most of the films that try to convey imaginative heist encounter. How to best tell a story? This is a problem for writers: words conveying emotions, thoughts and pictures formed out of conventions of language. Film directors address these same concerns in respect to time and visuals. In a sensually desensitized age, hollow visual images are enough to entertain some people. But there are exemptions. Andrei Tarkovsky's films and *2001: A Space Odyssey* come to mind as films that convey poetic imagery.

Art, like human existence, ought to possess a translucent and transcendent quality that enlightens without the need for self-consciousness. Human existence may present itself as a spectacle of sight and sound in its immediacy, but to refuse to go beyond this level merely suggests a fool's tale. Unfortunately, like children, whose initial aesthetic stage of engagement with reality is limited to the sensual—one of color and sound—most films do not transcend the sensual. What is so captivating about cinema as visual art is its inherent—even though, accidental humanistic quality. By this, I mean that in looking at the world through a mirror called cinema, we are given a golden opportunity to decipher the bits and pieces of reality that normally would escape our attention. From these neglected details and vignettes of daily existence one can awaken to the greater unseen order of human life. Georg Simmel points this out when he argues in his essay from 1908 entitled "Subjective Culture" that "thus far at least, historical development has moved toward steadily increasing separation between objective cultural production and the cultural level of the individual."[1] The importance of this realization is nowhere better played out that in the aesthetic, cultural, and life forms of contemporary man.

Seven Thieves is comparable in theme to such other effective heist films: *Topkapi*, which revolves around the stealing of precious jewels from a national museum in Turkey; the *Thomas Crown Affair*, a film that has to do with the masterminding of a bank heist by a bank executive, except this film does not concentrate on the unforeseen ironical twist that is so central to *Seven Thieves*, and *Shoot the Piano Player*, a moral tale of a soft-headed man who drags his brother into the underworld of crime. In *The Detective*, Alec Guinness, playing the role of G. K. Chesterton's Father Brown, spends his time running after an art thief who curiously steals paintings for his love of art, not profit, the thief's contention being that art belongs not so much to he who owns it, but rather to he who enjoys it. Chesterton's social commentary is never more subtle, yet poignant.

The dominant theme of *The Detective* is resentment, as is also the case in *Seven Thieves*. The professor is an old man who understands that time is the universal equalizer. He plans the heist as a last chance to perform a task that seems commensurate with his vision of life. Heist films that maintain motives other than mere profit are always more appealing because they justify the actions of the characters on what appear to be loftier terms. Some critics have described this genre as being simple cops and robbers. When we pay attention to the better films in this genre, we notice a profound undercurrent that usually goes undetected by casual viewers. Action in film, while remaining a central ingredient in the development of the narrative, can be effective as a sensual dimension. The failure of most action films, though, is that they are only that: a saturation of action. Unfortunately, in many cases mere gratuitous action is what makes a film watchable for some viewers and a strong justification for making them.

Just before the two men discuss the plan, Paul looks around the small café and witnesses a well-dressed woman sitting in a nearby table, eating while her white poodle eats from another plate. This is a case of witty and observant social commentary that, like Chesterton's wit, falls short of ideology. This is a significant scene becomes it sets the stage for what will be another prominent theme of the film: to steal from the morally decrepit rich, is in fact, no crime at all. This is the rallying point from which the film springs, even though we get the impression that stealing itself would not be dismissed by most of these characters. For example, take the professor's reasoning: "Look Paul, everyone's rich and they want to be richer." This line is enough to have some viewers rally them on. Later in the scene he utters "when boardinghouses, casinos, insurance companies go under no one cares." This is a case of self-justification. The strength of the professor's argument is that people do not care about the losses that a casino will have. In fact, he is counting on that bit of practical wisdom.

The German philosopher Max Scheler (1874–1928) makes a valid argument in his work, *Resentment in the Structuring of Ethics* (*Das Ressentiment im Aufbau der Moralen*) by suggesting that resentment comes about through a self-analysis, where one sees oneself trapped in a situation that we dislike. This leads to vindication in extreme cases, but often settles as a sense of entitlement. This is part of the emotional baggage that the professor carries with him. The professor is convinced that this action will only cause the average person to rejoice. Does he associate the casino with the people who expelled him from the university?

The motives that entice the seven characters to take part in the heist are all different and, in some respects, unique. Paul, for instance, is reluctant to accept the job, but decides to do it only in reverence for the professor, who begs for his help for a final time. Theo needs a confidant who he can trust, but also a witness to his life. Paul's reason for taking on the casino job is not truly made manifest until the end of the film. In his behalf, we can argue that he makes a sacrifice for the well-being of the professor. Raymond, the executive secretary of the casino, who happens to be a coward, becomes involved in order to ingratiate himself with Melanie, a nightclub dancer. Raymond's desire for Melanie is not exactly clear, just that, like a young boy, he will do anything for the attention of a girl. While most of the other characters are doing it strictly for the money, it is a fundamental staple of the major themes of the film that the main two characters, the professor and Paul, who mastermind the entire operation, have more profound motivations. These are the only two characters that are not doing it strictly for the money. This leads the active viewer to the realization that cinema has a viewpoint. The viewpoint is the director's vision, which allows for a unified meaning to flow from the narrative. The viewpoint does not have to be a grand vision of human reality, but it must move the drama along toward a definite resolution. A film like *It's a Mad, Mad, Mad, Mad World* embraces a form of zaniness that can only exist as cinema, and yet the characters all embody a particular take on human reality that is in keeping with some actual human types.

It is my experience that in watching films there should be some directed meaning—a stylistic coherence, though not necessarily a moral that organizes the visual and sensual experience. Simple cohesion will do. One of the demands that most people make of cinema is that it offers a unified vision of any given angle of human reality.

Paul accepts the job because Poncho (Eli Wallach) convinces him that the group is "to gamble with higher stakes than the casino is used to seeing." They are banking on a blitzkrieg technique, an assault on reality so remarkable—that the traditional "it can't be done" that the casino has come to expect will prove to be its greatest weakness. Complementary to this methodical and calculated risk is Paul's thorough background check of the other five, excluding the professor whom he knows intimately. The degree of rigorous preparation that goes into this heist disqualifies the average common thief. The professor has planned the entire operation for a year. He has secured detailed maps of the inside of the casino as well as the schedule of the intricacies of its day-to-day operation. The heist is to take place on the night of the Governors' Ball. Theo intuits, "the casino will be too full and busy" to look for their kind. For instance, he makes sure that the baron, whom they are to impersonate, will be gone at the time of the heist in Brazil taking care of oil business. They purchase a Rolls-Royce and paint the baron's code of arms on the doors. Later, Poncho, who impersonates the baron, throws a temper tantrum as the wheelchair-bound baron is known to do. When the professor asks if perhaps Poncho is overdoing it, Paul replies, "You ever heard of a millionaire being thrown out of a casino because his manners were bad?" *Seven Thieves* exploits the folly, hypocrisies and half-truths of a large number of human relationships.

The viewpoint of this film, which is also a strong observation of human existence, is founded on the overall understanding that the regular casino goers are not exactly moral people. This is best exemplified in the scene when a tuxedo-wearing gentleman who is a guest at the Governors' Ball recognizes Melanie from previously having seen her dance in a nightclub. Perhaps, like attracts like.

Theo gives the distinct impression that dreams and the will to make them real are a main ingredient in our drive to live. Compare the professor's desire to "make the world gasp a little" to the panache of Jean-Pierre Sarti (Ives Montand) in *Grand Prix* that spectators come to the race to see someone get killed. Why does he race? To put life in proper perspective. This is similar to the anxiety felt by Guido (Marcello Mastroniani) in Fellini's *8½* in trying to reconcile his artistic vision with the pressure exerted on him by the producer.

Reading too much into characterization of any type often serves to destroy the conventions of the on-screen character. There exists a sphere of interiority, in fiction and is often the case in life itself, that remains impenetrable. This sacred space cannot be violated by overindulgent analysis and theory.

Existential longing is beautifully placed on display at the end of *Seven Thieves*, when the job is successfully completed and the professor dies of a heart attack in the back of a delivery van. The human impact of this scene and the film become manifest when we find out from Paul that the professor is his father. This is one of several memorable scenes in the film. At this point, the question of immorality is effectively juxtaposed with immortality. This latter theme takes precedence at the end of the film, but its centrality to the film is rendered from the very start. Because the professor has such a strong desire for avenging the wrongs that he has suffered, some may come to question his moral makeup. From the start, we know little about the professor: he lost his teaching position as a chemist. Is this enough for us to take a moral stance on his entire life? The casino owners don't think so.

When the professor exclaims to Paul early in the film that he has no friends, it is not clear if this is entirely his fault or the result of life's contingencies. It is a common observance that very good people often have few friends. Many films in the action/adventure genre have traditionally suffered from myopia; their guiding raison d'être is dependent on visuals.

The professor's planning the heist for the duration of a year signifies that a great deal of thought has gone into the project. A heist film like *Ocean's Eleven* works both as entertainment and a plausible storyline, because all of the men that Danny Ocean (Frank Sinatra) brings together are ex-army companions. This is a significant plotting device because it explains their respective level of expertise as well as the necessary human bond they enjoy. It is a common thread found in this type of film that it takes either fate or a malicious will in the form of an envious outsider to foil what meticulous planning and cohesion can accomplish.

The situation in *Seven Thieves* is different. As an example of frail and vitally unfounded human relations, the heist brings together a series of strangers that even though possessing a specialized skill, do not respect each other, as is made evident at the end. Paul's is astute. He checks out all of the members beforehand. The problem is not the inherent complexity of the heist itself, but rather trust. Poncho cannot bring himself to take the cyanide pill that the professor has created. The libidinal reason for Raymond, the executive secretary of the casino, to accept the project is his infatuation with a nightclub dancer. How far this quasi-romance will keep him committed to the heist is a question that concerns Paul and Theo. The close-up shot of Raymond's face as he looks at Melanie dance at the club is one of a man mesmerized by an unattainable fantasy. The gleam in his eyes speak volumes of a man that would do almost anything to attain what he does not possess.

Melanie lies to Paul about her past as they sit in the casino during a trial run of the heist. Paul confronts her and tells her that he checked her out and that her parents were not what she told him. Melanie is shocked by the extent of Paul's meticulous planning. She is also impressed. She is desperately in need of creating a background of decency to her life. In an earlier exchange, after Paul accuses Melanie of bitterness, she replies, "Not bitter Mr. Mason. Just tired." Late in the film, Melanie comes to the realization, "I used to believe that having a lot of money may let me be born again." She believes she will give up her nightclub act and shady associations in exchange for instant respectability.

The social themes in *Seven Thieves* never deteriorate into ideological diatribe. Early in the film we witness Paul telling Theo not to indulge himself in talk about the rich people that frequent the casino, for they too want those same riches. Paul goes to great lengths to remind the professor that perhaps his justification for the heist is not so grand. Paul does not allow Theo the luxury of justifying the casino heist. Theo is an interesting character, because he is a man who is feeling the bite of time. He is older and understands his time to be limited. However, age is not the sole reason for Theo's crisis. Theo's life has taken a particular path that has delivered him to his predicament. Let us apply the following Gabriel Marcel contention to Theo's existential crisis: "I wonder if nothingness does not play a kind of intermediary and suspect role between two positions of being—an initial position and an ultimate one."[2] Theo's longing addresses the nothingness that rules his life. He tells Paul that he has the urgent need to see a friendly face.

The second nightclub scene is supremely revealing about the emotional condition of Theo, Paul, and Poncho. Paul looks around the nightclub, and turns to Theo, "You mix with some peculiar company." Theo, using language from his previous career as a chemist, then tells him, "In an experiment like this you take human beings as we find them. Why be interested in their private life?" This exchange is particularly important not only to the film, but also to this genre. This is best exemplified by Jacques Barzun and Wendell Hertig Taylor in the introduction of their book, *A Catalogue of Crime*:

> For the seasoned reader, tales of crime fulfill the definition that Dr. Johnson gave in another context: "the art of murdering contrary to what is often said, the pleasure is not the symbolic satisfaction of aggressive desires. The pleasure of reading crime fiction is intellectual and exploratory—the world seen under a special light."[3]

Paul's reticence is manifested in his ability to rattle the other characters in order to test their strength of character. In other words, Paul is testing them through his standoffish manner. He and the professor act as wise old men who understand the intricacies of the criminal underworld. They are both outsiders who have not come to this juncture in their lives through a natural disposition. This is very evident when Paul forces Raymond to decide if he can get them invitations to the Governors' Ball. Raymond is literally seen sweating in his indecision. Paul's rigorous manner presses Poncho to think about what they are planning to undertake. Poncho comes across as too sure for Paul's liking. When Poncho challenges Paul about the nature of the job, the following exchange takes place:

Paul: "Because it has the smell of insanity."

Poncho: "Daring is not insanity. All we need is to gamble with higher stakes than the casino is used to and to have faith in each other."

Paul: "Cemeteries are full of people who had faith."

Poncho: "Obviously, Professor, your friend is a very nervous man."

Paul: "Oh, my friend that is the understatement of the evening. I am worse than nervous. You know something glib, positive characters like you scare me."

Paul's meticulousness, leave-nothing-to-chance attitude is again manifest when Melanie assures him that "there isn't any reason to worry." To which he replies, "Oh, uh. Who's going to guarantee it, you?" Paul's manner cuts through the other's optimism because he understands the complexity of the job. Later she asks him if he dislikes her. Paul answers, "You have to be conscious of people to like or dislike."

Seven Thieves' plot is replete with insightful nuances on the nature of irony. Paul tells Poncho, who is passing himself off as Baron von Roelitz and fears that he may be overacting, not to worry of acting convincingly; the count acts badly enough to cover whatever mistakes Poncho can make. The dramatic irony that drives the film serves as a kind of catharsis; the characters cannot anticipate the final surprise. *Seven Thieves* dramatizes a nuanced discernment of everyday experience. Again, I stress that we bring to and extract from drama whatever condition we deem necessary in our own existential condition.

The dramatic scope of *Seven Thieves* is too complicated and sophisticated to offer a synopsis. The trouble truly begins after the heist goes off according to plan. This is a cinematic anticlimax that illustrates the film's ironic end. The gang takes the four million francs out of the casino in a false compartment of the baron's wheelchair. Theo's existential exigency finally reaches an impasse when the heist is over, and they are driving away. He cannot contain his excitement. He tells Paul: "Can't wait until morning to see what the newspapers say." Shortly after, his life seemingly complete, he has a heart attack and dies. At this point we witness Paul crying, as it is revealed that Theo is his father.

The drama that frames the final sequences of the film has Paul becoming more stringent with his patience. The others are anxious to get their hands on their portion of the money, but Paul shocks them by revealing that the money has been serialized by the bank of France, thus effectively making the money useless. At this point the fragile functional unity that the group once enjoyed begins to disintegrate. Paul's discomfort with the other members and his reluctance to take part in the heist takes over him. We realize he took part in the job solely for the love of Theo, his father.

NOTES

1. Georg Simmel. *On Individuality and Social Forms*. Chicago: University of Chicago Press, 1971, 234.

2. Marcel, Gabriel. *Tragic Wisdom and Beyond*. Translated by Stephen Jolin and Peter McCormick. Evanston: Northwestern University Press, 1973, 75

3. Barzun, Jacques, and Wendell Hertig Taylor. *A Catalogue of Crime*. New York: Harper & Row, Publishers, 1989, p. xiii.

Chapter 8

Curse of the Demon
Evil, Myth, and Reason

CURSE OF THE DEMON

Synopsis

Jacques Tourneur's classic yarn of psychological terror is a work about the supernatural realm that man does not understand. The film contrasts demonic forces with rational perspective on human reality that attempts to establish security in the use of reason. Tourneur suggests that regardless of reason, man lives in fear of diffused forces that we can't understand. The investigation into the demonic that *Curse of the Demon* explores yields a surprising ending, especially for the positivistic age when the film was created.

When Professor Harrington (Maurice Denham) is seen driving frantically through the woods at night trying to reach Julian Karswell's (Niall MacGinnis) mansion in Jacques Tourneur's *Curse of the Demon* (1958), he does so out of the hope that Karswell can control the supernatural. This is a concession on behalf of Dr. Harrington, the psychologist, that perhaps there are realities in the universe that cannot easily be quantified. His fear is certainly strong enough that he tries to assuage it by whatever means possible. Karswell, even though a devoted Satanist, surprises him with a confession of impotence.

Dr. Harrington rushes into Karswell's home and demands: "Call it off, Karswell. Stop this thing that you've started, and I'll admit publicly that I was totally wrong and you were totally right." Karswell's response is anything but reassuring: "That's very gratifying to hear, but some things are easier started than stopped." Once opened, the satanic contents of Karswell's Pandora's box rule over its proprietor. Dr. Harrington continues: "I've seen it. I know it's real." At this point Karswell merely begins to humor him so that Dr. Harrington may leave him alone. Karswell looks up at the clock and realizes that it is 9:00 p.m.; immediately his countenance turns serious. He tells Dr. Harrington that he will call it off and sends the man home much more subdued than when he first arrived. The significance of this scene, in light of what occurs later in the film, is that Karswell has inadvertently passed Harrington a parchment, a small piece of paper with runic symbols on it that marks one to die demonically. This is an important early sign that Karswell, too, fears the demon, and does not want the man to die on his property because he does not want to confront the evil that he has cast.

What is the importance of the parchment? On one level, we can suggest that the parchment represents a kind of entailment between evil and those who venerate its existence. As such, this is an example of the black arts, and how evil forces are used to perform evil acts. But in a broader sense, the parchment can be seen as a form of magical thread that binds one to destiny. Consider how this idea plays out in classical mythology: Clotho is regarded as creating, or spinning man's fate, and Lachesis is the caretaker, the weaver of man's luck; finally, there is the snapping of the string by Atropos at the time of death.[1]

In *Curse of the Demon*, the parchment serves as the rite of passage of the devil into the affairs of man, a process that, as Karswell alludes to, cannot be stopped once it is begun. Evil is summoned, invited even, Karswell appears to suggest. But this is only one form that evil manifests itself to man, as we witness in the film.

Since its beginning in 600 B.C.E., philosophy is the first discipline to use reason to uncover the underlying principles of human reality. Philosophers have sought to ground human existence in the interplay of reason and a rational universe. This essentially comes down to the discovery of form and logos as its implementation. Up to Thales's time, Homeric mythological cosmogony served to explain the universe.

Throughout the ancient world, myth served as the epitome of such explanations. This aspect of human reality cannot be easily refuted. For this same reason, the value and raison d'être of myth has not totally disappeared. Myth has to do with the ability of supernatural beings and their power to affect man's fate. Another way of conveying this is to suggest that myths are most effective when they specifically address human concerns.

The meaning of the ancient Greek word mythos can be understood in several ways, including: fable, tale, and talk. But myth also means that which cannot really exist. The latter meaning suggests a rather playful explanation that allowed the Greeks the luxury of believing, tongue-in-cheek, in the gods that made up the Greek pantheon. Pre-Socratic thinkers differentiated philos-sophia from mythos by demonstrating that the former convincingly showcased man as an agent of reason—that is, as the recipient of universal form. For instance, Xenophanes rejected all manner of man's anthropomorphism. He argued that the gods curiously always took the shape of man, if not man's thought. Euhemerus, a thinker who lived in the third century B.C.E., argued that the gods were no more than ancient kings who had been glorified through the bad memory and romanticism of subsequent civilizations. In addition, myth is centered around the notion of being and becoming, good and evil, and eternal principles that have not been exhausted through religion, philosophy or science. This is the historical point at which myth becomes scrutinized by reason.[2]

Dr. Harrington drives back home through the dark woods. When he arrives at his home, he drives the car into the garage. However, when he is about to close the garage doors, he sees a white cloud of mist rapidly approaching, at which point he gets back in the car and backs up in a hurry. In the process, he knocks down a utility pole and is electrocuted. This is the first time that the demon makes an appearance in *Curse of the Demon*. The demon is briefly seen moving toward the Professor. The next time that the demon shows up is at the very end of the film.

Jacques Tourneur (1904–1977), director of *The Leopard Man*, *Out of the Past*, and *Berlin Express* does not waste time setting up the storyline in *Curse of the Demon*. The film's plot revolves around a satanic cult, its leader Julian Karswell and an American positivist psychologist named Dr. Holden (Dana Andrews), who is in Britain attending an international conference on the topic of "International Reports from Paranormal Psychology."

Dr. Harrington was involved in an investigation of Karswell's demon cult and subsequently brought his findings to the press exposing Karswell and his followers. Sometime during their meeting, Karswell passed the parchment with the runic symbols to Dr. Harrington. This takes place prior to Dr. Holden's arrival in England. Dr. Holden is out to disprove the validity of any claims concerning the existence of the supernatural. The film employs a superbly intelligent and engaging plot. *Curse of the Demon* demonstrates a well-crafted regard for its major themes: the nature of evil, supernatural forces beyond man's control, scientific materialism, and the expansion of reason into the nonrational.

Curse of the Demon was released in Britain under the alternate title *Night of the Demon*. The latter version is twelve minutes longer and contains some plot development that was cut from *Curse of the Demon*. Having viewed both films many times, I will refer to the longer version.

The film opens with a shot of Stonehenge as the narrator is describing man's timeless belief in a world framed by twilight. From the beginning, *Curse of the Demon* is fraught with symbols and symbolism. Stonehenge is seen as both a physical monument that issues from another time and people but also as a repository of the vital beliefs of people from long ago. But what was the motivating factor behind these early renditions of man's concern with his inner world? This seems a pertinent question, if for no other reason than that symbols point to reality, even though they may not be reality proper.

When Dr. Holden arrives in London, he is greeted by some members of the press who ask him questions about the nature of the supernatural. He meets Dr. Harrington's secretary who is the first to inform him of Dr. Harrington's death. This is important because it involves Dr. Holden in Dr. Harrington's investigation of Karswell's sect directly. This also has the effect of removing Dr. Holden from his ivory tower and forcing him to try to make sense of a concrete example of alleged evil, which he spends most of the film negating.

In his hotel room, Dr. Holden is greeted by two other scientists who will attend the conference: Dr. O'Brien and Dr. Kumar, both men are cognizant of the Karswell investigation. At this point in the film a fine conversation on the nature of the supernatural takes place. Tourneur's direction is never heavy or pedantic, but neither is it superficial. The dialogue that makes up the conversations on the nature of the supernatural is never forced. These conversations take place in spontaneous ways that revolve around the action of any given scene. Tourneur does not create artificial situations to highlight a particular point.

The first of these exchanges occurs when Dr. Holden is coming out of the shower and the conversation at hand turns to Rand Hobart, one of Karswell's followers, a clinical patient who is incarcerated for murder. When one of the scientists present supplies a picture of a demon drawn by Hobart, Dr. Holden suggests that what they really ought to be doing is compiling data on the psychological makeup of Karswell's followers. The problem begins when someone mentions that Hobart is an alleged murderer, at which time Dr. Holden, taking up the picture, says, "You don't mean to suggest that that thing made him do it?" After Dr. Holden gives them a lecture on the value of scientific reason, Dr. O'Brien answers him: "I know the value of the cold light of reason, but I also know the dark shadows that that light can cast. The shadows that can blind men to truth." Dr. Holden quickly rebuts: "What truth? Demonology and witchcraft have been discredited since the Middle Ages. I wrote a book about it. That's why I am here." This exchange further demonstrates how self-absorbed Dr. Holden is with scientific facts. This scene is indicative of Tourneur's meticulous attention to detail, facts, and language. At this point an allusion is made to some historical manifestations of the devil. Dr. O'Brien asks: "Explain how an uneducated farmer like Hobart can know anything about this creature whose legend has persisted from civilization to civilization." It is at this juncture in the film that mention is made of the incarnations of evil as Asmodeus, Baal, Moloch, and Seth-Typhon.

Jacques Tourneur goes to great pains to offer a sophisticated script that raises the level of the film to more than just a tale of spooks in the night. When Dr. O'Brien mentions four ancient representations of the devil, this is convincingly tied to the picture that Hobart drew of the demon. It is interesting that the film mentions the Persian devil Asmodeus given that it is a spirit that represented storms, rage, and revenge. This is equally conveyed by Karswell when out of the outrage that he feels towards Dr. Holden's incredulity, he conjures up a powerful and menacing windstorm. According to the Lemegeton, Asmodeus often shows itself riding a dragon and holding a spear. He is said to have three heads. Baal, too, is a god of rain and storm that makes its first appearance in ancient Palestine. The sixteenth-century demonologist John Wier argues that Baal also had three heads: that of a cat, man and toad. His central characteristic? Guile. None of this comes about as coincidence, for Jacques Tourneur was a serious student of the occult.

For the Egyptians, demons were viewed as the messengers of the goddess Sekhmet. They were the embodiment of evil, always spreading disease. A fine example of this is the Egyptian creature known as the Eater of Hearts, who crouches besides the scales during the weighing of the heart ceremony. *The Book of the Dead* depicts this entity also as containing three heads: crocodile, lion, and hippopotamus. He belongs in the Hall of Judgment.[3]

Reflection on demons and evil is a central component of Zoroastrianism, a sophisticated ancient Persian faith that predates the Achaemenid dynasty in 550 B.C.E. The Zoroastrians viewed the universe as dualistic. The interesting factor of good and evil is that the Zoroastrian's perceived good and evil to exist as separate entities. Presiding over good is Ahura Mazda; Ahriman over the forces of evil. Ahriman's goal is to create dissension in mankind. His goal is to foster lies and the continuation of death and suffering for man. Ahriman has at its disposition a host of agents, evil spirits. The Zoroastrians conceived of six good spirits (Amesha Spenta) that do the work of Ahura Mazda and six evil powers that are Ahriman's aides. The main agent of evil in the terrestrial realm is Angra Mainyu. S. A. Nigosian explains in his book *The Zoroastrian Faith*: "Thus, the phenomenal world consists of pairs of conflicting opposites: light/dark, truth/falsehood, health/sickness, rain/drought, pure/impure, good creatures/noxious creatures, life/death, heaven/hell."[4]

Curse of the Demon is a subtle exploration of the terror conveyed by the supernatural on the imagination. Holden comes to the Karswell devil cult investigation armed with the tools of the hardened positivist: a regard for hard facts, the materialist affirmation that human reality is only made up of matter, and lack of genuine awe and wonder that would enable him to confront the sublime. The film does more than entertain, for it also interrogates the relationship between good and evil. The balance and interaction of these two realms is today perhaps more than ever before in the history of man seen as a paradox and contradictory.

Evil has appeared paradoxical from time immemorial. The crux of human attention has been on positing the existence of God, whose distinguishing characteristics, include: omniscience, benevolence, and omnipotence. Hence, comes about the problem of evil.

This paradox is founded on the seeming incomparability of these two forces. The existence of evil, witnessed in the tragedies that occur to unsuspecting benevolent people, as well as the overbearing reality of existential suffering, cannot be denied. The problem of evil is what I refer to as a local concern of man, even though it rightfully takes on colossal metaphysical proportions. If man could afford to entertain a cosmic viewpoint—the realization that evil is the price to pay for self-awareness would take center stage. Dr. Holden is oblivious to this concern. Pictures of Earth taken from Voyager's I and II, as both of these sister satellites left the heliopause reveal a chillingly cold, even though sublime human condition. The problem is that man cannot easily accommodate such a viewpoint emotionally.

When Dr. Holden goes to ask Karswell for a classic text on the supernatural, it is Karswell who instructs the calculating positivist. Karswell asks, "How much do you know about this book you're after?" Dr. Holden simply views the text as a book, a container of knowledge in the contemporary sense of research. On the other hand, Karswell guards the book as a record, a testament to a more ample reality than quantifiable and cataloged material reality. Dr. Holden answers, "Not very much, just what Professor Harrington referred to in his notes." This scene is a confrontation between positivism and the nonrational—the burden of proof is reversed—thus forcing Dr. Holden to broaden his scope or find adequate counterproofs. It would be incorrect to assume that this exchange is merely a clash of science and the supernatural. The problem merely involves aspects of the scientific method, and the arrogance that subjugating reality to any singular method presuppose.

Issac Newton was the last of a long line of thinkers who were willing to embrace the limits of experimentation and quantification. Newton was also one of the last of the alchemist/scientists. His discoveries, however, are not the worse off because of his ample curiosity. Pythagoras and Ptolemy (Claudius Ptolemaeus) too, were rationalists of the first degree who did not close themselves off to what may exist beyond their scientific scope. Paracelsus (Theophrastus Bombastus Von Hohenheim), a thinker who is credited with the discovery of ether as an anaesthetic, did so because his belief that body and spirit are dual components of man. He writes in his work *Traité' des trois essence premiéres*: "If the spirit suffers the body suffers also."[5] Karswell's answer to Dr. Holden is interesting: "Do I believe in witchcraft?" He goes on to add: "Where does imagination and reality begin? What is this twilight?

This half world of the mind that you professor know so much about? How can we differentiate the powers of darkness and the powers of the mind?" Karswell's point is pertinent to a neurotic age that professes both, a staunchly arid philosophical materialism and the likes of psychoanalysis.

Equally important is Karswell's suggestion that perhaps man has implemented a hyperrationality—if this is a fitting word—that destroys any relevance that belief can have in ordinary life. What Karswell seems to be admonishing raises the question of just what kind of vital understanding scientists possess when they take off their lab coat. The significance of this question is best exemplified by the Spanish philosopher Ortega y Gasset's distinction between ideas and beliefs, where an idea is something we possess, while beliefs are convictions that we embody. This is evidenced during the scene when Karswell and Dr. Holden are seen walking outside Karswell's house. Karswell entertains the village children during his annual party for them. This scene is the second time that Dr. Holden encounters anything remotely strange, the first being the invisible writing that is found in the personal card that Karswell hands him in the British Museum. Dr. Holden cannot make sense of the dramatic and visually stunning windstorm that Karswell evokes. Karswell is moved by the natural disposition that children have for understanding. He says: "If only we grown-ups could preserve their capacity for simple joys and beliefs." *Curse of the Demon* confronts us with a profound notion of human experience than that offered by stale materialism.

In many circles today, good and evil are no longer embraced as dual aspects of the human condition. The problem is multifaceted. Good and evil are vital components of man's lived experience. To negate one—even when their import is merely considered psychological—is to destroy the coherency of the other. This is Dr. Holden's position and dilemma. In the absence of conviction, as trivial as this may seem—only abstraction can save the day. This is the contradictory mindset that does not allow itself the sublime privilege of seeing the forest because the trees are in the way. Nietzsche's willful irreverence captures this point best in book V of *The Gay Science*:

"How far we too are still pious. In science, convictions have no rights of citizenship, as is said with good reason. Only when they decide to descend to the modesty of a hypothesis, of a provisional experimental point of view, of a regulative fiction, may they be granted admission and even a certain value within the realm of knowledge—though always with the restriction that they remain under police supervision, under the police of mistrust."[6]

As a scientific investigator, the question for Dr. Holden remains one of securing a degree of understanding that is complementary to man as a psychical and material being, and thus one that can be understood based on the power of the available scientific evidence. To this, Nietzsche adds: "But does this not mean, more precisely considered, that a conviction may obtain admission to science only when it ceases to be a conviction? Would not the discipline of the scientific spirit begin with this, no longer to permit oneself any convictions? Probably that is how it is."[7]

Dr. Holden's character is believable because of his being closed off to any notion of the existence of the supernatural. When Dr. Holden walks to his hotel room through the long, tunnel-like hall, he stops for no apparent reason and looks around. Eerie music is heard, and one has to wonder if this is in fact the demon taunting him or merely part of the mood created by the film's soundtrack. This scene is brilliantly shot. The viewer is offered just enough suspense to keep the story moving along without necessitating shock value. The scene is interrupted when Dr. O'Brien and Dr. Kumar walk out of a room; Dr. Holden invites them for a drink.

The conversation quickly turns to the clash between reason and the supernatural. Dr. Holden asks: "O'Brien, don't you think that skepticism is the proper scientific attitude?" O'Brien concedes by answering: "Sometimes." To this Dr. Holden, pouring a drink, answers: "I say show me." This raises the question of just how much "seeing" is sufficient evidence. Is "seeing" without a proper, all-encompassing explanation enough to quench the doubt of the skeptic? Dr. Kumar realizes this and asks Dr. Holden: "And if you are shown?" Dr. Holden answers, "Then look twice." Dr. Holden concludes this statement by adding: "The reality of the seeable and the touchable. That's what convinces me."

William James critiques this austere and stubborn intellectualizing in *The Varieties of Religious Experience* by arguing against the limitations of institutionalized religion and positivistic science. Of course, as a matter of artistic convention Dr. Holden's turnaround can only take place due to his scientific obstinacy. Yet the film does not conclude with a total abandoning of his previous mindset or a new acceptance of belief in the supernatural. The film delivers Dr. Holden to a neutral ground, where he might be further predisposed to consider the realm of the nonrational in human existence. James offers a corrective:

> Philosophy lives in words, but truth and fact well up into our lives in ways that exceed verbal formulation. There is in the living act of perception always something that glimmers and twinkles and will not be caught, and for which reflection comes too late. No one knows this as well as the philosopher. He must fire his volley of new vocables out of his conceptual shutgun, for his profession condemns him to this industry, but he secretly knows hollowness and irrelevancy. His formulas are like stereoscopic or kinetoscopic photographs seen outside the instrument; they lack the depth, the motion, the vitality.[8]

The subtlety and suspense employed by *Curse of the Demon* cannot fully be appreciated in a sensually satiated culture at a time when lack of imagination rules the day. Dr. Holden's facial expression in the hotel and his awakening to some presence around him suggest mystery. The film is indicative of a broader ontological reality than empiricism is ready to accept. Works of art cannot convey more than our sensibility and temperament demand. What type of people take interest in opera? How many people identify existential themes and logos in Hieronymus Bosch's canvases? If audiences today find it entertaining and sensually gratifying to have films become catalogs of visual horrors, it is due to an inability to contemplate the formal and conceptual in its purity. This is exemplified in the way that language, sex, imagination, the sublime and vulgarity are construed in contemporary cinema. Perhaps Jacques Barzun is vindicated in arguing that we have the culture we deserve. The horror film genre has evolved from the naive and juvenile to well-crafted supernatural films like *Curse of the Demon, Carnival of Souls, The Haunting, The Changeling,* and *The Omen*. It was not until the excesses of *The Exorcist* in the early 1970s that audiences were first served roller-coaster rides at the expense of the power of suggestion.

How embracing is Dr. Holden of the supernatural halfway through the film? The answer to this becomes clear when he storms out of a séance that Joanna Harrington, Dr. Harrington's niece, takes him to. Dr. Holden becomes disoriented again when he is caught by Karswell in his study, sifting through the older man's papers. Tourneur conveys great anticipation when Dr. Holden is seen walking alone at night through the woods adjacent to Karswell's house. The quality of the black and white contrast with the shadows in the woods creates a long suspense scene that continues with his search in Karswell's study, and culminates with his return to Joanna, who waits for him in the car.

Perhaps the most chilling but subdued example of suggestion in the film is the scene when the camera is angled from the top of the staircase. Dr. Holden is searching through Karswell's study when a hand is seen holding on to the banister. This scene only lasts a few seconds, yet the viewer is left guessing if it is Karswell's hand or that of some more sinister entity. The answer is never given away by anything that occurs prior to this scene. Even when Karswell does come into the room, one cannot be sure that it was he who looks down from the top of the stairs. This portion of the film conveys the idea that Karswell is always protected and aided in his activities by an evil force.

Another masterful example of Tourneur's sense of horror takes place when Dr. Holden is attacked by a black panther while searching through Karswell's study. When the lights are turned on by Karswell, Dr. Holden asks what kind of animal it was that attacked him. Karswell smiles and tells him that it was the black cat that is seen sitting nearby. The height of Dr. Holden's fright comes when he is followed by a series of lights and mist as he walks back from Karswell's home through the woods. Dr. Holden, a purveyor of conventional realism, has his calm nature shattered by the disorienting experience. The next scene takes place in a Scotland Yard office. This is effective counterpoint. This is an important scene because it symbolizes a clash between the supernatural and the tangible reality that is required of any criminal investigation. What was it that followed him? Even though the detectives are patient and tolerant of his claim, Scotland Yard has very little to go on. Dr. Holden seems to make a turn toward acceptance of the supernatural when he finds himself telling three members of the police that he was followed in the woods.

Serious questions lurk in our understanding films that dwell in the reality of realms that depart from our everyday world. If *Curse of the Demon* is to effectively engage us, we must be willing to accept its artistic conventions. Dr. Holden's world, to use positivistic jargon, has been conditioned by a self-limiting regard for reality. While the other three paranormal investigators are busy investigating, Dr. Holden is merely out to debunk any claims. Because Dr. Holden has closed off his beliefs only to the staunchest materially quantifiable experiences, his level of cultural engagement becomes limited by his chosen method. Thus, confronted with what would naturally seem an opportunity for further exploration and knowledge, Dr. Holden instead opts for the easy security of negation. Ortega y Gasset recognized this in his book, *Man and Crisis*. Ortega writes in a chapter titled, "On Extremism as a Form of Life":

> The withdrawal by man into a corner of the world is an accurate symbol of the first stage of desperation. It means that man, in effect, reduces life and the world to a corner, to a single fragment of what it was formerly. This is simplification in the face of desperation, in the face of feeling lost in an excessive richness of life—all that knowledge and none of it enough; all those appetites and possible pleasures, but none of them full and complete; that too great piling up of necessary occupations, but no one of them with meaning which is absolute or satisfactory.[9]

What is missing from Dr. Holden's investigation is genuine awe-inspired wonder. His method is that of a hard-boiled positivist. He opts for a narrow conception of human reality and overemphasis on proof. The question can be posed: What constitutes proof in the field of the paranormal? Even in parapsychology one is open to the charge that if the phenomena under investigation are non-physical, what instrument, regardless of its sensitivity can measure it? There is also the charge that just because some "energy" has been detected, this does not ensure the existence of paranormal activity. What is called for, then, is not blind and irresponsible adherence to sensual autosuggestion or a narrowly defined scientific method. Instead, it is the responsible vision of the wise investigator to uncover how and when paranormal phenomena occur.

Dr. Holden wants nothing to do with the mindset of the paranormal investigator. He is tricked into attending a séance, only to storm out when the medium begins relating messages from Dr. Harrington. One of the many reasons *Curse of the Demon* is an interesting and enjoyable film is its varied and brilliantly paced sense of drama. A lot takes place from the time Dr. Holden arrives in London, to the final scenes when he encounters Karswell on the train. The film's action is not gratuitous or purely physical. Some of the action of the film takes place when Hobart is placed in a hypnotic trance in front of the scientists attending the convention, after he is awakened from a catatonic sleep. Dr. O'Brien asks him: "What is the order of the true believer?" Hobart answers, "That evil is good." Then, Dr. O'Brien follows through by asking him to remember the night of the demon. Hobart replies, "I see it in the trees. The light, the fire." He tells Dr. O'Brien that he passed back the parchment to the one who gave it to him and "the demon took him." This is the entailment of the alleged murder. At this point, he shocks those present by jumping out of a window.

Hobart is a central character, even though he remains in the periphery of the on-screen action. Hobart stands at the symbolic crossroads between what is deemed mental illness and diabolical influence. The scene where Hobart is surrounded by medical doctors and is given medicine creates the illusion that the men of science present are totally in control. This scene is similar to the one in *The Exorcist* when the doctors can no longer explain what is happening to Megan in strictly medical terms. Hobart's impulse to jump out of the window is decidedly an example of man's ignorance about human consciousness. Dr. Holden and the other doctors fail to offer a convincing explanation of Hobart's mental condition. This is confirmed when Dr. Holden runs to take the 9:45 p.m. train to South Hampton to find Karswell. This is a decisive moment in the film, not solely because it launches the film into its denouement, but because Dr. Holden reverts to a genuine concern for the "passing of the parchment." The finality of Hobart's death and Dr. Holden's return to grappling with Karswell's notion of a realm of twilight suggests a broadening of Dr. Holden's perspective.

Curse of the Demon is not so much a film about a particular kind of supernatural phenomena, i.e., devil worship and the power of evil, rather an exploration of the possibility of such a realm. Dr. Holden's resistance is not indicative of a particular scientist and his own brand of skepticism, but that of a world that has lost the ability for imagination and a sense of wonder. If it is true that ancient cultures turned to the supernatural to assuage their daily fears, the opposite is reasonable: material complacency and moral nihilism rob man of his capacity for imagination. The question arises whether man can violate the natural balance between volition and reason, vital life and self-aware existence and continue to exist as a rational being? Jung's insight serves to illustrate this point:

> Rationalism and superstition are complementary. It is a psychological rule that the brighter the light, the blacker the shadow; in other words, the more rationalistic we are in our conscious minds, the more alive becomes the spectral world of the unconscious. And it is indeed obvious that rationality is in large measure an apotropaic defence against superstition, which is ever present and unavoidable.[10]

Dr. Holden finds Karswell on the train along with Joanna, who is in a quasi-hypnotized state. The film's thematic climax is reached when Dr. Holden tells Karswell: "I want to thank you for convincing me of the existence of a world I never thought possible." No further discussion ensues. Karswell needs to get away. The two men begin a cat-and-mouse game that culminates in Dr. Holden's passing off the parchment to Karswell, when he hands him his coat. Surprisingly, Karswell is apprehended by two policemen who have been tailing him. Before they can whisk him away the parchment flies from Karswell's hands. He follows it desperately through the train and out onto the tracks.

What transpires next is an example of the sophisticated suspense that Jacques Tourneur has accomplished in *Cat People* and *I Walked with a Zombie*, in addition to *Curse of the Demon*. The film's ending is scripted in such a way that Karswell finds himself running after the parchment on one side of the tracks, while Dr. Holden, Joanna and two Scotland Yard officers remain on the other. The film does not give away its secrets at the end. When the demon comes running through the tracks preceded by mist and fire, Karswell initially does not take notice. Soon thereafter, he does acknowledge it; he has no choice. While the demon tramples on him, none of the others directly witness this. To add to the suspense, an oncoming train passes them speeding by on the adjacent track. Karswell is found on the tracks. The policemen go up to him. Dr. Holden and Joanna stay behind. Dr. Holden tells her that there are some things that are better left unknown. This awe and wonder-inspired pathos is the main point of the film. This is a significant turn of events for Dr. Holden—the positivist. Most importantly is the acceptance that perhaps the realm of evil and demons is not fully understood by man. Belief and rational thought do not have to be mutually exclusive.

Man is a holistic being that cannot be easily compartmentalized into rational and emotive components. Jung is correct in arguing that man's natural dispositions cannot readily be turned on and off. He explains: "One of the most fatal of the sociological and psychological errors in which our time is so fruitful is the supposition that something can become entirely different all in a moment; for instance, that man can radically change his nature, or that some formula or truth might be found which would represent an entirely new beginning."[11] *Curse of the Demon* takes us a long way toward a more reflective understanding of the human condition.

NOTES

1. See: John Melhuish Strudwick (1849–1935), British Pre-Raphaelite painter. *The Golden Thread* (1885) captures in oil the pathos of this metaphysical rendition of fate.

2. Otto, Rudolf. *The Idea of the Holy: An Inquiry into the Non-Rational Factor in the Idea of the Divine and its Relation to the Rational.* Translated by John W. Harvey. New York: A Galaxy Book, 1958.

3. *The Book of the Dead.* Introduction by E.A. Wallis Budge. New York: Gramercy Book, 1960.

4. Nigosian, S. A. *The Zoroastrian Faith: Tradition & Modern Research.* Montreal: McGill-Queen's University Press, 1993.

5. Natof, Andre. *The Occult.* Edinburgh: Chambers, 1991, 161.

6. Nietzsche, Friedrich. *The Portable Nietzsche.* Edited by Walter Kaufman. New York: Penguin Press, 1982, 448.

7. Ibid., 448.

8. James, William. *The Varieties of Religious Experience.* New York: Collier Books, 356.

9. Ortega y Gasset, José. *Man and Crisis.* New York: W.W. Norton & Company, 1962, 139.

10. Jung, C. G. *Psychology and the Occult.* Princeton: Princeton University Press, 1977, 144.

11. Ibid., 137.

Chapter 9

The Uninvited and Dead of Night
The Transcendent Other

THE UNINVITED AND DEAD OF NIGHT

Synopsis

A ghost story. A tale of a disembodied soul seeking revenge. These may seem as cinematic staples of the ghost story today, especially after the long history that cinema now enjoys. *The Uninvited* and *Dead of Night* are classic tales of the world of shadows, a world where man must decipher what is real from illusion. These are two films about the supernatural, an aspect of the human experience that makes its appearance in human history, dating back to prehistory. Immortality of the soul raises questions about the nature of man, making the meaning and purpose of life an inexhaustible subject rife for philosophical reflection.

Lewis Allen's film *The Uninvited* opens with Roderick Fitzgerald (Ray Milland) narrating the story. He explains how locals in this British coastal town have come to live with and even accept ghosts. The narration quickly establishes the lyrical quality of this film. As the camera pans across the rough sea, the viewer gets a sense of isolation and the timeless primitive conditions that shape these shores.

The isolation serves to hide the many secrets that the house and its former inhabitants keep. The setting of *The Uninvited* is in keeping with traditional conventions of haunted mansions. The house contains sinister secrets, but these secrets are kept obscured by time itself. The film explores the mysteries inherent in the passage of time and how it relates to human consciousness. Missing from *The Uninvited* are the overdone staple ingredients of today's horror genre: grotesquely deformed entities, houses coming apart, psychopaths waving knives, and flying objects that are intent on creating a visual candy store of sorts.

Roderick continues his narration: "If one listens to the pounding of the waves long enough in these haunted shores, all your senses are sharpened, you come by strange instincts." This line of thinking immediately suggests a comparison with city people anywhere, but most of all in London. Roderick and his sister, Pamela Fitzgerald (Ruth Hussey), are transplanted Londoners. This early disclaimer helps set the stage for what will be an interesting look at modern life and whether modernity in fact desensitizes man to the subtle essences that inform the human condition. Clearly, the fact that Roderick and Pamela are not quick to grasp the early signs of the strange occurrences that take place in the house demonstrates that being a Londoner, that is, a city dweller, is a marked disadvantage when dealing with the supernatural. My suggestion should not be lost on a literal juxtaposition between country and city people, however. London, too, is said to be filled with active ghosts, if not ghost stories. Instead, what is at stake here is whether man has lost the ability to see beyond the daily demands of mundane reality.

The story takes place in 1937. The house that Roderick and Pamela are interested in purchasing has been vacant, on and off, for the last twenty years. The two encounter the house by chance, as they are walking along a deserted beach with their dog, Bobby. Bobby runs to the house; following him, they climb a cliff and encounter a mansion. The house is referred to as "Windward House." The dog enters the house through an open window, as it runs after a squirrel. They follow the dog inside. It turns out that the house belongs to an old man, referred to simply as Commander Beech (Donald Crisp). When they meet the commander the next day, he tells them that five years before, some tenants had complained about strange occurrences in the house, and moved out. This comes as a warning that the house is sold "as is." Roderick and Pamela play down this exchange. During their meeting with the old man, they decide to purchase the house for what both parties consider to be a very reasonable price. The commander is reluctant to sell, but eventually does so, given that he cannot afford to keep it. He tells them that he bought the house for his daughter over twenty years earlier. His granddaughter, Stella Meredith (Gail Russell), does not approve of his selling the property because it reminds her of her dead mother.

The first sign that something is wrong in the house is seen right after Roderick and Pamela move in. They enter an upstairs room with a huge glass window that overlooks the sea. The room is damp and cold and will remain so throughout the film. Roderick, who is a music critic for a newspaper, will use this room to compose his own music on the piano. The room is intended to serve as inspiration, given its expansive vista of the sea.

The next day, as Roderick is about to enter a small shop in town, he sees young Stella Meredith, the commander's granddaughter. She informs him that she lived in that house until the age of three. When her mother died, the family moved out. Early on in the story the viewer is informed that her mother died by falling over the cliff in front of the house. The young woman tells Roderick that she can communicate with her deceased mother. Roderick is shocked by this statement, but he accepts it at face value.

The Uninvited is considered by many critics to be the very first Hollywood ghost story. It is also one of the best films in this genre. What some critics may view as a lack of sustained horror and fright is more than compensated for by its lyrical content. Such criticism, one suspects, may be more indicative of postmodern critics' bias for the roller-coaster effect of films of the last forty-odd years. Filmed in 1944, and based on a novel by Dorothy Macardle, the film offers a sense of sophistication and measured suspense that has all but disappeared from most post-1970s filmmaking.

The main virtue of this film, as is also true of another film in this genre, *Dead of Night* (1945), is effective storytelling. Storytelling, what amounts to narrative, is precisely what is missing from most of the films of the last forty years. The drama and leisurely pace of older films resemble literature more closely than their slash and shock counterparts. Gratuitous horror—that is, gore, dismemberment, on-camera murder, and excess blood—has been the bread and circus offered to moviegoers for over the last four decades. This is a significant cultural shift from what was once a higher popular culture, to what has today essentially become the leveling of most art forms. Bread and circus never fail to work well as formulaic filmmaking. The danger in this is that while popular culture used to run parallel with high culture, today high culture has lost its ability to guide and inspire the lower forms of arts, especially when popular culture has descended to the lowest common denominator of aesthetic and moral vulgarity. Given a lack of historical perspective, art loses the notion of an aesthetic reference point.

What is most exciting and rewarding about supernatural films is that they transplant discerning viewers to man's primal condition. Once removed from the relative safety and security of our postmodern perspective, we are essentially forced to exercise our imagination.

The idea of ghosts is a central and timeless aspect of many diverse cultures, still in this day and age. This is not entirely difficult to see, if we engage our imagination in stripping our contemporary consciousness of its modern amenities. As we continue to conquer our physical world, it might be necessary to take refuge in the inner mystery that informs the human condition. The aesthetic possibilities for art forms that embrace the *mysterium tremendum* are truly enlightening, for what is essentially today a world-weary and bored mankind. What remains of paramount importance to this genre is the question of how much history is consulted by writers and directors. Film has a limited capacity to engage in commentary, when the primary purpose of this medium is storytelling entertainment. Depending on how a particular film uses temporal sequences, themes and the overall impact of its written narrative, so too, will its correlation to our active imagination. Interestingly, the less consideration that is given to the aforementioned elements, the more that film must rely on purely visual effects—to the great detriment of coherence.

Writing, as expressed in the narrative of film, continues to be a central component of all cinematic genres. The camera must sooner or later choose—to use a phenomenological term—intend what it films. Regardless of what some critics view as the role of action in cinema, let us consider that if narrative is absent in the supernatural genre, what remains is pointless and essentially vacuous action. Suspense is not garnered through action but through the direction and pace of the narrative. Even more important, what remains in the absence of effective writing is excessive reliance on the purely visual that, more often than not, cancels itself out on at least three counts: 1) an overabundance of directionless action, 2) the overlapping of the visual and the narrative, and 3) visual sequences that actually work to detract from all semblance of believability.

The Uninvited is believable precisely because it leaves a region of reality intact—unexplored—for the viewer to complete on his own terms. The film is suggestive but does not exhaust the possibilities of the real. This is true as well in Alberto Calvacanti's direction in *Dead of Night*, a film that is often compared to *The Uninvited.* However, *Dead of Night* is not a ghost story, like *The Uninvited*. It is instead an excellent story that explores the nature of the paranormal and evil.

Dead of Night is the story of five people who come together in a country house to exchange ghost stories. One character, a race car driver who had a near-fatal accident tells of his constant premonitions of dying. He has a vision where a hearse driver outside his hospital window tells him that there is "room for one more inside." After his release from the hospital, he sees this same man, as he is about to board a city bus. He decides not to take the bus. He stares at the bus in astonishment when, several blocks later, the bus is involved in an accident and falls from a bridge.

Both of these films are portrayals of normal people who encounter a dimension of the bizarre and evil that they do not solicit. For horror to be convincing in cinema it must not only frighten, it must do so as a result of sinister intent. In *Dead of Night,* the main character tells those gathered around him that he has vivid visions. He even goes on to predict several actual events that will take place in that house in the following hours. Because the better films in this genre try to separate characters who believe from the naysayers, there is always the necessary tension that allows for a real-world situation.

For instance, this is perhaps nowhere more in evidence than in *Curse of the Demon* and the film's overly scrutinizing positivist psychologist. *Dead of Night*, too, employs a doctor who explains away the experiences of the other characters as either coincidences or downright irrational misperceptions. Where *The Uninvited* concentrates on questions of the spirit world and evil, *Dead of Night* spreads out these two themes throughout the five episodes with added attention to the nature of dreams. The latter film explores the question of whether dreams can foretell the future. As they sit around the room, the psychologist asks Mr. Craig, who claims that he has dreamt this exact moment, to tell them more about his dream. Mr. Craig answers: "Trying to remember a dream is like . . . how should I put it? Being out at night in a thunderstorm. There's a flash of lightning and for one brief moment everything stands out vivid and starkly." Yet whether in a dream or in a waking state, the insights that the dream reveals are comparable to what Maslow describes as a peak experience, where "the peak experience is felt as a self-validating, self-justifying moment that carries its own intrinsic value with it."[1]

Both of these films feature a spirit that tries to communicate something to the living. In one of the episodes of *Dead of Night*, a young woman tells how she was once playing hide and seek in a house that she was visiting, where she encountered a little boy in a second-floor bedroom. The boy was crying and she tried to console him, but before she could find out what was wrong, she was called and went back downstairs. When she told her story to the owners of the house, they were shocked and told her that the little boy had been deceased for quite a long time.

Another interesting aspect of ghost stories and stories where dreams and premonitions are conveyed in cinema is how effectively the relationship between past and present is conveyed. In most films, ghosts are portrayed as trying to undo a past wrong that was done to them or other parties. In this respect, what these ghosts desire is justice more than revenge. Films that deal with dreams are more concerned with predicting future events. In these films, dreams are utilized as the medium between the present, and the immediacy that is lived-time, and time as a projection: the future. *The Medusa Touch* is a particularly disturbing example, as a man, played by Richard Burton, not only sees the future but can also control it to a terrifying degree.

We also encounter a character's ability to predict the future in *Dead of Night*, wherein a woman tells the story of an experience that took place several weeks after she became engaged to be married. In this case, the future is predicted in the reflection of a mirror that she bought from an antiques dealer as a gift to her fiancé. When the man looks in the mirror, he sees the room behind him become transformed into another room. This goes on whenever he looks in the mirror. The illusion is of a dark room with a fireplace. The man tells his fiancé, "Every time I look in it, I see that room." The mirror also has a debilitating effect on him that makes him lose his will. In this episode, the spirit of the dead and the premonition of the future come together. At first, the woman begins to doubt the man's sanity and tries to correct the matter by forcing him to look into the mirror and see that there is only the expected reflection behind him. She succeeds, and shortly thereafter they are married and move into another house. Soon after, the man begins experiencing the same thing once again. The woman finds out that the antiques dealer had purchased the mirror and the bed at an estate sale. A man who was viciously and pathologically jealous of his wife murdered her and then cut his own throat. When the newlywed woman returns home, the man, who by now has become possessed by the spirit of the dead man, tries to strangle her. As this is going on, she looks in the mirror and actually sees the room that her husband has described many times before. Meanwhile, the doctor tries to explain away her experience by negating that people can become possessed by objects, and by negating the possibility of the supernatural altogether.

The signature episode in *Dead of Night* has to do with the psychologist conveying a story of a murder case that has puzzled him for some time. In the story a ventriloquist named Maxwell blames his problems on his dummy, Hugo. In a nightclub act, Hugo takes over the show, as the audience is amazed at Maxwell's proficient skill. After several minutes of rude and aggressive behavior, people begin to dislike the show and wonder if the ventriloquist is not insane. Once inside the dressing room, Hugo bites Maxwell.

Another staple characteristic of encounters with the paranormal in cinema is the isolation that is felt by the character who cannot tell anyone what he has seen because he does not quite believe it himself. This is not very different from ordinary, real-world experience, where the most commonplace existential communication can often prove to be difficult or impossible. As we watch a character attempt to communicate what in reality seems absurd, we also explore our own understanding of what it is that we feel and think, and how we, too, from time to time, have become trapped by the failure to make ourselves understood. The French philosopher Louis Lavelle has left a lasting contemplative legacy of this vital human concern. Lavelle writes in *The Dilemma of Narcisssus:*

> It is a mistake to think that the world of bodies is common to all, while the world of the spirit is private and individual. For in the first place, the world of bodies is public only because it is a spectacle readily apprehended by our minds; our physical being, on the other hand, is eternally isolated from the physical being of everyone else, and is continually shot through by impulses which are ours alone, impulses which we cannot dominate, and which we cannot wholly

communicate, nor completely hide, or perfectly know, nor can we remain entirely unconscious of them.²

The inability to communicate our experiences to others is a question of private versus public existence. In today's postmodern milieu, where there is an excessive and incessant desire to blur the lines of demarcation of these two modes of existence, it becomes impossible to believe that perhaps what others experience might actually be very different from what we witness. The impossibility of this vital conviction is exacerbated by the destruction of metaphysics by positivistic epistemology and the politicization of all aspects of human existence.

While in a London hotel, Maxwell receives the visit of an amateur ventriloquist who was present at the aforementioned show. The visitor, a man named Sylvester, has become enthralled by Maxwell's talent—even though he comes to suspect that the ventriloquist might in fact be insane. He has witnessed too many of Maxwell's unexplainable skits. Maxwell becomes increasingly frustrated by Hugo's behavior and what the dummy is doing to his sanity. The next morning Maxwell finds Hugo inside Sylvester's room. Maxwell accuses Sylvester of theft and shoots him. The fact that Sylvester does not die is an important factor in communicating the awkwardness of these events to the psychologist who is telling the story.

When Hugo is brought to Maxwell, in his prison cell, the dummy tells him that he wants to start working with the wounded man. Maxwell proceeds to destroy the dummy. What makes this even more bizarre, although it is a "merely interesting psychological case study" according to the doctor, the psychologist and a prison attendant witness this exchange through a small glass window in the door of the prison cell. In a final attempt to restore Maxwell's sanity, Sylvester is brought into the prison cell. When Maxwell answers some questions posed to him, the voice that is heard is not Maxwell's but Hugo's. Hugo gets the upper hand in this story, and the case is closed as one of insanity. Maxwell is in fact possessed by an evil spirit, Hugo's, as is Stella in *The Uninvited*, when she attempts to run off the cliff.

Dead of Night ends with a brilliant portrayal of suspenseful suggestion; Mr. Craig kills the psychologist in the living room of the country house where the stories are being told. In an unexpected plot twist, Craig is awakened by a telephone call from the owner of the country home he had dreamt about, asking him if he could come for the weekend to go over some architectural plans. It turns out that he was actually dreaming. *Dead of Night* ends where it begins, in a maze of premonitions that the subject himself has not solicited.³

Consider that technological development tends to create the misguided impression that somehow, man has changed the basic composition of human existence. One has only to imagine the world of primitive man and wonder how they viewed supernatural phenomena. A sensible and open-minded approach to this concern can enlighten us as to what we know for certain about the essence of human life. Placing the scientific method aside, however, existence exhibits a stubborn acumen that displaces the best of our rational conceptions. The nonrational is as central an element of human existence as rationality and science. It is important to realize that the nonrational does not mean the irrational, what is commonly considered contrary to reason. Perhaps it is due to the fact that science has given us tremendous comfort, lengthened our lives and answered many riddles of a materialistic bent, that man has seemingly turned his back on such questions. T. K. Oesterreich best explains this in his seminal work, *Possession: Demoniacal and Other*:

> The dominant conception of the present time is that no psychic life supervenes except in the presence of a material vehicle and that no spirit, either pure or possessed only of an etheric body, exists in this world. Now this idea, which has become one of the most firmly established constituents of our present-day outlook on life, is completely new as measured by the standard of history.[4]

This is a question that the French philosopher, Gabriel Marcel (1889–1973), may help us to shed some light on. Marcel conceives the nature of thinking to be twofold. On one hand, we have what he refers to as primary, and on the other, secondary reflection. Primary reflection is always of a conceptual nature. It is analytical and possesses an objective character. Here, the thinker serves as a rather neutral recipient of the concerns, as it were, of mind and intelligence itself acting as an autonomous entity. The main focus of this kind of thinking revolves around the idea of objectivity. By objectivity it is meant the act of judging the structure of reality in such a manner that this can be encountered and thus verified by anyone. The nature of a problem, then, is what Marcel has in mind in this respect. The problem can be set up so that anyone with the proper ability, if not method, can dissect it, effectively solving it. On the other hand, problems, Marcel argues, are always solvable regardless of their complexity. A problem can be defined as being made up of a question, to which man lacks a technique. Knowledge comes about through the possession of technique, whether this involves gardening or astrophysics. Hence, whatever cannot be solved is not technically considered a problem for the scientist. On the contrary, problems are those that admit of a solution. Of course, optimism is always a central component of this rational process. Frankly speaking, there ought to be no denying this condition of reason, given that this is part of the spirit of discovery. However, this rational process should contain space for questions that are not readily exhaustible. A refusal to admit this becomes delusional arrogance: "If only we come to possess the proper technique, then we can overcome any problem."[5]

This is not exactly what takes place in *The Uninvited*, though. It is true to say that initially Roderick and Pamela are faced with a kind of problem in the disturbances that they experience in the house. The rumblings that take place throughout the house bring about a practical level of annoyance that require a solution. Most of the film revolves around seeking an answer to the concern that Stella has in regard to her communication with her departed mother. It is correct, then, to say that Roderick and Pamela do eventually come to an understanding of what is maligning the new inhabitants of the house. That is, they come to believe that the presence is Stella's mother. In a greater sense, and this is where the epicenter of the film lies, the whereabouts of the disembodied departed is never solved.

The supernatural genre depicts problems by which the main characters are affected and which they attempt to solve. In the better films, the protagonists go blindly and naively searching for answers that eventually overwhelm them. It is important to keep in mind that even when these strange occurrences are understood and solved there nevertheless remains the question of why this other dimension exists in the first place. This is more a question of cinematic convention than intent. If we consider that Roderick and his sister Pamela do not accept the existence of ghosts at the beginning of the film, we are then prepared to witness how their convictions change. Yes, it is true that they are scared at first, but they learn to live with the ghosts that inhabit their home. Eventually, it is important for the film to shift the dramatic attention from the fact that there are ghosts in the house to what they are trying to communicate to young Stella. This change of mind and acceptance of the spirit world is also a change of conviction. Roderick and Pamela are thus confronted with the sublime. Oesterreich adds: "Together with consciousness of the presence of spirits it produces an impression of horror, of something sinister, and in general all the sentiments of tremendum of which Rudolf Otto offers an excellent analysis, demonstrating also their importance in primitive religion."[6]

This is what Marcel refers to as the difference between the nature of a problem per se and a mystery. The nature of the mystery is such that it always assumes the reality of essences, which intuition uncover. Marcel's thought begins by presupposing that there may be a limit to what reason can uncover. He writes in *Metaphysical Journal*:

April 2nd, 1916

> This morning, on a clear and marvelous springtime day, I glimpsed that the notions of so-called "occult" knowledge, against which "reason" claims to revolt, are in reality at the root of the commonest day to day experiences which we take for granted: the experiences of feeling, of will or of memory. Who would be prepared to question that the will "acts" as suggestion, as magical suggestion? Does not the experience of memory imply the real and effective negation of time? It is all obvious—too obvious for the twilight condition of our psychology.[7]

Is this not also Hamlet's problem, when he says: "There are more things in heaven and Earth, Horatio, than are dreamt in your philosophy?" Marcel has written a great deal about the possibility of communicating with the dead. For instance, in an article entitled "The Origins of My Philosophy" in a book edited by Martin Ebon, *Communicating with the Dead*, Marcel speaks about a particular personal experience. He tells of how he went along with the family of a deceased French soldier to a medium and how the dead man communicated startling information, insight which no one present at the table could have possessed. The soldier described how he had died, along with two other soldiers in his company, whom were later identified by French authorities.

The Uninvited is a classic supernatural whodunit in that it initially attempts to get to the bottom of a supernatural problem using rational means. This is important in setting up the total puzzlement, that will beset the protagonists later on in the film. For instance, during their first night at the house, cries are heard coming from a room in the second floor. Roderick walks out of his room followed seconds later by his sister. This scenario is probably enough to scare any viewer. Given that it is an early scene, in order to have some degree of realism, the director has Roderick calmly state, "There's a logical explanation for this." His sister counters by asking, "What is it?" To which he answers, "I can't give it to you right now." This fair amount of incredulity must be allowed to take place in order to set the stage for a further conversion of the protagonist to take place. How this conversion takes place is a central component of this film, as a dramatic work.

Stella, who is twenty years old, has not returned to Windward House since her grandfather took her away. He does not want her to return to that old house because, as he tells Roderick, "A house can be filled with malignancy, malignancy directed at a certain child." Roderick does not ignore this ominous admonition. Even though Roderick cannot be certain of any complicity between the commander and a ghost, he realizes that things do not add up. He begins to think that perhaps this ghost has something to say and is seeking an audience. Disregarding her grandfather's advice, the young woman returns to the house on the invitation of Roderick and his sister. In a scene where Roderick plays a serenade for her, as the piece turns sad, she gets up and runs away. This room is always frigid, the flowers wilt, and Roderick complains of having lost his inspiration for writing music whenever he enters it. At about this very same time, Lizzy, the caretaker, screams, saying that she's seen the ghost of a woman.

This story, like *The Changeling*, for example, is about a ghost that seeks justice—that the truth be known—but which it cannot readily communicate. We can say that the disembodied spirit in both of these films is encapsulated in its own spirit world without being able to liberate itself from its past life in the physical plane. We witness this same solipsism in Enrique Anderson Imbert's wonderful short story "El Fantasma," in which the soul of a dead man cannot contact the living members of his family or communicate with the souls of the dead.

In *The Uninvited*, we learn that Stella's father was a painter who had an affair with a Spanish gypsy and portrait-model named Carmel, who posed for the painter. As the story progresses, we come to realize that Stella's grandfather is the bearer of a terrible secret that the ghost wants known. Roderick sets up a séance at the house along with a Dr. Scott, his sister, and Stella in order to attempt to communicate with the ghostly woman. During the séance Stella goes into a deep trance and assumes the voice of Carmel, who tells the party present to go and talk to Ms. Mary Holloway, who was the family nurse at the time. Ms. Holloway is currently running a nursing home, even though she is insane.

In effect, this film does great justice to the ancient Greek philosophical quip about appearance and reality. There is always an investigative angle to the better supernatural films that employ reason and deduction, until the protagonist becomes convinced that this is a fruitless approach and something else must be at work. The protagonists in these films rarely come out at the beginning proclaiming alliance to the supernatural in any form or guise. Instead, there is always a reluctance to accept what cannot be easily explained by buying time, consulting experts and utilizing common sense and reason. *The Uninvited* is inspired by a superbly intelligent script that asks: can such disembodied entities actually exist? The film works from the assumption that spirits exist, and if they ever return, they do so from a need to communicate. Pamela makes this clear when she says, "If a spirit comes back is for some particular purpose."[8]

After the séance, all present, including Stella, fall under the impression that Stella's mother, Mary Meredith, will protect the young woman from the evil that Carmel is perpetrating. Subsequently, Roderick, Pamela and Dr. Scott decide to visit Ms. Holloway at the asylum. At that moment, they discover that Stella had been staying there at the behest of her grandfather. While Ms. Holloway stares at a painting of Mary Meredith, she tells them that the young woman has taken a train to return to Windward House—knowing full well that the house will be uninhabited at the time. They leave Ms. Holloway in a delusional frenzy and come to the realization that she sent the young woman there so that she would jump off the cliff.

As they arrive at the house, Roderick and his sister hear screams and immediately see Stella running for the edge of the cliff. Roderick manages to grab her, as Stella holds on to the roots of a tree. Once inside the house, the ghostly apparition of a woman shows up. This ghost is probably one of the most believable and toned-down examples of apparitions found in films in this genre. Of course, the suspense reaches its climax at the discovery that Stella's mother is not Mary Meredith but Carmel. After his affair with the portrait model, Stella's father shipped his mistress to Paris, where she could deliver the child in the absence of scandal. The child was brought back to Windward House. However, Carmel could not live without her child and returned to claim the baby girl. Mary Meredith tried to wrestle the baby away from Carmel and throw the child over the cliff, but it was she who fell to her death The film effectively solves the problem of the interaction between the two ghosts present in Windward House and their affliction of the human inhabitants.

What remains as an accepted cinematic convention is the idea that spirits exist in ways that perhaps the protagonists cannot explain. Of course, this latter concern cannot be addressed in detail without turning the film into a documentary on the supernatural. The film ends with Roderick telling the ghost of Mary Meredith that they now know the truth and that she should leave Windward House. This suggests a meeting of the two realms: the visible and supernatural, but also a realization that lack of understanding does not have to be synonymous with fear.

NOTES

1. Maslow, Abraham H. *Toward a Psychology of Being*. New York: D. Van Nostrand Company, 1968.

2. Lavelle, Louis. *The Dilemma of Narcissus*. Translated by William Gairdner. Burdett, New York: Larson Publications, 1993, 210.

3. Greenhouse, Herbert B. *Premonitions: A Leap into the Future*. Bernard Geis Associates, 1971, 244. Research into the diverse aspects of the paranormal made considerable inroads with the creation of laboratory experiments and controlled case studies in the early 1960s. Also, see: *Psychic: A Challenge for Science*. Edited by

John White. New York: G.P. Putnam's Sons, 1974. In this insightful encyclopedia, twenty-nine aspects of research into the paranormal are brought together.

4. Oesterreich, T. K. *Possession: Demoniacal and Other Among Primitive Races, in Antiquity, The Middle Ages, and Modern Times*. Secaucus, New Jersey: The Citadel Press, 1974, 376.

5. Barrett, William. *The Illusion of Technique: A Search for Meaning in a Technological Civilization.* New York: Anchor Press, 1978.

6. Oesterreich, 377.

7. Marcel, Gabriel. *Metaphysical Journal*. Translated by Bernard Wall. Chicago: Gateway Edition, 1952, 130.

8. See: Arthur S. Berger. *Aristocracy of the Dead: New Findings in Postmortem Survival.* Jefferson, North Carolina: McFarland & Company, Inc., Publishers, 1987. Mr. Berger argues in a chapter of this informative work titled, "The Neglected Angle" that perhaps at the center of all arguments that negate the immortality of the soul lies the fallacy that survival after death is a universal phenomenon. He writes, "A pair of widely held assumptions, however, like blinders, seem to have narrowed the view of survival researchers and prevented them from studying the attributes of communicators. One of these assumptions are that, if there is survival after the grave, all people will survive equally. There will be no exceptions. In the words of one respected student of the subject 'survival' is automatic and universal." He then goes on to say "Both these assumptions are not only unnecessary for the investigation of the survival problem, but, if false, either or both may have severely retarded the search for evidence, 23.

Chapter 10

Jacques Tati
Last Bastion of Innocence in Modernity

PLAYTIME AND MR. HULOT'S HOLIDAY

Synopsis

Tati offers viewers a comedic perspective on life. However, his films are not comedies, properly speaking. Instead, films like *Playtime* and *Mr. Hulot's Holiday* contrast innocence with a mechanized world that keeps the characters from developing a sense for life. Monsieur Hulot is constantly stumbling unto a world that turns him into an unsuspecting cog in the wheel of rapid technological change. Yet, Mr. Hulot retains his innocence, a form of temporal purity and salvation that enables him to cherish the immediacy of his lived-experience in modernity.

If it is true that God is in the details, as Ludwig Mies van der Rohe asserts, then Tati's films are architectonic temples.[1] Tati's work is replete with images of the anonymity that seems so prevalent in modern technological life. Anonymity in Tati's films can be interpreted as a reflection of the status and relative position of objects in the lived experience of his characters.

The comic nature of objects is viewed as such because there are human subjects from which they are differentiated, and which they ultimately affect. Tati infuses his films with a brilliant array of broken objects, curious trinkets, and overly complicated hardware. This is what fills Hulot's universe with meaning. Mr. Hulot is something of a magnifying glass that amplifies the importance of everyday objects through his insatiable curiosity. Hulot walks the city armed with the curiosity that only children and poets possess. His gaze is always glued to the mundane and seemingly trivial nuances of everyday life. Yet he does not give this impression when we are first introduced to him. At first, we see a quirky character who is witness to a multitude of simultaneously occurring phenomena. As Tati's films develop, we begin to notice that Hulot is always the main focus of attention, not always physically but through his ability to draw the viewer's attention. For instance, in *Playtime* there is the difficulty of regulating the air conditioner/heater just right in the restaurant that is about to debut, hilarity in the crown imprint that is left on the back of people's shirts, and objects falling out of Hulot's pockets when he hangs upside down from a tree in *Traffic*. In addition, there is the scene of Hulot's sister turning on a gaudy fish-fountain only when her guests are arriving in *Mon Uncle,* and his smoking, backfiring old car in *Mr. Hulot's Holiday*.

Hulot is the consummate outsider looking in. While he is not totally inept at modern life, his is a poetic view of the details that form such a world. Hulot is also an antidote to the cynical view that takes technical or material progress for granted. In appearing to be behind the times he is able to take in the full splendor of the meaning of the things that surround him. Hulot's confusion works well as a vehicle for modern technology and gadgetry. He is shy and unassuming and always out of place. We witness him going about disoriented and interacting with people and things. However, Hulot shows no antipathy toward technology. He is simply amused by it all. In this respect, he is no different than most people and thus fits the bill of being everyman. Being in strange surroundings does not cause him strife. His manners are jovial and friendly, always bursting with curiosity.

PLAYTIME

Playtime opens with a shot of white puffy clouds in an infinitely blue sky. Angelic music is playing. There is also a shot of an ultramodern glass structure. It is hard to believe that the entire cityscape is a movie set. Tati's attention to detail is admirable. This is also especially interesting given that Tati declared bankruptcy after *Playtime* was completed. A reflection of the Eiffel Tower in a plate of glass alerts viewers that the film takes place in Paris. Is one to gather that this modern Paris can in fact be any modern city? More anonymity. This is conceivable, given that Tati, much like Jean-Pierre Melville, is a poet of moving pictures. The set itself serves as an arena for the theme of the film: Do we control technology or vice versa? Another recurring theme in Tati's work is confusion in modernity. Hulot pokes fun at what appears to be a humanity lost in its own glowing material progress. Yet Tati does not offer an ideological format in which to reject technology and science. Instead, he cites examples of how human beings have become, whether consciously or not, dependent on machinery. Part of this confusion, not alienation as some more politically minded critics would argue, comes about due to the dynamic and vibrant nature of the modern world. Hulot possesses that most characteristic quality of man: adaptability.

For example, in the airport terminal in *Playtime* people are parading across the terminal floor. One is left to reflect as to the final destination of the masses of humanity. Tati poeticizes the human environment. Perhaps there is no greater indication of this than to witness how the melancholic musical score at the start of *Mr. Hulot's Holiday* and the quote that entices viewers to enjoy themselves, create a mood of renunciation of life. At the start of *Playtime*, a group of lively female tourists is led down an escalator and out to a waiting bus. They are vibrant and excited to see Paris. Tati's work has very little dialogue. This technique, which can be said to be half taken from mime and half from the era of the silent film, emphasizes the often mute and unnoticed qualities of everyday life. This is highlighted by focusing on the nature of travel. Instead of dialogue, Tati employs incidental background sounds of ongoing conversations. Tati's films can be likened to the sounds of an orchestra warming up. Most of the sounds and conversations are muffled and undecipherable.

The quiet and muffled world of Tati's films is a central ingredient in his ability to call attention to everyday things. It is a nuanced stroke of genius that in a world of excessive noise, Tati should concentrate on the seemingly unimportant facets of modern life. He strips the human environment to its bare minimum. He exorcises conversation, as if to suggest that today there is already too much talking. Also gone is the capacity to know any character from the inside out. Tati hardly makes use of the close-up. Is it not one of the central characteristics of the twentieth century, and especially of the post–World War II world, that few people seem willing to know themselves or others from within? Consider what Rilke has to say about this point in one of his letters dated October 3, 1907: "Is it really true when the whole world now pretends to understand him and his pictures? Must not the art-dealers and art-critics feel hopelessly bewildered or indifferent towards this dear zealot, in whom something of St. Francis had come to life again?"[2]

Do these characters ever actually converse? Do they try to make sense of the coming and goings of the people who they encounter? In *Playtime*, Hulot greets a man at the lobby of the office building while they wait for their respective appointments. They notice each other only because of the strange noises made by the air in the cushions in the modern black chairs.

Stripping the loud, modern world down to comic and incoherent sounds, Tati focuses the attention of the viewer on aspects of modern life that are readily taken for granted. Hulot walks the streets and experiences the beach in *Mr. Hulot's Holiday* with the vibrant freshness of one who does so for the first time. An interesting question that surfaces in Tati's work is: Who notices all of this? Mass confusion is part of the intrinsic charm of his work.

When we take into consideration all of the nuances that fill Tati's screen, besides the specific activity that Hulot is engaged in, we come to realize that few people notice much about the reality that surrounds them. This is undeniably true of his films—and one suspects this might be equally true of the modern world in general. The absence of sensibility raises the question—to whom is the action occurring? Undoubtedly some of the attention is centered on Hulot, but a great amount goes unnoticed by the other characters. For instance, there is a sense that any alert person would notice the crown imprints on the backs of people's shirts in *Playtime*. When the American tourist finally notices it, he uses it to make it a condition for admission to his "private club" at the back of the Royal Garden restaurant. No one seems to notice or wonder where the crown marks originate. Who is the American man who allows people to enter based on this distinguishing mark? Are we so self-absorbed not to realize that the doorman of the restaurant in *Playtime* in fact does not have a door to hold open, given that the glass was smashed? This lack of attention is what garners the laughs in Tati's work.

Tati's films suggest that such things take place everywhere and at all times, except that most people do not notice them. Philosophically, this line of thinking leads to the question of what the world is really like when it is not being observed. Tati establishes this by making the viewer the omniscient observer who witnesses all, but who cannot interfere in the action. If we could only tell the restaurant patrons that the ice bucket is really filled with pieces of glass from the shattered front door, not ice.

Once we see the buses driving away from the airport, we are treated to a lovely shot of a modern world that could really be anywhere, even though we see French-language signs. Throughout his films, Tati uses arrows as symbols to suggest confusion. The endless array of arrows that guide drivers to their respective destinations are exaggerated in order to convey the sense of spatial confusion. The signs are also visual symbols of the handing over of our responsibility and freedom to technology. It is reasonable to argue that the more arrows, the more confused that the characters become. For example, in *Traffic* the arrows are strewn throughout the entirety of the film and are often directly responsible for creating havoc. The beauty of this mass disorientation is that everyone eventually finds their way.

Tati's films resemble Fellini's at least in one sense: both directors depict a the world as a circus-like spectacle. Fellini develops the spectacle theme more than Tati; both directors demonstrate a poetic respect for the chaotic contingencies of human reality. Both possess a Borges-like desire to view human existence as if it is always in motion, as if we are moving through a maze. In both cases, we find that at every bend we encounter the radiance of possibility, literally and figuratively. For both directors light plays a central role in the discernment of reality. In Tati's films the contrast between light and dark is nonexistent given that most scenes take place outdoors. The brilliant splendor of *Playtime* promises a level of joviality and optimism that is admirable. The interior of the tour bus is bright and modern, with a partial glass roof. The camera is angled in such a way as to view hundreds of cars in the airport's parking lot. Tati treats the viewer to a slow-moving procession of cars and buses on the highway that becomes a kind of ballet of modernity, a ballet of motion that resembles the one in *2001: A Space Odyssey*, where Strauss's music accompanies the movement of the space station as it generates artificial centrifugal force. *Playtime* is a film replete with chance encounters—couple this with the brightness of cityscapes, and one begins to see Hulot as a restless poet, while the other characters comfortably settle into daily existence.

Mr. Hulot, who is always played by Tati, is greeted by an old doorman at another modern building. The doorman can't seem to figure out how the highly complicated electrical switchboard works. He refers to this device as an "electrical thingamajigs." I can't help but imagine that the advanced age of the doorman is significant, juxtaposed as he is with an ultramodern electrical control panel. This scene carefully captures the passage of time by reminding us that while today it is an old man that looks on in bewilderment at the electrical panel, tomorrow we will be struggling to deal with some as yet unforeseen creation.

The doorman has Hulot wait in the lobby for an official, who in turn walks him over to a modern and austere waiting room that is decorated with pictures of old men, presumably the board of directors of the corporation. While there, Hulot begins to fidget with the cushions of the furniture that appear to be air-filled. Hulot passes the time waiting by studying the demeanor of another gentleman who is also waiting. Later, he walks into a tiny room to view an eye-catching "painting" that turns out to be an elevator. In the next scene, we see Hulot opening a door and unsuspectingly entering a roundtable meeting of some kind. This works well as a symbol that Hulot is constantly entering what appear to him as alien surroundings.

In a very funny scene, Mr. Hulot is seen flagging down a Mr. Griffin, the man whom we already met in the lobby. While he thinks that he is waving at Mr. Griffin, it turns out that Mr. Griffin is really behind him in the same building. What Hulot sees across the hall is only a reflection in a mirror. As this scene is unfolding, Hulot is dragged into a group of people visiting a space exposition. How best to experience reality than indirectly? The latter is one of the merits of Tati's films.

Viewing reality in this way, we come to see our world and ourselves in a detached, unified way that we rarely encounter in its immediacy. Cinema works best as a form of mirror to human life. Even when this mirror is not too accurate, it necessitates that we pay attention to ourselves and our surroundings. Art unifies the metaphysical field of possibility for us in a way that enriches our awareness of ourselves. This task is never exhaustive, for it is often merely representative of select aspects of human existence. Cinema can help to capture the essence of the atomic, temporal structure of life in a condensed, yet vital fashion.

What must viewers bring to cinema and art patrons to the value of art to make it enlightening and fulfilling? Tati's audience is made to exercise something of the Hulot in themselves, while watching him rediscover the world.

Parmenides's assertion that reality is objective, even though ambiguous, is based on the foundation that reality likes to hide. But to hide does not mean to trick, dissuade, or confuse man's capacity for reason. Reality's objectivity can be measured by its universal qualities. When we stand before a work of art, there is only so much that the work can convey to us. Music, too, can bring out exalted emotions. These experiences speak to the sublime in the human condition. Yet these are lived-experiences that cannot easily be explained. Our desire to communicate our experiences, whenever this is possible, is a secondary process that has little to do with the immediately lived aesthetic experience. It is a futile and pretentious notion to pretend to understand wholeheartedly the sublime underpinning of aesthetic intuition.

Parmenides writes in fragment 1: "Who come to our house with mares that carry you, welcome; for it is no ill fortune that sent you forth to travel this route (for it lies far indeed from the beaten track of men)."[3] That truth may lie so far from the beaten path suggests the embrace of metaphysics of the difficult. This is a philosophical attitude that asks: What is the role of rational individuals in the search for truth and understanding? In Parmenides's poem the decision to transcend the world of seeming, of appearances for that of truth is a vital decision that rewards seekers with truth.

What viewers take from Tati's films is proportionate to our ability to engage with human reality. Tati's films resemble a primal formalism; subjects trying to make sense of objective aspects of human reality. Unlike traditional films that employ dialogue and narrative to tell a story, Tati's films force us to operate at an inquisitive level. Anyone who has ever watched a Tati film alongside a child quickly realizes this. In spite of the absence of dialogue, Tati's films convey a great deal of meaning, even though the meaning is not articulated at the patent level.

When an American tourist named Barbara goes out of her way to take a picture of a flower vendor whom the tourist considers to be an authentic display of French culture, the comedic suggestion is that this applies to tourists everywhere. Barbara is called by another woman in her tour group to enter the exposition with her. "Barbara, come on, look how modern it is, they even have American stuff." As she opens the glass door, a beautiful reflection of the Eiffel Tower momentarily distracts Barbara's attention. She is quickly reminded that she is in Paris. Once inside the exposition, the women are treated to an electric room, which has headlights, a fluted column that turns out to be a garbage can, and totally silent doors. One vendor says: "Our motto—slam your door in total silence." An oxymoron, some may suggest. Perhaps? A modern one, at that. While inside the exposition, two women mistake Hulot for an employee and ask him to fix their lamp. Of course, Hulot does not protest. His curiosity and willingness to help often get the best of him. Hulot is marveled by the many objects at the expo.

Implicit in Tati's films is a sense of timing. His characters never really converse with each other. Instead, they are often involved in giving or taking directions, pointing and gesticulating in the manner of Mediterranean people. Movement is a staple of Tati's work, albeit movement in Tati's films is a meticulous, macrocosmic tribute to the ant world. Viewed from a distance, ants seem to know where they are going. Everyone is always in motion, people entering or leaving buildings, doors opening and closing—always, there is motion.

Tati's films can be described as a poetic depiction of dynamic processes. Because Mr. Hulot appears in what are considered Tati's best four films, his character is well developed. However, none of the films are sequels. Each film has Hulot undergoing new adventures, what amount to a new set of comedic circumstances. We know that he has been in the army and he has a sister. Surprisingly, if we are to judge from his quirky walk, he also knows how to drive a car. Whether Tati intended to have Mr. Hulot star in all of his full feature films is not important. It is great fun watching his exploits.

This is also the case in *The Thin Man* series. The sophisticated and well-scripted comedy team of William Powell and Myrna Loy appeared in six films as Nick and Nora Charles, beginning with *The Thin Man* in 1934 and culminating with *Song of the Thin Man* in 1947.[4]

MR. HULOT'S HOLIDAY

Hulot's character is made clear at the start of *Mr. Hulot's Holiday*. Already, in his first embodiment as Mr. Hulot, Tati informs us that a central aspect of Hulot's character serves as a study in leisure. *Mr. Hulot's Holiday* begins with a long shot of waves breaking in a deserted sea accompanied by a melancholic jazz score. From the very beginning a caption informs the viewer:

> Mr. Hulot is off for a week by the sea to take a seat behind his camera and you can spend it with him. Don't look for a plot, for a holiday is meant purely for

fun and if you look for it you will find more fun in ordinary life than in fiction. So, relax and enjoy yourselves. See how many people you can recognize. You might even recognize yourself.[5]

Leisure is one of a handful of themes that Tati's films explore. There is a correlation between leisure and the gentle, slow and deliberate movements that Tati is so fond of portraying. The mesmerizing slow procession of cars leaving the airport, and the street scene when Hulot is called by a former army friend in *Playtime* are fine example of this theme. From the outset of *Mr. Hulot's Holiday*, Tati equates the idea of a holiday with everyday existence. If fun is what we seek, Tati suggests, all we have to do is become better attuned to ordinary life. This is the sense of timelessness that is so pervasive in Tati's body of work. However, Mr. Hulot is much more than a symbol of leisure. He is a poet of the everyday. Hulot is like a perpetual child, always allowing himself to be surprised by the nuances of daily life. In children, natural curiosity is rewarded by understanding, in adults it is renewal. Havelock Ellis reminds us of this in *The Dance of Life* when: "By revealing the spectacular character of reality he restores the serenity of its innocence. We see the face of the world as of a lovely woman smiling through her tears."[6]

Leisure surfaces again as a prominent theme in a shot of the Arc de Triomphe reflected on a glass door. The doorman tells another worker inside the hotel lobby, "Hey George, here comes group E." Group E refers to a group of tourists entering the hotel lobby, presumably coming back from touring Parisian sites. One of the men in the group is carrying a small rendition of the Eiffel Tower. A woman is heard saying, "I am going straight to bed," as they go up on the escalator. Simultaneously another group is descending. Tourists in, tourists out. Everyone in this group is dressed up. One woman says, "There we go, out on the town." The implication is that the tourists visit old Paris but always return to their modern comforts.

Hulot is not an artist, but the curiosity that informs his engagement with the daily world is that of the poet. We do not think of Hulot as a poet because he does not create, but his lack of being a creator is not necessarily because he lacks curiosity. Tati tells us very little about Hulot. He rarely utilizes the technique of the close-up. Just what does Hulot think and feel?

The close-up shot can work to depict the internal make up of a character. Because Hulot is always seen surrounded by objects and people, one can only imagine what he thinks. This is in keeping with Tati's ability to showcase reality through sound and physical gags. We only know Hulot from watching him interact with his environment. *Mr. Hulot's Holiday* and *Playtime* express the passage of time. These two films have a melancholic feel that is indicative of an intuitive understanding of some moments of human reality that clearly cannot be replicated. *Playtime* conveys a sad sense of finality. At the end *Playtime* the characters disperse from the drugstore and retreat into the anonymity of the city. In order for Tati's work to have a sense of finality, it must also have a vivid starting point. At the beginning of the film, we are introduced to quite a few colorful people that unexpectedly turn out to be main characters in the film. While it may appear that Tati's plots do not have a linear development, vis-à-vis other films, this is not the case.

The finality of *Playtime* is evidenced in that, at the end of the film, the characters come together at the Royal Garden restaurant. The many characters who, up to that time, have seen busily undertaking different tasks, are now united. This gives the film a sense of coherence and irony. Seeing the different characters separately creates the sensation that something is about to happen to all these people. The course of events leading up to their eventual reunion is as infinite as the categories that define human existence. As Maurice Merleau-Ponty writes in *The Primacy of Perception*, "We never cease living in the world of perception, but we go beyond it in critical thought—almost to the point of forgetting the contribution of perception to our idea of truth."[7] At the center of it all, we encounter Hulot and his foibles.

The combination of situations coupled with the choice of musical scores gives Tati's films a distinct pathos that enlightens everyday affairs. Tati avoids intellectualizing his themes, thus preserving the freshness and innocence that is such a staple of his films. For instance, one can take a cynical and ideological stance, as is so often the case in postmodern film criticism, and argue that Hulot is a poor man lost in the world of the rich in *Mr. Hulot's Holiday*. His nondescript automobile puffs and shakes along the road, moving at minimum speed, while other people pass him by in newer and fancier automobiles. Consider the view from Hulot's hotel room: there is none. While others enjoy oceanfront views, Hulot is perched in an attic room that, because of the angle of the roof, has only one window that faces the sky. The point is that Hulot does enjoy his holiday regardless of his surroundings.

There is a sense in which Hulot is more than an actual character. Rather, he is an amalgam of character traits. Always, Hulot comes closest to resembling a child. In *Mr. Hulot's Holiday*, he dances around uninhibitedly while playing table tennis in the hotel lobby. This is confirmed quickly thereafter when the other player, a child, emerges from behind a wall that covers the view of half the table. At this time, a woman says to Hulot in English: "It was very good of you to play with him. You see, his father is so busy." This scene is bisected by a young intellectual trying to woo a young woman with a pompous political diatribe.

Hulot is always polite and willing to please. His desire to help often gets him in trouble. When he tries to mount a horse, the animal kicks a car's rumble seat, trapping a man inside. David Bellos elaborates in *Jacques Tati: His Life and Art*:

> Though most of his attempts to do so go awry, Hulot embodies the abstract intention of making amends, irrespective of context. But he never does so by taking direct initiatives, or by entering into real interaction with the other characters in the lobby, in the dining room, or on the beach. Hulot exists at one remove. An idea, an emotion, an insubstantial presence. Hulot is more like a ghost of *Sylvie* than the mumbling postman of *Jour de fete*.[8]

The first nighttime scene in *Playtime* is a lovely display of ritualistic and timeless choreography, as the buildings light up, floor after floor, in a patented sequence. The apartments in the city are ultramodern and people waste no time in showing off their gadgets. In *Playtime* and *Mon Uncle*, there is a fair amount of respect and fascination for all that is new. In one particularly telling scene the people in four different apartments are all seen watching television through wall-size glass windows. These scenes are silent, thus placing the people inside their homes in a somewhat zoological perspective. A particularly magical scene takes place when Hulot leaves his friend's ultramodern apartment and is walking alone in the street at night. He looks up at the buildings in wonderment, as a musical interlude accompanies his contented walk.[9]

The second part of *Playtime*, as I am to refer to it, begins with the opening night of a new restaurant, "The Royal Garden." The owner and managers of the restaurant have great expectations for their flashy new operation. Of course, as irony would have it, everything goes wrong, partly because the restaurant is not finished by the time the first patrons arrive. The band begins to play a Cuban cha-cha. As the first dancers take to the dance floor, the crown imprints begin to appear on the back of people's shirts. The architect continues his frenetic measuring of all the dimensions that are not to specification. In an early scene, one of the waiters rips up a floor tile with his shoe. The planning goes wrong, partly because the owners of the restaurant are more concerned with looks than substance. Hulot enters the restaurant by chance. He is taken there by an army friend whom he met in the street as the man was about to deliver flowers to the restaurant. The glass door breaks and the doorman uses the round handle to pretend that he is opening a phantom door. This matters to the patrons, most whom are too stuffy to notice their surroundings. As Barbara enters the restaurant, a French couple sitting at a nearby table murmurs, "Did you see her shoes?"

Inside the restaurant, the air conditioner and heater are not well regulated, so that an ice cream cake and a plastic toy airplane melt. The tempo of the music picks up into a conga beat, so does the overall mood of the clients. As the dancing begins, the restaurant is beginning to fall apart, but few people take notice. The electrical system goes awry. Pieces of glass that were collected from the broken front door are used as ice for the champagne bucket. Waiters trip, rip their uniforms and serve cold food as the manager walks around with the architect trying to correct the many mishaps. Again, no one seems to notice.

The party eventually winds down. The culmination of the destruction occurs when the American tourist jumps to grab a piece of the décor and makes a portion of the ceiling cave in. At first there is a gasp of anticipation from the patrons, but the party resumes quickly thereafter. The band gives up and leaves, prompting the American tourist to call out for a piano player. Barbara volunteers and begins to play a slow piece that saves the animated mood. The party breaks up at dawn. Some of the partygoers stop at a drugstore across the street as the sun comes up. Then, as if to emphasize the cyclical nature of a normal day in the city, activity begins to mount once again. The city comes alive in the morning. The day progresses and people go about their usual business. These last scenes tie in beautifully to the everyday activity of the city prior to the restaurant scene. The tourists are picked up by their bus, which joins the procession of cars and buses. Hulot is seen once again walking about, umbrella in hand. He comes very close to meeting Barbara, but as his luck would have it, he gets trapped in a turnstile at a store. Day again begins to give way to night. Tati alludes to life as a carousel; a maze of automobiles becomes caught in a European circular boulevard. The music at this point is that of the circus. *Playtime* is a fine example of Tati's uncanny ability to suspend the immediacy of everyday events to enable us to take a fresh look at life.

Michel Chion best explains this. He concludes his marvelous book *The Films of Jacques Tati*:

> Poetry rises from cars clogging up, and more clogging up. How to end? Cars finally gather in the town's traffic circle and create a jam. Traffic is hell, but a simple little trigger—a certain sense of slipping brought on by the music coming from a barrel organ—can change everything and ultimately release the enchantment. The resounding music is all it takes to have cars hopelessly turning in circles and become part of a merry-go-round, around which metaphors flourish and brighten our vision. Unexpectedly a person slips a coin in the parking meter and it is as if the drop of the coin starts the music and the merry-go-round all over again.[10]

NOTES

1. Chion, Michel. *The Films of Jacques Tati.* Toronto: Guernica, 1997, 44. Chion writes: "When dealing with Tati's films, it is good to be on the look out for amusing details. Which is precisely the point of his films."

2. Wyndenbruck, Nora. *Rilke: Man and Poet.* New York: Appleton-Century-Crofts, 143.

3. Parmenides of Elea. *Fragments.* Translated by David Gallop. Toronto: University of Toronto Press, 1984, 53.

4. Quirk, Lawrence J. *The Complete Films of William Powell.* New York: Carol Publishing Group, 1990.

5. *Mr. Hulot's Holiday* (1953).

6. Ellis, Havelock. *The Dance of Life.* Random House, 333.

7. Merleau-Ponty, Maurice. *The Primacy of Perception.* Evanston: Northwestern University Press, 1964, 3.

8. Bellos, David. *Jacques Tati: His Life and Art.* London: The Harvill Press, 1999, 171.

9. Maslow, Abraham H. *Toward a Psychology of Being.* New York: D. Van Nostrand Company. In a chapter from this book titled, "Creativity in Self-Actualizing People" Maslow argues that creativity can be viewed as an attitude that some people take toward reality, and not a narrow definition of "creative" people. He seems to be describing Hulot when he writes: "Such people can see the fresh, the raw, the concrete, the idiographic, as well as the generic, the abstract, the rubricized, the categorized and the classified. Consequently, they live far more in the real world of nature than in the verbalized world of concepts, abstractions, expectations, beliefs and stereotypes that most people confuse with the real world," 137.

10. Ibid. *The Films of Jacques Tati,* 160.

Conclusion

SUMMING UP

Human reality is truly indomitable.

W. Somerset Maugham suggests in his poignant philosophical work *The Summing Up* that people, the "plain man," look to philosophers for suitable clarity about life, even if this is often incomplete. In effect, Maughan's uncommon perspicuity describes the role of philosophical thought's ability to uncover the framework of human reality. This has been the case since the time of the pre-Socratic philosophers, for the lifeline and raison d'être of philosophical reflection is contemplation of man in the cosmos, and the purpose and meaning of human existence. Clear and simple, this task is the responsibility of every inspired life. That the latter today has been lost in self-referential analytic jargon and bloated academic lingo is at best, a case of squandered opportunities, at worst, a colossal tragedy.

At the end of every day, thoughtful persons find it necessary, in one way or other, to sum up their lived-experience of the day that has just ended. We sum up the end of the year in worldwide celebrations; anyone who creates and builds something does the same after the work is completed. This is truly a practical task, for it enables us to attain understanding and guide our lives in a direction that is in keeping with our ability for self-reflection; an intellectually honest and life-affirming process that must take into consideration unforeseen contingencies, and that ultimately reward us with an authentic existence.

Self-reflection is essential because life is transparent to itself, always fleeting before our eyes, often much too fast to be fully appreciated in its immediacy. Oftentimes, all we can do is assess our lived experiences after the fact. The realization that the latter frustrates existential longing necessitates a pro-active stance on life.

This is why poets and intuitive persons attempt to capture human experience and reality in a bottle, as it were. This is also why a metaphysical/

existential approach to the lived experience is a worthy contemplative approach to human existence, especially in the ebb and flow of daily life. A metaphysical/existential undertaking of human existence best safeguards the capture and appropriation of the essences that inform human reality.

The strength and value of metaphysical/existential contemplation is the ability to corral sensual experience, as it were, while simultaneously bringing perspective to spurious interactions between persons, and man and the objectifying forces that form the structure of objective reality. Metaphysical/existential contemplation offers man a fighting chance to comprehend the intricate manifestation of essences in human reality. The other alternative leaves us with sheer biological life that lacks all semblance of rhyme and reason.

Summing up the correlation between metaphysical/existential reflection, which is a philosophy of existence, and cinema reminds us of the archival mirror effect that cinema can have on thoughtful persons. In the preceding chapters, I have taken a metaphysical/existence perspective on cinema that makes visual and sensual storytelling a viable centerpiece for philosophical reflection through cinema's ability to capture time.

Appendix

FURTHER READING

Ambrogio, Anthony. "What if the Uninvited Had Haunted Universal or RKO?" *Midnight Marquee: The Magazine of Classic Horror, Science Fiction, Suspense and Noir Cinema*, Issue 53, Spring 1997.
Andrew, Christopher. *The Sword and the Shield: The Mitrokhin Archive and the Secret History of the KGB*. New York: Basic Books, 1999.
Aries, Philippe. *The Hour of Our Death*. Translated by Helen Weaver. Oxford: Oxford University Press, 1991.
Arnheim, Rudolf. *Film as Art*. Berkeley: University of California Press, 1971.
Atkins, John. *The British Spy Novel: Styles in Treachery*. London: John Calder, 1984.
Baudelaire, Charles. *Paris Spleen*. New York: New Directions, 1970.
Baxter, John. *Sixty Years of Hollywood*. London: The Tantivy Press, 1975.
Bazin, André. *Orson Welles: A Critical View*. Los Angeles: Acrobat Books, 1991.
———. *Jean Renoir*. New York: Da Capo Press, 1992.
Bertin, Celia. *Jean Renoir: A Life in Pictures*. Baltimore: The John Hopkins University Press, 1991.
Bjorkman, Stig. *Bergman on Bergman: Interviews with Ingmar Bergman*. New York: Simon and Schuster, 1973.
Blatty, Peter William. *Legion*. New York: Simon and Schuster, 1983.
Bloom, Harold. *Omens of Millennium: The Gnosis of Angels, Dreams, and Resurrection*. New York: Riverhead Books, 1996.
Bookbinder, Robert. *Classic Gangster Films*. New York: A Citadel Press Book, 1993.
———. *The Films of the Seventies*. New York: A Citadel Press Book, 1993.
Bordwell, David, Janet Staiger, and Kristin Thompson. *The Classical Hollywood Cinema: Film Style & Mode of Production to 1960*. New York: Columbia University Press, 1985.
Bowker, Gordon. *Pursued By Furies: A Life of Malcolm Lowry*. New York: St. Martin's Press, 1995.

Bradbury, Ray. *The Martian Chronicles*. New York: Bantam Pathfinder Editions, 1975.

Breindel, Eric. *A Passion for Truth*. Edited by John Podhorezt. New York: HarperCollins Publishers, 1999.

Brode, Douglas. *Lost Films of the Fifties*. New York: Citadel Press, 1991.

Bruccoli, Matthew J., and Richard Layman. Editors. *Hardboiled Mystery Writers Raymond Chandler, Dashiell Hammett, Ross Macdonald: A Literary Reference*. New York: Carroll & Graf Publishers.

Calderon de la Barca, Pedro. *Life is a Dream*. New York: Hill & Wang, 1970.

Cameron, Ian. *Adventure in the Movies*. New York: Crescent Books, 1974.

Capek, Karel. *Three Novels: Hordubal, Meteor, An Ordinary Life*. Highland Park, N.J.: Catbird Press, 1990.

Cavell, Stanley. *The World Viewed: Reflections on the Ontology of Film*. Cambridge: Harvard University Press, 1979.

Cavendish, Richard. Editor. *Man, Myth & Magic: An Illustrated Encyclopedia of the Supernatural*. Italy: BPC Publishing Ltd., 1970.

Cela, Camilo José. *La Colmena*. Barcelona: Editorial Bruguera, 1985.

Chandler, Charlotte. *I, Fellini*. New York: Random House, 1995.

Chierichetti, David. "Death Takes a Holiday." *Scarlet Street: The Magazine of Mystery and Horror*, No. 32, 1999.

Clifford, Irving. *Fake! The Story of Elmyr de Hory the Greatest Art Forger of Our Time*. New York: McGraw-Hill Book Company, 1969.

Clute, John. *The Illustrated Encyclopedia of Science Fiction*. London: Dorling Kindersley, 1995.

Cocteau, Jean. *Diary of an Unknown*. Translated by Jesse Browner. New York: Paragon House, 1991.

Daniels, George C. *The Swing Era: The Movies: Between Vitaphone and Video*. New York: Time-Life Books, 1972.

Danks, Adrian. "Together Alone: The Outsider Cinema of Jean-Pierre Melville." *Senses of Cinema*, March 12, 2004.

De Assis, Machado. *Philosopher or Dog?* New York: Avon Books, 1982.

Djilas, Milovan. *Conversations with Stalin*. Translated from the Serbo-Croat by Michael B. Petrovich. New York: Harcourt, Brace & World, Inc., 1962.

Dostoyevsky, Fyodor. *A Raw Youth*. Translated by Constance Garnett. New York: Dell Publishing co., 1959.

Dowling, William C. "Paul Ricoeur: A Philosophical Journey." *Providence: Studies in Western Civilization*. Volume 8, Number 2; Fall/Winter 2004.

Drane, James. *Pilgrimage to Utopia*. Milwaukee: The Bruce Publishing Company, 1965.

Eisentein, Sergei. *The Film Sense*. San Diego: Harcourt Brace & Company, 1975.

Emerson, Ralph Waldo. *Essays*. Philadelphia: David Mckay, Publisher, 1893.

Everson, William K. *The Bad Guys: A Pictorial History of the Movie Villain*. New York: Cadillac Publishing Co., Inc.1964.

———. *Hollywood Bedlam: Classic Screwball Comedies*. New York: Citadel Press, 1994.

———. *Classics of the Horror Film: From the Days of the Silent Film to the Exorcist.* New York: Citadel Books, 1995.
———. *The Detective in Film.* New York: Citadel Books, 1972.
Fallaci, Oriana. *The Egotists: Sixteen Surprising Interviews.* Chicago: Henry Regnery Company, 1968.
Fearing, Kenneth. *The Big Clock.* London: Xanadu Publications Limited, 1994.
Ferry, Luc and Alain Renaut. *French Philosophy of the Sixties: An Essay on Antihumanism.* Translated by Mary Schnackenber Cattani. Amherst: The University of Massachusetts, 1990.
Flynn, Daniel J. *Intellectual Morons: How Ideology Makes Smart People Fall for Stupid Ideas.* New York: Crown Forum, 2004.
Garmon, Ronald Dale. "Stalking the Blue-Chip Nightmare: The Two Legacies of Cornell Woolrich." *Scarlet Street: The Magazine of Mystery and Horror.* No. 21/Winter 1996.
Geduld, Harry M. Editor. *Film Makers on Film Making: Statements on their Art by Thirty Directors.* Bloomington: Indiana University Press, 1973.
Gerould, Daniel. *The Witkiewicz Reader.* Evanston: Northwestern University Press, 1992.
Gombrich, E. H. *Art and Illusion: A Study in the Psychology of Pictorial Representation.* Princeton: Princeton University Press, 1989.
Gorman, Ed. Editor. *The Fine Art of Murder: The Mystery Reader's Indispensable Companion.* New York: Carroll & Graf Publishers, Inc., 1993.
Grillet-Robbe, Alain & Rene Magritte. *La Belle Captive.* Translated with an Essay by Ben Stoltzfus. Berkeley: University of California Press, 1995.
Guardini, Romano. *The End of the Modern World.* Wilmington, Delaware: ISI Books, 2001.
Guitton, Jean. *El Trabajo Intelectual.* México: Editorial Porrua, S.A., 1994.
Haining, Peter. Editor. *London After Midnight: A Tour of its Criminal Haunts.* Great Britain: Barnes & Noble Inc., 1996.
Halligan, Benjamin. "The Long Take that Kills: Tarkovsky's Rejection of Montage." *Central European Review: The Forthnightly Journal of Central and East European Politics, Society and Culture*, Vol, No. 39, November 13, 200.
Healy, Raymond J., and Francis Mccomas. *Famous Science Fiction Stories: Adventures in Time and Space.* New York: The Modern Library, 1957.
Hirsch, Foster. *Acting Hollywood Style.* New York: Harry N. Abrams, Inc., Publishers, 1996.
Horsley, Carter B. "Last Year at Marienbad: Beautiful and Indelible Incongruity." *The City Review*, March 21, 2004.
Hughes, H. Stuart. *Oswald Spengler: A Critical Estimate.* New York: Charles Scribner's Sons, 1952.
Huxley, Aldous. *Brave New World.* New York: Perennal Library, 1971.
Infante, Guillermo Cabrera. *Holy Smoke.* New York: Harper & Row, Publishers, 1985.
Irving, Clifford. *Fake! The Story of Elmyr de Hory the Greatest Art Forger of Our Time.* New York: McGraw-Hill Book Company, 1969.

Jacob, Gilles, and Claude de Givray. *François Truffaut: Correspondence 1945–1984*. New York: Cooper Square Press, 2000.

James, William. *The Will to Believe and Other Essays in Popular Philosophy*. New York: Dover Publications.

Jung, C. G. *The Spirit in Man, Art, and Literature*. Translated by R. F. C. Hull. Princeton: Princeton University Press, 1978.

———. *The Portable Jung*. Edited by Joseph Campbell. New York: Penguin Books, 1971.

———. *Memories, Dreams, Reflections*. Translated by Richard & Clara Winston. New York: Vintage Books, 1989.

Kessler, Ronald. *Moscow Station: How the KGB Penetrated the American Embassy*. New York: Charles Scibner's Sons, 1989.

Kimball, Roger. *Experiments Against Reality: The Fate of Culture in the Postmodern Age*. Chicago: Ivan R. Dee, 2000.

Kinney, Harrison. *James Thurber: His Life and Times*. New York: Henry Holt and Company, 1995.

Kipling, Rudyard. *The Science Fiction Stories of Rudyard Kipling*. John Brunner. Editor. New York: Carol Publishing Group, 1994.

Kolakowski, Lescek. *Religion*. London: Fontana Press, 1993.

Kracauer, Siegfried. *From Caligari to Hitler: A Psychological History of the German Film*. Princeton: Princeton University Press, 1966.

Kronenberg, Steve. "Whom the Gods Would Destroy. Part Two: Surgical Psychos of the Silver Age." *Monsters from the Vault*, No.6, 1998.

Kundera, Milan. *Immortality*. Translated by Peter Kussi. New York: HarperPerennial, 1992.

Laertius, Diogenes. *Lives of the Eminent Philosophers*. Volume I. Translated by R. D. Hicks. Cambridge: Harvard University Press, 1972.

———. *The Unbearable Lightness of Being*. Translated by Michael Henry Heim. New York: HarperPerennial, 1991.

Le Fanu, Sheridan. *In a Glass Darkly*. Wordsworth Classics. Hertforshire, 1995.

Lem, Stanislaw. *Hospital of the Transfiguration*. San Diego: Harcourt Brace Jovanovich, Publishers, 1988.

Levi-Strauss, Claude. *Structural Anthropology*. Translated by Claire Jacobson and Grundfest Schoepf. New York: Basic Books, 1963.

Lewis, C. S. *The Dark Tower and Other Stories*. San Diego: Harcourt Brace & Company, 1977.

Lorentz, Pare. *Lorentz on Film: Movies 1927–1941*. Norman: University of Oklahoma Press, 1986.

Lurker, Manfred. *The Gods and Symbols of Ancient Egypt*. Translated from the German by Barbara Cummings, 1986.

Marcel, Gabriel. *Man Against Mass Society*. Chicago: A Gateway Edition, 1952.

———. *Problematic Man*. New York: Herder and Herder, 1967.

Marías, Julián. *Tratado Sobre La Convivencia: Concordia Sin Acuerdo*. Barcelona: Ediciones Martinez Roca, 2000.

Marnham, Patrick. *The Man Who Wasn't Maigret: A Portrait of Simenon.* New York: Farrar, Straus and Giroux, 1992.
Maugham, Robin. *Conversations with Willie: Recollections of W. Somerset Maugham.* New York: Simon and Schuster, 1978.
Maugham, W. Somerset. *Ashenden: The British Spy.* New York: Avon Books, 1966.
May, John R., and Michael Bird. Editors. *Religion in Film.* Knoxville: University of Tennessee Press, 1998.
McDonough, Michael. *Malaparte: A House Like Me.* New York: Clarkson Potter Publishers, 1999.
Meyer, David N. *The 100 Best Films to Rent You've Never Heard Of.* New York: St. Martin's Press, 1997.
Miller, William Max. "Of Gods and Monsters: A Pathology Report on Dr. Pretorius." *Midnight Marquee,* Issue 56, Spring 1998.
Miłosz, Czesław. *The Captive Mind.* New York: Vintage International, 1981.
More, Thomas. *Utopia.* Translated by Robert M. Adams. New York: W.W. Norton & Company, Inc, 1975.
Nobile, Philip. *Favorite Movies: Critics' Choice.* Editor. New York: Macmillan Publishing Co., Inc., 1973.
Nolan, Tom. *Ross Macdonald: A Biography.* New York: Scribner, 1999.
Nozick, Robert. *The Examined Life: Philosophical Meditations.* New York: Touchstone Books, 1990.
O'Neill, Edward R. "Notes on the Long Take in George Cukor's *A Life of Her Own.*" *Cineaction,* Issue No. 50, 1999.
Ortega Y Gasset, Jose. *Phenomenology and Art.* Translated by Philip W. Silver. New York: W.W. Norton & Company Inc., 1975.
———. *The Modern Theme.* New York: Harper Torchbooks, 1991.
Pacepa, Ion Mihai. *Red Horizons: Chronicles of a Communist Spy Chief.* New York: Regnery Gateway, 1987.
Piaget, Jean. *Insights and Illusions of Philosophy.* Translated by Wolfe Mays. New York: Meridian Books, 1971.
Pieper, Josef. *Leisure: The Basis of Culture.* Translated by Alexander Dru. Indianapolis: Liberty Fund, 1999.
Porter, Burton. *Philosophy Through Fiction and Film.* Upper Saddle River, New Jersey: Prentice Hall, 2004.
Pronzini, Bill, and Martin H. Greenberg. Editors. *13 Short Detective Novels.* New York: Bonanza Books, 1987.
Quirk, Lawrence J. *The Complete Films of William Powell.* New York: Citadel Press, 1990.
Renaut, Alian. *The Era of the Individual: A Contribution to a History of Subjectivity.* Princeton: Princeton University Press, 1997.
Ribas, Armando P. *El fin de la idiotez y la muerte del hombre nuevo.* Miami: Ediciones Universal, 2004.
Rickman, H. P. Editor. *Dilthey: Selected Writings.* Cambridge: Cambridge University Press, 1976.

Rhode, Eric. *Tower of Babel: Speculations on the Cinema*. New York: Chilton Books, 1966.
Robbe-Grillet, Alain, and René Magritte. *La Belle Captive: A Novel.* Berkeley: University of California Press, 1995.
Rosmini, Antonio. *Conscience*. Durham: Rosmini House, 1989.
———. *The Origin of Thought*. Durham: Rosmini House, 1989.
Rubenstein, Leonard. *The Great Spy Films*. New York: Citadel Books, 1979.
Russell, Burton Jeffrey. *The Devil: Perceptions of Evil from Antiquity to Primitive Christianity*. Ithaca: Cornell University Press, 1977.
———. *Satan: The Early Christian Tradition*. Ithaca: Cornell University Press, 1981.
———. *Lucifer: The Devil in the Middle Ages*. Ithaca: Cornell University Press, 1984.
———. *Mephistopheles: The Devil in the Modern World*. Ithaca: Cornell University Press, 1986.
———. *The Prince of Darkness: Radical Evil and the Power of Good in History*. Ithaca: Cornell University Press, 1988.
Samuels, Charles Thomas. "François Truffaut: Encountering Directors." *Industry Central*, September 1970.
Scheler, Max. *Problems of Sociology of Knowledge*. Translated by Manfred Frings. London: Routledge & Kegan Paul, 1980.
Schoeck, Helmut. *Envy: A Theory of Social Behavior*. Indianapolis: Liberty Press, 1981.
Schopenhauer, Arthur. *The Wisdom of Life* and *Counsels and Maxims*. New York: Prometheus Books, 1995.
Seligmann, Kurt. *Magic, Supernaturalism, and Religion*. New York: The Universal Library, 1968.
Sertillanges, A. D. *La Vida Intellectual*. México: Editorial Porrua, S.A., 1994.
Shariff, Stefan. *Alfred Hitchcock's High Vernacular: Theory and Practice*. New York: Columbia University Press, 1991.
Shaw, Dan. Editor. *Film and Philosophy*. Volume 8. 2004.
Shelden, Michael. *Graham Greene: The Enemy Within*. New York: Random House, 1994.
Shevchenko, Arkady N. *Breaking with Moscow*. New York: Alfred A. Knopf, 1985.
Simmel, Georg. *On Individuality and Social Forms*. Edited by Donald N. Levine. Chicago: The University of Chicago Press, 1971.
Singer, Marilyn. Editor. *A History of the American Avant-Garde Cinema*. New York: The American Federation of Arts, 1976.
Smith, John. M. and Tim Cawkwell. *The World Encyclopedia of the Film*. Editors. New York: Galahad Books, 1972.
Steene, Birgitta. *Ingmar Bergman*. New York: Twyane Publishers, Inc., 1968.
Stone, Alan A. "8½: Fellini's Moment of Truth." *Boston Review: A Political and Literary Forum* Summer, 1995.
Stein, Gertrude. *How to Write*. New York: Dover Publications, Inc., 1975.
Taffel, David. *Nietzsche Unbound: The Struggle for Spirit in the Age of Science*. St. Paul: Paragon House, 2003.

Thomas, Tony. *The Films of the Forties*. New York: Citadel Press, 1975.
Thompson, David. *Rosebud: The Story of Orson Welles*. New York: Alfred A. Knopf: 1996.
Thompson, Frank. *Lost Films: Important Movies That Disappeared*. New York: A Citadel Press Book, 1996.
Tyler, Parker. *Early Classics of the Foreign Film*. New York: Citadel Books, 1962.
Vahanian, Gabriel. *The Death of God: The Culture of Our Post-Christian Era*. New York: George Braziller, 1967.
Verdes-Leroux, Jeannine. *Deconstructing Pierre Bourdieu: Against Sociological Terrorism from the Left*. New York: Algora Publishing, 2001.
Verne, Jules. *The Mysterious Island*. New York: Bantam Books, 1976.
Vincendeau, Ginette. *Jean-Pierre Melville: An American in Paris*. London: BFI Publishing, 2003.
Voegelin, Eric. *Anamnesis*. Columbia: University of Missouri Press, 1978.
———. *Order and History: The Ecumenic Age*. Volume Four. Baton Rouge: Louisiana State University Press, 1986.
Unamuno, Miguel de. *Paisajes Del Alma*. Madrid: Alianza Editorial, 1979.
Weales, Gerald. *Canned Goods as Caviar: American Film Comedies of the 1930s*. Chicago: University of Chicago Press, 1985.
Weil, Simone. *Lectures on Philosophy*. Cambridge: Cambridge University, 1995.
Weiss, Paul. *Cinematics*. Carbondale: Southern Illinois University Press, 1975.
Williams, Charles. *Witchcraft*. Cleveland: Meridian Books, 1966.
———. *Many Dimensions*. Grand Rapids, Michigan: William B. Eerdman's Publishing Company, 1949.
Wilson, Colin. *The Occult: A History*. New York: Barnes & Noble, 1995.
Witkiewicz, Stanislaw Ignacy. *The Mother and Other Unsavory Plays*. New York: Applause, 1993.
———. *The Madman and the Nun and The Crazy Locomotive*. New York: Applause, 1989.
Wolf, Markus. *Man Without a Face: The Autobiography of Communism's Greatest Spymaster*. New York: Times Books, 1997.
Woodall, James. *Borges: A Life*. New York: Basic Books, 1996.
Woolrich, Cornell. *I Married a Dead Man*. New York: Penguin Books, 1982.
———. *Waltz into Darkness*. New York: Penguin Books, 1995.

Films Cited

COMEDIES

You Can't Take It with You (1938); English, Black & White, 126 minutes.
Director: Frank Capra
Cast: James Stewart, Lionel Barrymore, Jean Arthur, Edward Arnold, Spring Byington, Mischa Auer, Ann Miller.
Playtime (1967); French, Color, 120 minutes.
Director: Jacques Tati.
Cast: Jacques Tati.
Mr. Hulot's Holiday (1953); French, Black & White, 86 minutes.
Director: Jacques Tati.
Cast: Jacques Tati, Nathalie Pascaud.
Traffic (1971); English language version, Color, 89 minutes.
Director: Jacques Tati.
Cast: Jacques Tati, Maria Kimberly, Marcel Fraval, H. Bostel, Tony Kneppers
Mon Uncle (1958); French, Color, 116 minutes.
Director: Jacques Tati.
Cast: Jacques Tati, Jean-Pierre Zola.
The Thin Man (1934); English, Black & White, 93 minutes.
Director: W. S. Van Dyke II.
Cast: William Powell, Myrna Loy, Maureen O'Sullivan, Nat Pendleton, Minna Gombell, Porter Hall, Cesar Romero.
Another Thin Man. (1939); English, Black & White, 113 minutes.
Director: W.S. Van Dyke II.
William Powell, Myrna Loy.
Illusion Travels by Streetcar (1953); Spanish, Black & White, 90 minutes.
Director: Luis Buñuel.
Cast: Lilla Prado, Carlos Navarro, Agustín Isunza.

SCIENCE FICTION

The Illustrated Man (1969); English; Color, 102 Minutes.
Director: Jack Smight.
Cast: Rod Steiger, Claire Bloom, Robert Drivas.
Panic in the Year Zero (1962); Black & White; 95 minutes.
Director: Ray Milland.
Cast: Ray Milland, Joan Freeman, Frankie Avalon, Jean Hogan, Richard Garland.
Colossus: The Forbin Project (1969); English; Color; 100 minutes.
Director: Joseph Sargent.
Cast: Eric Braeden, Susan Clark, William Schallert.
Seconds (1966); English; Black & White; 106 minutes.
Director: John Frankenheimer.
Cast: Rock Hudson, Salome Jens, John Randolph, Will Geer, Jeff Corey, Murray Hamilton, Wesley Addy.
Fahrenheit 451 (1966); English, Color, 111 minutes.
Director: François Truffaut.
Cast: Julie Christie, Oskar Werner, Cyril Cusack, Anton Diffring, Jeremy Spenser, Bee Duffell, Alex Scott, Mark Lester.
Stalker (1979); Russian, Color/Black & White, 160 minutes
Director: Andrei Tarkovsky.
Cast Alexander Kaidanovsky, Nikolai Grink, Anatoli Solonitsyn, Alice Friendlich.
Solaris (1972); Russian, Color, 165 minutes.
Director: Andrei Tarkovsky.
Cast: Nataly Bondorchuk, Donatos Banionis, Yuri Yarvet, Anatoly Solonitsyn.
1,000 Eyes of Dr. Mabuse (1960); German, Black & White, 99 minutes.
Director: Fritz Lang.
Cast: Gert Frobe, Dawn Addams, Peter Van Eyck, Wolfgang Preiss.
Alphaville (1965); French, Black & White, 95 minutes.
Director: Jean-Luc Godard.
Cast: Eddie Constantine, Anna Karina, Akim Tamiroff.
2001: A Space Odyssey (1967); English, Color, 139 minutes.
Director: Stanley Kubrick.
Cast: Keir Dullea, William Sylvester, Gary Lockwood, Daniel Richter, voice of HAL; Douglas Rain.
The Medusa Touch (1978); English, Color, 110 minutes.
Director: Jack Gold.
Cast: Richard Burton, Lee Remick, Gordon Jackson, Harry Andrews.
Blade Runner (1982); English, Color, 117 minutes.
Director: Ridley Scott.
Cast: Harrison Ford, Rutger Hauer, Sean Young, Edward James Olmos, M. Emmet Walsh, Daryl Hannah.
Man Facing Southeast (Hombre Mirando al Sudeste) (1987); Spanish, Color.
Director: Elise Subiela
Cast: Lorenzo Quinteros, Hugo Soto, Inés Vernengo.

The Day the Earth Stood Still (1951); English, Black & White, 92 minutes.
Director: Robert Wise
Cast: Michael Rennie, Patricia Neal, Hugh Marlowe, Sam Jaffe, Billy Gray.
Enemy From Space (1957); English; Black & White; 85 minutes.
Director: Val Guest
Cast: Brian Donlevy, William Franklyn.
Invasion of the Body Snatchers (1956); English; Black & White; 80 minutes.
Director: Don Siegel
Cast: Kevin McCathy. Dana Wynter, Carolyn Jones, King Donovan.
The Last Man on Earth (1964); English, Black & White; 86 minutes.
Director: Sidney Salkow.
Cast: Vincent Price, Franca Bettoia, Emma Danieli, Giacomo Rossi-Stuart.
Logan's Run (1976); English, Color, 120 minutes.
Director: Michael Anderson.
Cast: Michael York, Jenny Agutter, Peter Ustinov, Richard Jordan.
Soylent Green (1973); English, Color; 97 minutes.
Director: Richard Fleischer.
Cast: Charlton Heston, Edward G. Robinson, Joseph Cotton, Chuck Connors.
Things to Come (1936); English, Black & White; 92 minutes.
Director: William Cameron Menzies.
Cast: Raymond Massey, Cedric Hardwicke, Ralph Richardson.
The Time Machine (1960); English, Color; 103 minutes.
Director: George Pal.
Cast: Rod Taylor, Yvette Mimieux, Alan Young, Sebastian Cabot.
Metropolis (1926); Black &White, Silent, 120 minutes.
Director: Fritz Lang.
Cast: Brigitte Helm, Alfred Abel.
The Twilight Zone (1959); English, Black & White, Television Series.
Director: Several.
Cast: Several.
Watership Down (1978); English, Color animation, 92 minutes.
Director: Martin Rosen.
Cast: Animated.
Westworld (1973); English, Color, 88 minutes.
Director: Michael Crichton.
Cast: Yul Brynner, Richard Benjamin, James Brolin.
X (The Man with X-Ray Eyes) (1963); English, Color, 80 minutes.
Director: Roger Corman.
Cast: Ray Milland, Diana Van Der Vils, Harold J. Stone, John Hoyt, Don Rickles.
Brainstorm (1965); English, Black & White, 105 minutes.
Director: William Conrad.
Cast: Dana Andrews, Viveca Lindfors, Stacy Harris, Jeffrey Hunter.

SUPERNATURAL HORROR

The Uninvited (1944); English, Black & White, 98 minutes.
Director: Lewis Allen.
Cast: Ray Milland, Ruth Hussey, Donald Crisp, Gail Russell, Cornelia Otis Skinner, Dorothy Stickney, Barbara Everest, Alan Napier.
The Omen (1976); English, Color, 111 minutes.
Director: Richard Donner.
Cast: Gregory Peck, Lee Remick, Billie Whitelaw, David Warner, Harvey Stephens, Patrick Froughton, Leo McKern.
The Haunting (1963); English, Black & White, 112 minutes.
Director: Robert Wise.
Cast: Julie Harris, Claire Bloom, Richard Johnson, Russ Tamblyn, Lois Maxwell, Fay Comption.
The Changeling (1979); English, Color, 109 minutes.
Director: Peter Medak.
Cast: George C. Scott, Trish Van Devere, Melvyn Douglas, John Colicos, Jean Marsh, Madeleine Thornton-Sherwood.
Dead of Night (1945); English, Black & White, 102 minutes.
Director: Alberto Cavalcanti
Cast: Basil Dearden, Pobert Hamer, Charles Crichton, Mervyn Johns, Roland Culver, Antony Baird, Judy Kelly, Miles Malleson, Sally Ann Howes, Googie Withers, Ralph Michael, Michael Redgrave, Basil Rodford, Naunton Wayne, Frederick Valk.
Curse of the Demon (1958); English, Black & White, 83 minutes.
Director: Jacques Tourneur.
Cast: Dana Andrews, Peggy Cummins, Niall MacGinnis, Maurice Denham, Athene Seyler.
Cabinet of Dr. Caligari (1919); German with English subtitles, Black & White, 69 minutes.
Director: Robert Wiene.
Cast: Werner Krauss, Conrad Veidt, Lil Dagover.
The Other (1972); English, 100 minutes.
Director: Robert Mulligan.
Cast: Uta Hagen, Diana Muldaur, Chris Udvamoky, Martin Udvamoky, John Ritter.
Rosemary's Baby (1968); English, Color, 136 minutes.
Director: Roman Polanski.
Cast: Mia Farrow, John Cassavetes, Ruth Gordon, Sidney Blackner, Maurice Evans, Ralph Bellamy, Elisha Cook Jr., Patsy Keller, Charles Grodin.
The Exorcist (1973); English, Color, 121 minutes.
Director: William Friedkin.
Cast: Ellen Burstyn, Max von Sydow, Linda Blair, Jason Miller, Lee J. Cobb, Kitty Winn, Jack MacGowran.
The Exorcist III (1990); English, Color, 110 minutes.

Director: William Peter Blatty.
Cast: George C. Scott, Ed Flanders, Brad Dourif, Jason Miller, Nicol Williamson, Scott Wilson, Nancy Fish, George DiCenzo, Viveca Lindfors.
Don't Look Now (1973); English, Color, 110 minutes.
Director: Nicolas Roeg.
Cast: Julie Christie, Donald Sutherland, Hillary Mason, Clelia Mantania, Massimo Serato.
The Sentinel (1977); English, Color, 93 minutes.
Director: Michael Winner.
Cast: Christina Raines, Ava Gardner, Chris Sarandon, José Ferrer.
Burn Witch Burn (1962); English, Color, 87 minutes.
Director: Sidney Hayers.
Cast: Janet Blair, Peter Wyngarde, Margaret Johnson.
Carnival of Souls (1962); English, 83 minutes.
Director: Herk Harvey.
Cast: Candace Hillgass, Sidney Berger, Frances Feist, Herk Harvey, Stan Levitt, Art Ellison.
Blithe Spirit (1945); English, Black & White, 96 minutes.
Director: David Lean.
Cast: Rex Harrison, Constance Cummings, Kay Hammond, Margaret Rutherford.
Dr. Terror's House of Horrors (1965); English, Color, 98 minutes.
Director: Freddie Francis.
Cast: Christopher Lee, Peter Cushing, Max Adrian, Ann Bell, Michael Gough, Jennifer Jayne, Neil McCallum, Bernard Lee, Roy Castle, Alan Freeman, Peter Madden.
Burn Witch Burn (1962); English, Black & White, 87 minutes.
Director: Sidney Hayers.
Cast: Janet Blair, Peter Wyngarde, Margaret Johnson.

DRAMA

Lola (1961); French, Black & White, 90 minutes.
Director: Jacques Demy.
Cast: Anouk Aimee, Marc Michel, Jacques Harden, Alan Scott, Elina Labourdette, Annie Duperoux.
The Red Balloon (1956); French, Color, 34 minutes.
Director: Albert Lamorisse.
Cast: Pascal Lamorisse, Georges Sellier.
Vincent, François, Paul & the Others (1974); French, Color, 118 minutes.Director: Claude Sautet.
Cast: Yves Montand, Michel Piccoli, Serge Reggiani.
Treasure of the Sierra Madre (1948); English, Black & White, 126 minutes.
Director: John Huston.

Cast: Humphrey Bogart, Walter Huston, Tim Holt, Bruce Bennett, Barton MacLane, Alfonso Bedoya, Bobby Blake, John Huston, Ann Sheridan.
The Seven Thieves (1960); English, Black & White, 102 minutes.
Director: Henry Hathaway.
Cast: Edward G. Robinson, Rod Steiger, Joan Collins, Eli Wallach, Alexander Scourby, Michael Dante, Sebastian Cabot.
Last Year at Marienbad (1962); French, Black & White, 93 minutes.
Director: Alain Resnais.
Cast: Delphine Seyrig, Giorgio Albertazzi.
Le Cercle Rouge (1970); French, Color, 134 minutes.
Director: Jean-Pierre Melville.
Cast: Alain Delon, André Bourvil, Gian-Maria Volonte, Yves Montand, François Perier, André Ekyan.
Le Samurai (1967); French, Color, 100 minutes.
Director: Jean-Pierre Melville.
Cast: Alain Delon, François Perier, Nathalie Delon, Caty Rosier, Michel Boisrond.
Le Doulos (1963); French, Black & White, 108 minutes.
Director: Jean-Pierre Melville.
Cast: Jean-Paul Belmondo, Serge Reggiani, Jean Desailly, Rene Lefevre, Marcel Cuveilier.
Un Flic (1972); French, Color, 94 minutes.
Director: Jean-Pierre Melville.
Cast: Alain Delon, Richard Crenna, Catharine Denueve, Riccardo Cucciolla, Michal Conrad, André Pousse.
Bob Le Flambeur (1955); French, Black & White, 100 minutes.
Director: Jean-Pierre Melville.
Cast: Roger Duchesne, Isabelle Corey, Daniel Cauchy, Guy Ecomble, André Garret, Claude Cerval, Howard Vernon
Breathless (1959); French, Black & White, 89 minutes.
Director: Jean-Luc Godard.
Cast: Jean-Paul Belmondo, Jean Seberg, Daniel Boulanger, Liliane David.
Fort Apache, The Bronx (1981); English, Color, 125 minutes.
Director: Daniel Petrie
Cast: Paul Newman, Edward Asner, Ken Wahl, Danny Aiello, Rachel Ticotin, Pam Grier, Kathleen Beller.
Battleground (1949); English, Black & White, 118 minutes.
Director: William Wellman
Cast: Van Johnson, John Hodiak, Denise Darcel, Ricardo Montalban, George Murphy, James Whitmore.
8½ (1963); Italian, Black & White, 135 minutes.
Director: Federico Fellini.
Cast: Marcello Mastroianni, Claudia Cardinale, Anouk Aimee, Sandra Milo, Barbara Steele, Rosella Falk, Madeleine Le Beau, Caterina Boratto, Edra Gale, Mark Herron.
La Dolce Vita (1960); Italian, 175 minutes.

Director: Federico Fellini.
Cast: Marcello Mastronianni, Anouk Aimee, Anika Ekberg, Barbara Steele, Nadia Gray.

Citizen Kane (1941); English, Black & White, 119 minutes.
Director: Orson Welles.
Cast: Joseph Cotton, Everett Sloane, Agnes Moorehead, Dorothy Camingore, Ray Collins, George Coulounis, William Alland, Paul Stewart, Ruth Warrick, Erskine Sanford.

Odd Man Out (1947); English, Black & White, 115 minutes.
Director: Carol Reed.
Cast: James Mason, Robert Newton, Kathleen Ryan, Robert Beatty, Cyril Cusak, F. J. McCormick, William Hartnell, Fay Compton, Dennis O'Dea, Dan O'Herlihy.

The Man on the Eiffel Tower (1949); Color, 97 minutes.
Director: Burgess Meredith.
Cast: Charles Laughton, Franchot Tone, Burgess Meredith, Robert Hutton, Jean Wallace, Patricia Roc, Wilfrid Hyde White, Belita.

The Man Who Loved Women (1977); French, Color, 119 minutes.
Director: François Truffaut.
Cast: Charles Denner, Brigitte Fossey, Nelly Borgeaud, Lesli Caron, Genevieve Fontanel.

To Have and Have Not (1944); English, Black & White, 100 minutes.
Director: Howard Hawks.
Cast: Humphrey Bogart, Walter Brennan, Lauren Bacall, Hoagy Carmichael, Dan Seymour, Marcel Dalio, Dolores Moran, Sheldon Leonard.

Wages of Fear (1952); French, Black & White, 156 minutes.
Director: H. G. Clouzot.
Cast: Yves Montand, Charles Vanel, Peter Van Eyck, Vera Clouzot, Folco Lulli, William Tubbs.

The Third Man (1949); English, Black & White, 104 minutes.
Director: Carol Reed.
Cast: Orson Welles, Joseph Cotton, Alida Valli, Trevor Howard.

Topkapi (1964); English, Color, 120 minutes.
Director: Jules Dassin.
Cast: Melina Mercouri, Peter Ustinov, Maximilian Schell, Robert Morley, Akim Tamiroff, Despo Diamantidou.

Save The Tiger (1973); English, Color, 101 minutes.
Director: John G. Avildsen.
Cast: Jack Lemmon, Jack Gifford, Thayer David.

The Spy Who Came in From the Cold (1965); English, Color, 112 minutes.
Director: Martin Ritt.
Cast: Richard Burton, Claire Bloom, Oskar Werner, Bernard Lee, George Voskovec, Peter Van Eyck, Sam Wanamaker.

Berlin Express (1948); English, Black & White. 86 minutes.
Director: Jaques Tourneur.
Cast: Merle Oberon, Robert Ryan, Charles Korvin, Paul Lukas, Robert Coote.

The Guns of Navarone (1961); English, Color, 167 minutes.
Cast: Gregory Peck, David Niven, Anthony Quinn, Anthony Quayle, Irene Papas, Gia Scala, James Darren.
Ocean's 11 (1960); English, Color, 127 minutes.
Director: Lewis Milestone.
Cast: Frank Sinatra, Dean Martin, Sammy Davis Jr., Peter Lawford, Angie Dickinson, Richard Conte, Cesar Romero, Patrice Wymore, Joey Bishop, Akim Tamiroff, Henry Silva.
The Colditz Story (1957); English, Black & White, 97 minutes.
Director: Guy Hamilton.
Cast: John Mills, Lionel Jeffries, Bryan Forbes, Ian Carmichael, Richard Wattis, Anton Diffring, Theodore Bikel.
The Great Escape (1963); English, Color, 168 minutes.
Director: John Sturges.
Cast: Steve McQueen, James Garner, Richard Attenborough, Charles Bronson, James Coburn, David McCallum, Donald Pleasence, James Donald, Gordon Jackson, John Leyton, Angus Lennie, Nigel Stack.
Grand Prix (1966); English, Color, 175 minutes.
Director: John Frankenheimer.
Cast: James Garner, Eva Maria Saint, Yves Montand, Toshiro Mifune, Brian Bedford, Jessica Walter, Françoise Hardy.
Sorcerer (1977); English, Color, 121 minutes.
Director: William Friedkin.
Cast: Roy Scheider, Bruno Cremer, Francisco Rabal, Amidou Ramon Bieri.
F For Fake (1973); English, Color, 98 minutes.
Director: Orson Welles.
Cast: Orson Welles, Elmyr De Hory, Clifford Irving, Oja Kodar, François Reichenbach.
The Magnificent Ambersons (1942); English, Black & White, 88 minutes.
Director: Orson Welles.
Cast: Tim Holt, Joseph, Dolores Costello, Anne Baxter, Agnes Moorehead, Ray Collins, Richard Bennett, Erskine Sanford.
The Shooting Party (1984); English, Color, 108 minutes.
Director: Alan Bridges.
Cast: James Mason, Dorothy Tutin, Edward Fox, Cheryl Campbell, John Gielgud, Gordon Jackson, Apharon Ipale, Rupert Frazer, Robert Hardy, Judi Bowker.
The Thomas Crown Affair. (1968); English, Color, 102 minutes.
Cast: Steve McQueen, Faye Dunaway, Paul Burke, Jack Weston, Biff McGuire, Addison Powell, Astrid Heeren, Gordon Pinsent, Yaphet Kotto, Sidney Armus, Richard Bull, Peg Shirley, Patrick Horgan, Carol Corbett, Tom Rosqui.
How to Steal a Million (1966); English, Color, 123 minutes.
Cast: Audrey Hepburn, Peter O'Toole, Eli Wallach, Hugh Griffith, Charles Boyer, Fernand Gravey, Marcel Dalio, Jacques Marin, Roger Treville, Edward Malin, Bert Bertram.
The Stranger (1946); English, Black & White, 95 minutes.

Director: Orson Welles.
Cast: Orson Welles, Loretta Young, Edward G. Robinson, Richard Long, Martha Wentworth.
A Man and A Woman (1966); French, Color, minutes.
Director: Claude LeLouch.
Cast: Anouk Aimee, Jean-Louis Trintignant, Pierre Barouh, Valerie Lefrange.
Quai Des Orfevres (1946); French, Black & White, minutes.
Director: Henri-Georges Clouzot.
Cast: Louis Jouvet, Simone Renant, Bernard Blier, Suzy Delair.
Rififi (1955); French, Black & White, 118 minutes.
Director: Jules Dassin.
Cast: Jean Servais, Carl Mohner, Robert Manuel.
Night and the City (1950); English, Black & White, 96 minutes.
Director: Jules Dassin
Cast: Richard Widmark, Gene Tierney
Laura (1944); English, Black & White, 88 minutes.
Director: Otto Preminger.
Cast: Gene Tierney, Dana Andrews.
The Man in the White Suit (1951); English, Black & White, 81 minutes.
Director: Alexander Mackendrick.
Cast: Alec Guinness, Joan Greenwood, Cecil Parker.
The Lavender Hill Mob (1952); English, Black & White, 77 minutes.
Director: Charles Crichton.
Cast: Alec Guinness, Stanley Holloway.
Ministry of Fear (1944); English, Black & White, 87 minutes.
Director: Fritz Lang
Cast: Ray Milland, Marjorie Reynolds.
Black Angel (1946); English, Black & White, 81 minutes.
Director: Roy William Neill.
Cast: Dan Duryea, June Vincent, Peter Lorre, Broderick Crawford.
Phantom Lady (1944); English, Black & White, 87 minutes.
Director: Robert Siodmak.
Cast: Franchot Tone, Ella Raines, Alan Curtis.
Farewell My Lovely (1975), English; Color, 98 minutes.
Director: Dick Richards.
Cast: Robert Mitchum, Charlotte Rampling.
The Killers (1946); English; Black & White, 113 minutes.
Director: Robert Siodmak.
Cast: Burt Lancaster, Ava Gardner.
Kiss of Death (1947); English; Black & White, 99 minutes.
Director: Henry Hathaway.
Cast: Victor Mature, Brian Donlevy, Coleen Gray, Richard Widmark.
Casablanca (1942); English; Black & White, 113 minutes.
Director: Michael Curtiz.

Cast: Humphrey Bogart, Ingrid Bergman, Paul Henreid, Claude Rains, Conrad Veidt, Sydney Greenstreet, Peter Lorre.
The Man in the Gray Flannel Suit (1956); English; Color, 152 minutes.
Director: Nunnally Johnson.
Cast: Gregory Peck, Jennifer Jones, Fredrick March.
The Naked Edge (1961); English; Black & White, 97 minutes.
Director: Michael Anderson.
Cast: Gary Cooper, Deborah Kerr.
Born To Be Bad (1950); English; Black & White, 94 minutes.
Director: Nicholas Ray.
Cast: Joan Fontaine, Robert Ryan, Zachary Scott, Mel Ferrer.
The Card (1952); English; Black & White, 91 minutes.
Director: Ronald Neame.
Cast: Alec Guinness.
Force of Evil (1949); English; Black & White, 82 minutes.
Director: Abraham Polonsky.
Cast: John Garfield.
The Ladykillers (1955); English; Color, 87 minutes.
Director: Alexander Mackendrick.
Cast: Alec Guinness, Cecil Parker, Herbert Lom, Peter Sellers, Danny Green.
Kind Hearts and Coronets (1950); English; Black & White, 110 minutes.
Director: Robert Hamer.
Cast: Alec Guinness, Dennis Price, Valerie Hobson.
Pitfall (1948); English; Black & White, 84 minutes.
Director: André de Toth.
Cast: Dick Powell, Jane Wyatt, John Litel, Raymond Burr, Dick Wessel.
Port of Shadows (1942); French Black & White, 90 minutes.
Director: Marcel Carne.
Cast: Jane Wyatt, Jean Ganin, Michel Simon.
Z (1969); French, Color, 127 minutes.
Director: Costa-Gavras.
Cast: Jane Wyatt, Yves Montand, Irene Papas.
Pepe Le Moko (1937); French, Black & White, 93 minutes.
Director: Julien Duvilier
Cast: Jane Wyatt, Jean Gabin, Mireille Balin.
Union Station (1950); English, Black & White, 80 minutes.
Director: Rudolph Mate.
Cast: Jane Wyatt, William Holden, Nancy Olson.
La Bête Humaine (1938); French, Black & White, 99 minutes.
Director: Jean Renoir.
Cast: Jean Gabin, Julien Carette.
Crime Wave (1954); English, Black & White, 74 minutes.
Director: André de Toth.
Cast: Sterling Hayden, Gene Nelson.
The Mountain (1954); English, Color, 105 minutes.

Director: Edward Dmytryk.
Cast: Spencer Tracy, Robert Wagner, Claire Trevor, William Demarest, Richard Arlen, E. G., Marshall.

Bibliography

Arenas, Reinaldo. *Celestino antes del alba*. Ediciones Universal, 1996.
Assouline, Pierre. *Simenon*. New York: Alfred A. Knopf, 1997.
Barrett, William. *The Illusion of Technique: A Search for Meaning in a Technological Civilization*. New York: Anchor Press, 1978.
Barzun, Jacques, and Wendell Hertig Taylor. *A Catalogue of Crime*. New York: Harper & Row, Publishers, 1989.
Bazin, André. *Orson Welles: A Critical View*. Los Angeles: Acrobat Books, 1991.
Bellos, David. *Jacques Tati: His Life and Art*. London: The Harvill Press, 1999
Berger, Arthur S. *Aristocracy of the Dead: New Findings in Postmortem Survival*. Jefferson, NC: McFarland & Company, Inc., Publishers, 1987.
Bradbury, Ray. *Fahrenheit 451*. New York: Ballantine Books, 1996.
Budge, E. A. Wallis. *The Book of the Dead*. New York: Gramercy Book, 1960.
Cassirer, Ernst. *An Essay on Man: An Introduction to a Philosophy of Human Culture*. New Haven: Yale University Press, 1972.
Chion, Michel. *The Films of Jacques Tati*. Toronto: Guernica, 1997.
Clarke, Arthur C. *The Sentinel*. Barnes and Noble Books: New York, 1996.
Couteau, Robert. "The Romance of Places: An Interview with Ray Bradbury." *Quantum: Science Fiction & Fantasy Review*. (Gaithersburg, Maryland: Thrust Publications). Spring 1991.
Cowie, Peter. *Seventy Years of Cinema*. New York: Castle Books, 1969.
Ellis, Havelock. *The Dance of Life*. New York: Random House, 1929.
González, Pedro Blas. "Jacques Tati: Last Bastion of Innocence." *Senses of Cinema*. Issue no. 37, Oct.–Dec. 2006, 1–11.
Greenhouse, Herbert B. *Premonitions: A Leap into the Future*. Bernard Geis Associates, 1971.
Huxley, Aldous *Brave New World*. New York: Perennial Library, 1989.
Infante, Guillermo Cabrera. *Arcadia Todas Las Noches*. *Bogota*: Editorial La Oveja Negra, Ltda, 1987.
James, William. *The Varieties of Religious Experience*. New York: Collier Books.
Jaspers, Karl. *Socrates, Buddha, Confucius, Jesus: The Paradigmatic Individuals*. Translated by Manheim, Ralph. San Diego: Harcourt Brace & Company, 1990.
Jung, C. G. *Psychology and the Occult*. Princeton: Princeton University Press, 1977.

Lavelle, Louis. *The Dilemma of Narcissus*. Translated by William Gairdner. Burdett, New York: Larson Publications, 1993.

Lem, Stanislaw. *Solaris*. Translated by Joanna Kilmartin and Steve Cox. San Diego: A Harvest Book, 1970.

M. August. Associated Press. October 13, 2000.

Madariaga, Salvador de. *Don Quixote: An Introductory Essay in Psychology*. London: Oxford University Press, 1961.

Marcel, Gabriel. *Tragic Wisdom and Beyond.* Translated by Stephen Jolin and Peter.

Marías, Julián. *Philosophy as Dramatic Theory.* University Park: The Pennsylvania State University Press, 1971, 237.

Maslow, Abraham H. *Toward a Psychology of Being*. New York: D. Van Nostrand Company, 1968.

McCormick. Evanston: Northwestern University Press, 1973.

———. *Tragic Wisdom and Beyond*. Translated by Stephen Jolin and Peter McCormick. Evanston: Northwestern University Press, 1973.

———. *Metaphysical Journal*. Translated by Bernard Wall. Chicago: Gateway Edition, 1952.

Merleau-Ponty, Maurice. *The Primacy of Perception*. Evanston: Northwestern University Press, 1964.

Montaigne, Michel de. *Selected Essays*. Roslyn, N.Y.: Walter J. Black, 1943.

Natof, Andre. *The Occult*. Edinburgh: Chambers, 1991.

Nietzche, Friedrich. *The Portable Nietzche*. Edited by Walter Kaufman. New York: Penguin Press, 1982.

Nigosian, S. A. *The Zoroastrian Faith: Tradition & Modern Research.* Montreal: McGill-Queen's University Press, 1993.

Oesterreich, T. K. *Possession: Demoniacal and Other Among Primitive Races, in Antiquity, The Middle Ages, and Modern Times.* Secaucus, NJ: The Citadel Press, 1974.

Olander, Joseph D., and Martin Harry Greenberg. *Arthur C. Clarke*. Editors. Taplinger Publishing Company: NY, 1977

Ortega y Gasset, José. *The Dehumanization of Art*. Princeton: Princeton University Press, 1972, 25.

———. *The Revolt of the Masses*. New York: W.W. Norton, 1960.

———. *History as a System*. New York: W.W. Norton, 1961.

———. *The Dehumanization of Art and Other Essays on Art, Culture, and Literature*. New Jersey: Princeton University Press.

———. *Ideas y Creencias*. Colección Austral. Espasa-Calpe, S.A., 1976.

———. *Man and Crisis*. New York: W.W. Norton & Company, 1962.

Orwell, George. *Nineteen Eighty-Four*. Penguin Classics, 2003.

———. *Animal Farm*. Signet 50th Anniversary Edition, 2004.

Otto, Rudolf. *The Idea of the Holy: An Inquiry into the Non-Rational Factor in the Idea of the Divine and its Relation to the Rational.* Translated by John W. Harvey. New York: A Galaxy Book.

Parmenides of Elea. *Fragments*. Translated by David Gallop. Toronto: University of Toronto Press, 1984.

Plato. *The Collected Dialogues of Plato*. Edith Hamilton and Huntington Cairns. Editors. Princeton: Princeton University Press, 1985.
Popper, Karl. *The Open Society and its Enemies*. Princeton University Press: Princeton, New Jersey, 2020.
Quirk, Lawrence J. *The Complete Films of William Powell*. New York: Carol Publishing Group, 1990.
Schopenhauer, Arthur. *The Wisdom of Life* and *Counsels and Maxims*. New York: Prometheus Books, 1995.
Shevchenko, Arkady N. *Breaking with Moscow*. New York: Alfred A. Knopf, 1985.
Simmel, Georg. *On Individuality and Social Forms*. Chicago: University of Chicago Press, 1971.
Solovyov, Vladimir. *Crisis of Western Philosophy: against Positivism*. Lindisfarne Books, 1996.
Tarkovsky, Andrei. *Sculpting in Time*. Translated from the Russian by Kitty Hunter Blair. Austin: University of Texas Press,1986.
Truffaut, François. *Correspondence 1945–1984*. Edited by Gilles Jacob and Claude de Givray. New York: Cooper Square 3 Press, 2000.
Voltaire. *Candide*. Penguin Classics. New York, 1977.
Witkiewicz, Stanislaw Ignacy. *Insatiability*. Evanston: Northwestern University Press, 1996.
Whitehead, Alfred North. *Modes of Thought*. New York: The Free Press, 1968.
Wyndenbruck, Nora. *Rilke: Man and Poet*. New York: Appleton-Century-Crofts.
Zamyatin, Yevgeny. *We*. New York: Penguin Books, 1993.

Index

Alētheia, 32
Allen, Lewis; Phenomenology and Life After Death, 112; *The Uninvited*, 107
Alien, 12
Ambler, Eric; *A Coffin for Dimitros*, 64
Anderson, Imbert Enrique; *El Fantasma*, 119
Anderson, Michael; *Logan's Run*, 30
The Appropriation of Human Reality, xi
Asmodeus, 99
The Asphalt Jungle, 66, 75

Baal, 99
Barzun, Jacques and Wendell Hertig Taylor; *A Catalogue of Crime*, 92
Bazin, André; *Orson Welles: A Critical View*, 73
Bellos, David; *Jacques Tati: His Life and Art*, 132
Blade Runner, 16
Borges, Jorge Luis; Life as Labyrinthine Maze
Bradbury, Ray, 25, 29

Cabrera-Infante, Guillermo, 39
Capra, Frank; *You Can't Take It with You*, xv
Carnival of Souls, 103
The Changeling, 103

Charles, Nick; *The Thin Man* Series, xv
Chesterton, G. K.; *The Detective*, 88; Resentment, 88
Chion, Michel; *The Films of Jacques Tati*, 133
Clarke, Arthur C., 6; "The Sentinel," 4
Colossus: The Forbin Project, 31
Communism, 25

Dead of Night, 106
Descartes, Rene; Cogito ergo sum, 16
Dickens, Charles; *The Personal History of David Copperfield*, 33

Ellis, Havelock; *The Dance of Life*, 49, 130
Egyptians; The Book of the Dead, 99
Essence, xi
Euhemerus; The Gods, 99
The Exorcist, 103
Existential dramas, 2; *Le Cercle Rouge*, 74; *Le Deuxième Souffle*, 75; *Le Doulos*, 75; *Le Samourai*, 69; *Un Flic*, 79

Fellini, Federico; *8½*, 90
Ford, John; Visual images, 2

Godard, Robert; Liquid fuel rocket, 6

Grand Prix, 90

Hathaway, Henry; Existential longing, 90; Idealism and Optimism, 86; *Seven Thieves*, 83
The Haunting, 103
Homer; Mythological cosmogony, 96
Human Reality as Indomitable, xi-xvi
Huston, John, 49

It's a Mad, Mad, Mad, Mad World, 89

James, William; *The Varieties of Religious Experience*, 102
Jaspers, Karl, 51

Kubrick, Stanley, 3,6; Intelligent design, 5; HAL 9000 computer, 6,30; *2001: A Space Odyssey*, 1

Lamorisse, Albert; *Red Balloon*, xvi
Last Man on Earth, 30
Lavelle, Louis; *The Dilemma of Narcissus*, 114; The World of Spirit and Bodies, 114–15
Lem, Stanislaw, 12
Lived Experience, xi

Marcel, Gabriel; The Bite of Reality, xiii; HAL 9000 computer, 6, 30; *Metaphysical Journal*, 117–18; Problem and Mystery, 92, 116; *The Tragic Wisdom and Beyond*, 33
Maugham, Somerset; *The Summing Up*, xiv, 135
Madariaga, Salvador de
Mandelstam, Nadezhda; *Hope Against Hope*, 35
The Medusa Touch; Immediacy and Lived-Time, 113
Melville, Jean-Pierre; *Bob Le Flambeur*, 61
Merleau, Ponty Maurice; *The Primacy of Perception*, 131

Metaphysical/Existential Approach to Cinema, xii-xvi; Essence and Metaphysical/Existential appropriation of Human Reality, xi-xii

Nazism, 26
Newton, Issac, 100
Nietzsche, Friedrich; *The Gay Science*, 100
Nigosian, S. A.; *The Zoroastrian Faith*, 99

Ocean's Eleven, 91
Oesterreich, T. K.; *Possession: Demoniacal and Other*, 116
Omega Man, 30
The Omen; Metaphysical Horror, 103
Ortega y Gasset, José; *The Dehumanization of Art*; *Ideas and Beliefs*,72, 101; Lived Reality, 11; *Man and Crisis*, 104; The Nature of Biography, 44; *The Revolt of the Masses*, 34; Vital Reason, 44

Pal, George; *The Time Machine*, 30
Philosophy; Framework of Human Existence, 135; Reason and the Rational Universe, 96
Popper, Karl; *The Open Society and its Enemies*, 27
Paracelsus, 100
Parmenides, 1
Plato, 1; *Charmides*, 50,56
Postmodern life, *xv*
Pre-Socratics, 96–98
The Problem of Evil; Paradox of Evil, 99, 101
Ptolemy (Claudius Ptolemaeus), 100
Pythagoras, 1

Rand, Ayn, 35
Resnais, Alain; Existential Subjectivity, 41; *Last Year at Marienbad*, 41
Rififi, 75

Rosenberg, Alfred, 36

Sartre, Jean-Paul; Pour-soi, 16
Scheler, Max; *Resentment in the Structuring of Ethics*, 89
Shevchenko, Arkady, 25
Shoot the Piano Player, 88
Siegel, Don; *Invasion of the Body Snatchers*, 30
Simmel, George; "Subjective Culture," 87
Socrates; Know Thyself, 49
Solovyov, Vladimir; *The Crisis of Western Philosophy*, 35
Soylent Green, 30
Star Wars, 12
Subiela, Eliseo; *Hombre mirando al sudeste*, xvi

Tarkosvky, Andrei, 11; *Sculpting in Time*, 12; *Solaris*, 12; *Stalker*, 12, 20
Tati, Jacques; Innocence in Modernity, 123; Leisure, 130; *Mr. Hulot's Holiday*, 129; *Playtime*, 123; Subjectivity and Objects, 124; World Weariness, 2
Terminator, 12
Thales, 96
Topkapi, 75, 88
Tourneur, Jacques; *Berlin Express*, 97; *Cat People*, 106; *Curse of the Demon*, 95; Hyper-Rationality, 101; *I Walked with a Zombie*, 106; *Leopard Man*, 97; *Out of the Past*, 97; Rationalism and Superstition, 106; Satanic Contents of *Pandora's Box*, 95; Supernatural Phenomena, 97, 105
Travern, Bernard, 55
Truffaut, François; *Fahrenheit 451*, 25, 30; *The Man Who Loved Women*, xv, *Twilight Zone*, 31

Verne, Jules, 6
V-2 rocket, 6
Voltaire; *Candide*, 7

Wellman, William; *Battleground*, xv
Welles, Orson; *Citizen Kane*; *F For Fake*, 40–41
Wells, H. G., 6; *Things to Come*, 30; *War of the Worlds*, 41
Westworld, 31
Wise, Robert; *The Day the Earth Stood Still*, 30; *Enemy From Space, The Creeping Unknown, Five Years to Earth*, 30
Witkiewicz, Stanislaw Ignacy; *Insatiability*, 19
Whitehead, Alfred North; *Modes of Thought*, 32

Xenophanes; Anthropomorphism, 97
Xingjian, Gao; Communist China and the Nobel Prize, 36

Zoroastrianism, 99

About the Author

Pedro Blas González is a professor of philosophy at Barry University. He is the author of *Human Existence as Radical Reality: Ortega's Philosophy of Subjectivity* (2005); *Fragments: Essays in Subjectivity, Individuality and Autonomy* (2005); *Ortega's "The Revolt of the Masses" and the Triumph of the New Man* (2007) and *Unamuno: A Lyrical Essay* (2007). He has also published two e-book novels: *Dreaming in the Cathedral* (2010) and *Fantasia* (2012). In 1998 he translated and wrote an introduction to José Ortega y Gasset's last essay to be published in English to date: "Medio siglo de filosofía," (1951), "Half a Century of Philosophy" *Philosophy Today* (Vol.42:2), 115–25.

www.ingramcontent.com/pod-product-compliance
Lightning Source LLC
Chambersburg PA
CBHW021356300426
44114CB00012B/1259